WILMETTE PUBLIC LIBRARY

3 1239 00861 5905

WITHDRAWN
Wilmette Public Library

the
CHOICE
for
LOVE

WILMETTE PUBLIC LIBRARY
1242 WILMETTE AVENUE
WILMETTE, IL 60091
847-256-5025

Also by Barbara De Angelis, Ph.D.

*Soul Shifts: Transformative Wisdom for Creating a Life of Authentic Awakening, Emotional Freedom, and Practical Spirituality**

How Did I Get Here?: Finding Your Way to Renewed Hope and Happiness When Life and Love Take Unexpected Turns

Secrets About Life Every Woman Should Know: Ten Principles for Total Emotional and Spiritual Fulfillment

What Women Want Men to Know

Real Moments: Discover the Secret for True Happiness

Real Moments for Lovers: The Enlightened Guide for Discovering Total Passion and True Intimacy

Passion

Ask Barbara: The 100 Most-Asked Questions about Love, Sex, and Relationships

*Confidence: Finding it and Living It**

The Real Rules: How to Find the Right Man for the Real You

Are You the One for Me?: Knowing Who's Right and Avoiding Who's Wrong

Secrets about Men Every Woman Should Know

How to Make Love All the Time

Co-author of:
Chicken Soup for the Couple's Soul: Inspirational Stories about Love and Relationships

Chicken Soup for the Romantic Soul: Inspirational Stories about Love and Romance

*Available from Hay House
Please visit:

Hay House USA: www.hayhouse.com®
Hay House Australia: www.hayhouse.com.au
Hay House UK: www.hayhouse.co.uk
Hay House South Africa: www.hayhouse.co.za
Hay House India: www.hayhouse.co.in

the CHOICE *for* LOVE

Entering into a New, Enlightened Relationship with Yourself, Others & the World

DR. BARBARA DE ANGELIS

WILMETTE PUBLIC LIBRARY

HAY HOUSE, INC.
Carlsbad, California • New York City
London • Sydney • Johannesburg
Vancouver • New Delhi

Copyright © 2017 by Barbara De Angelis

Published and distributed in the United States by: Hay House, Inc.: www.hayhouse
.com® • *Published and distributed in Australia by:* Hay House Australia Pty. Ltd.: www
.hayhouse.com.au • *Published and distributed in the United Kingdom by:* Hay House UK,
Ltd.: www.hayhouse.co.uk • *Published and distributed in the Republic of South Africa
by:* Hay House SA (Pty), Ltd.: www.hayhouse.co.za • *Distributed in Canada by:* Raincoast
Books: www.raincoast.com • *Published in India by:* Hay House Publishers India: www
.hayhouse.co.in

Cover design: Charles McStravick • *Interior design:* Riann Bender

Hafiz, excerpt from "Awake Awhile," from the Penguin publication *I Heard God
Laughing: Poems of Hope and Joy.* Copyright © 1996 & 2006 by Daniel Ladinsky and used
with his permission.

All rights reserved. No part of this book may be reproduced by any mechanical, pho-
tographic, or electronic process, or in the form of a phonographic recording; nor may it
be stored in a retrieval system, transmitted, or otherwise be copied for public or private
use—other than for "fair use" as brief quotations embodied in articles and reviews—without prior written permission of the publisher.

The author of this book does not dispense medical advice or prescribe the use of any
technique as a form of treatment for physical, emotional, or medical problems without the
advice of a physician, either directly or indirectly. The intent of the author is only to offer
information of a general nature to help you in your quest for emotional, physical, and
spiritual well-being. In the event you use any of the information in this book for yourself,
the author and the publisher assume no responsibility for your actions.

Cataloging-in-Publication Data is on file at the Library of Congress

Hardcover ISBN: 978-1-4019-5197-9

10 9 8 7 6 5 4 3 2
1st edition, February 2017

Printed in the United States of America

170,
44
DE

For everyone I have ever loved
in this life
or another.

For everyone who has ever loved me.

For all of my Love Teachers
in this world
and in the invisible, unfathomable
Realms of Divine Love.

For you,
who has chosen to travel
the sublime path of the Heart.

CONTENTS

PREFACE

"There is only one path to Heaven. On earth, we call it Love."
— Henry David Thoreau

From my highest heart to yours, I welcome you to this miraculous journey of Love and Awakening.

From my highest heart to yours, I am overjoyed that you found your way to this book, to me, and to what is meant to be nothing less than an ecstatic reunion with the Love that you always have been, are, and always will be.

From my highest heart to yours, I recognize you as a great seeker. I honor you as a courageous seeker. Even though I don't know your name, I do know that, if you've chosen to read these words, you are, indeed, a sincere fellow traveler on the Great Path.

I deeply honor the vast inner distance you've already traveled to have arrived here. All seekers must traverse these invisible distances within ourselves, distances that cannot be measured in miles yet are the hardest and most challenging part of our human adventure—the passage from the habit of turning away to the insistence on turning towards; the passage from the frightened part of you that says, *"I don't want to look at myself, I don't want to face things, I don't want to feel things"* to the brave part of you that finally proclaims: *"I will do whatever it takes to be free."*

Once, you made a promise. You promised to be here now, when awakening was dawning on this planet. You promised to remember in this body, in this lifetime, who you really are. You promised to wake up first and be a beacon of light for others, in whatever way you can, to remind them of the way home. You promised to make the choice for love.

Feel this truth arrive in your heart. Open to it. Allow it to fill you with joyful recognition.

Right now, in this moment, if you're reading or hearing these words, you *are* fulfilling your promise. *I promise to remember who I am before I die. I promise to never be seduced for too long by negativity or forgetfulness. I promise to remember that I am of the light, no matter how many voices in me try to convince me otherwise. I promise to walk the path of Love.*

So this is my first offering to you: No matter how imperfect you've thought you are, no matter how many times you've gotten lost, no matter how difficult your road has been or still is, no matter how much you may be going through or struggling with now, no matter how many people have disappointed you, no matter how much time you're afraid you've wasted, you *have* kept your promise.

When you've fallen, you have risen up.

When you've despaired, you have reached for hope.

When you've forgotten, you have remembered.

You have not forsaken your highest vow—the promise to awaken as a soul and not go back to sleep in this lifetime.

And so, just for a moment, I invite you to stop, and to love yourself for how far you have already come . . .

Once, I too made a promise. I made a promise to live my life serving love, surrendering to love, teaching love, and living love. For over forty years, my life has been dedicated to keeping that soul promise, and helping others keep theirs—to wake up, to remember, and to find their way back to love. During all that time, this book was waiting for the right moment to be born. Now, I am able to fulfill even more of my promise as I humbly offer to you *The Choice for Love.*

Coming Home to Love, Now More Than Ever

*"We are all born for love,
it is the principle of existence and its only end."*
— Benjamin Disraeli

There is a power in your heart far greater than anything you can imagine. This power is your love. It is the limitless, sublime, cosmic life force that pulsates within you, bringing meaning to everything it touches.

When that love flows into your relationships, it brings true intimacy and unbroken connection.

When that love flows into your work, it brings limitless creativity and vision.

When that love flows into your spiritual journey, it carries you all the way to awakening.

As you travel life's difficult roads and meet unexpected challenges, it is this love that becomes your saving grace. Right now, love is offering you an invitation to rediscover it in its fullness, to open yourself to it in ways you didn't know were possible, to learn how to be *in* love, and live *as* love.

You do not need to be in a relationship to love. You do not need to have conquered your fears to love. You do not need to be fully healed from the past to love. All you need to do to love is to feel the love that is already burning inside you, a fire whose spark cannot be extinguished no matter how many storms have tried to swallow its light.

Love is the living antidote for everything.
When you touch the center of your heart,
even for a brief moment,
you are Home.

We live in what are undeniably very troubling, unsettling, and disturbing times on our planet. It's easy to despair or retreat, and it is tempting to tune out and turn away from so much harshness, hatred, and suffering. Many of us are also experiencing unexpected personal changes, challenges, or inner and outer events that leave us with more questions than answers.

Now more than ever, it is vital to keep your promise.

Now more than ever, the world needs you to live your highest consciousness.

Now more than ever, each of us is being called to accelerate our process of transformation, healing, and awakening.

Now more than ever, we need to wake up and stay awake.

Now more than ever, we need to learn what it means to make the choice for love.

**No matter how fast we think we are growing and shifting,
we can go faster.**

**No matter how much we think we are healing,
we can heal more deeply and let go of more.**

**No matter how much we think we are loving—
both ourselves and others—we can love more.**

**Now, more than ever, the Choice for Love is
an essential spiritual practice,
and the highest service to our planet and humankind.**

*"We don't receive wisdom; we must discover it for ourselves after a journey
that no one can take for us or spare us."*

— Marcel Proust

For me, writing is a devoted act of love. It is the final phase of what is a profound, mystical, and sacred process: the creation of a living vortex of transformational energy that will be called a "book."

**The words in this book are more than just words—
they are vibrational bridges created for you to cross over,
and vibrational gateways for you to pass through.**

This enlivened, vibrational content is what is going to activate your most awakened consciousness and allow you to experience your own personal revelations and openings. *Therefore, I invite you to read the book through many times at your convenience to give yourself a chance to experience all that is has to offer,* since it will be impossible to absorb everything by going through it only once.

Like any gift, a book such as *The Choice for Love* is meant to not just be looked at and admired, but to be unwrapped, used, and lived. Throughout the book, I will offer you many practices and exercises. As you start using some of the techniques I offer, you'll begin to understand the information you've read from the inside out, rather than only from the level of your intellect. **Your realizations and awakenings will happen not because of my words, but because of your own experiences of integrating the concepts into action, and because of the wisdom that has emerged from that integration.**

Your Sacred Pilgrimage

"There is only one royal road for the spiritual journey . . . Love."
— Sathya Sai Baba

My highest intention is that the experience of this book will be a deeply meaningful and illuminating pilgrimage for you. What is a pilgrimage? It is not the same as a trip or a visit. When you embark on a physical pilgrimage, you travel to a sacred place, or go somewhere to meet a wise teacher or a holy person, with one sincere and elevated intention: *that you will return from your quest transformed from the inside out.* You hope you will not be the same as you were when you departed, that you will emerge rearranged, reignited, recharged with inspiration, reverberating with clarity, and altered in a way that is permanent and cannot be undone.

How, then, can a book be a pilgrimage? This is possible because while most pilgrimages have an outer timeline and structure—a trip to India, a visit to a holy cathedral, a retreat in nature—*the true transformational journey and authentic shift that one hopes will take place can actually only happen within us, as we travel the inner road from forgetfulness to remembrance, from limitation to freedom, and from separation to love.*

**This is the pilgrimage I invite you to take with me on these pages—
the pilgrimage that has you as its sacred destination;
the pilgrimage that promises you a reunion with none other than
your own inner temple of Heart-Wisdom,
and your own infinite Field of Love.**

As we embark on this divine and destined journey together, I invite you to receive the love that is being delivered through this book, through these words; to allow the wisdom and guidance to touch you, embrace you, and gently and compassionately usher you toward the innermost part of yourself.

May my words serve you on your sacred journey to wholeness.

May they open you, heal you, lift you, and guide you back to your own glorious, unbounded ocean of Love.

Thank you for keeping your promise.

Offered with the highest love,

Barbara De Angelis
October 2016
Santa Barbara, California

PART ONE

A NEW RELATIONSHIP WITH LOVE

1

Love Is All There Is

Returning Home through the Exquisite Doorway of the Heart

"The heart is the hub of all sacred places. Go there, and roam."
— Bhagawan Nityananda

From the moment we were born into this world, and perhaps even before, each of us has been traveling on a mysterious, miraculous soul journey. No matter where we believed we were going, wanted to go, or tried desperately not to go, no matter how many detours we've regrettably taken or unexpected delays we've encountered, that path has inevitably been leading us to one place: the exquisite doorway of the Heart. There, upon entering, we will have the astonishing revelation that the love we've been seeking in countless ways has been inside of us all along.

Your whole life has been a spectacular love story. Love is the most powerful force in our lives. It is invisible, immeasurable, and incomprehensible, drawing us toward itself with a gravitational pull that's impossible to resist.

You were conceived and created from love, and as soon as you arrived here, you began reaching for more love and haven't stopped since. As a child, your first act of will was to reach for your mother. You reached out for contact, for comfort, and for nourishment. As you grew you reached for toys and treats and things you loved and wanted. You reached for approval from your parents. You reached for friendships to keep you company. You reached for affection from lovers. You reached for a partner with whom you hoped to spend your life. You reached for the continuation of that love with your children and grandchildren.

My hope is that you've had many beautiful experiences of love. Ultimately, however, you must redirect your search from reaching out to reaching within, so you can retrieve the invaluable treasure that's waiting there for you.

Here is a story for you about that journey home to the heart.

At the time before Time, the Supreme Source that we often call God created the Universe, and everything in it—all of the physical matter; the plants and animals; the stars, planets, and galaxies; and His masterpiece, the human beings. As soon as God saw the humans, He felt so much love for them, as you would love your own children, and so naturally, He wanted to give His precious human offspring the greatest gift He could think of, which was the remembrance of their own divinity. God made it so, and every human knew they were the ultimate love disguised in human form, and naturally they were all very happy. This made God happy, and He sat back, ready to enjoy the play of life.

God was just beginning to relax, when suddenly, a group of the higher lords, guides, and celestial creatures demanded an emergency meeting with Him:

"God, we have a real problem. You gave these human beings the knowledge of their true divine nature, and you know what's happening? Every time one of them comes up against a challenge or hits a rough spot in their relationship, they say: *'Wait a minute—don't I remember being told that I am the same as the Source of All? If that's so, then why should I have to deal with all this earthly nonsense? After all, I'm not really this human form I am living in. I'm one with God. I am pure love. These dramas are too annoying, not to mention exhausting. Why even bother having any relationships? I'll just sit here by myself immersed in my own infinite presence.'*"

"And that's what they're doing," the Council members confessed. "One by one, the humans are deciding they don't see the point of pretending they're not God, and as soon as they do, they stop doing everything. **They're not learning any human lessons, they're not growing, they're not developing any compassion, and they're not even speaking to each other. They've dropped out of the Cosmic Game.**"

"Well, this is very disturbing," God admitted. *"The whole purpose of Creation was for these human beings to learn how to find their way through the obstacle course of their humanity back to their Divinity.* I wanted them to have the most precious thing in the Universe, which is the remembrance of their true supreme nature as love. Yet it seems by remembering it, they have no interest at all in living an earthly life."

"This development calls for drastic measures. **We are going to have to hide the secret of who they really are so that they won't be able to easily find it, and they'll be motivated to keep searching.**"

"I have an idea," one of the divine beings said. "There are some really tall mountains on Earth. We could hide it there."

"That won't work," God replied. "Human beings have a wonderful quality of setting their minds to a task and accomplishing it no matter how difficult it may be. They will be resourceful and find a way to climb the mountains."

Another being suggested, "Hide it at the bottom of the sea. They can't breathe under the water."

"They're going to invent submarines," God answered. "They'll go down and they'll find it."

"I've got it—hide it in outer space!" an Angel offered. "They can't get off the planet." God shook His head. "Sorry—I created them to be smart and infinitely clever. They'll advance scientifically, and one day they'll design ships that will fly all over the solar system."

"I know where you can hide it," a soft voice offered. God looked up and saw a young female angel.

"Yes, my dear?" God asked. "Where do you think we should hide the secret of who they are?"

"Hide it deep within the human heart. They'll never look for the divine love there."

God smiled, for He knew they had found the perfect hiding place. And immediately God made it so, and everywhere human beings instantly forgot who they really were. *And since that time, people have been searching high and low for the love that is already there inside of them.*

This book is about entering into a new kind of enlightened relationship with the most powerful, extraordinary force in the Universe that will fill you, heal you, guide you, and awaken you—*the relationship with your own infinite field of love.* There in the spiritual heart, you discover this hidden, cosmic gift of love that is your own true source and original home.

What is love? We usually think of love as an emotion we experience, or a bond we share with someone close to us. In order to experience a new, enlightened relationship with love, we have to open to a new, enlightened understanding of what love actually is:

Love isn't an emotion, a behavior, or even the connection you feel with another person—*it's a supercharged, light-drenched, limitless vibrational field of infinite divine energy.*

It is the source energy of everything that is, and the very essence of your being. It is dynamic and alive. It is the most essential vibration, and the glue of the Universe.

It's everything you've been searching for.

THE GREAT REUNION

*"Faith is not the clinging to a shrine
but an endless pilgrimage of the heart."*
— Abraham Joshua Heschel

In so many religious and spiritual traditions throughout history, the circle with a divine center has been a symbol of oneness and wholeness that radiates out to form creation. Four thousand years ago, prehistoric peoples built stone circles. Many ancient cultures including the Egyptians, the Druids, the Celts, and the Mayans incorporated circular designs as a part of their spiritual rituals. Perhaps you've seen a picture of a mandala, a beautiful spiritual and ritualistic symbol common to Buddhism and Hinduism that represents the Universe. Mandalas depict the journey from the cosmic center out to the manifest world, as well as the journey from outside back in.

From the sacred space at the center of the circle, life emerges. This is actually the truth of our everyday existence. Emanating out from the center of our Sun is a tremendous power that creates light and heat, giving us life as it has for thousands of millions of years. Without it, we would not exist.

In the same way, out of the center of a cell, the nucleus, all living things manifest, including you. You grew out of a circle, a cell, into more and more cells, until you took the form you're in now. The sacred geometry of the circle is everywhere, from the cornea of your eye, to the crystals that make up water, the orange you ate for breakfast, a snowflake, and out to the spiral of the galaxy. **Everything starts in the center and moves out from there.**

You can see this principle in action by taking a pebble and throwing it into a pond. A little circle forms around the pebble. That circle interacts with the water and forms another circle, and that circle forms another circle until there are many concentric circles spreading farther and farther from the center. What are these circles? *They are all just expressions of one vibration. That one vibration created everything that is emanating from it.*

This is the nature of who you are. **At your core is the same divine spark, the great cosmic intelligence that is at the core of everything else.** From that divine source, different expressions of creative intelligence rippled out until there was an embryo, and then your body, then your personality, and then the events in your life, and the things you do and experiences you have. You conclude: *"This is who I am—these ripples."* **But who you really are is so much more.**

The original Source/Light/Consciousness/Divinity from which you expanded is still there at the very center of all the ripples, still creating those waves and pulsations like the pebble in the pond.

The center of your center is the pulsation of pure love. It is known as the Heart.

When we think of our physical heart, we know it's a muscle that is responsible for pumping blood through your body and keeping you alive. However, your true heart is a non-physical, metaphysical heart. **This inner heart is the seat of that ultimate reality. It serves as the entry point for the soul from the divine, unlimited, source energy into your physical individuality and form.** *It is the home from which all of the ripples of who you are originate.*

The spiritual heart is the vibrational space spoken about by mystics and referenced in ancient spiritual texts—*"the hub of all sacred places,"* as beautifully articulated by Bhagwan Nityananda, a renowned, enlightened Indian saint. It's the connecting link between heaven and earth, and between the universal consciousness and your consciousness.

What is the nature of this vibrational heart? *It is an infinite ocean of love.* So your true soul journey is the journey back to the perfection and wholeness of that center, which is not far away, but is your very source and your very essence.

**The journey back to the center of the heart is the journey
back to your true birthplace, to the source of all love.
It is the Great Reunion.
It is the journey Home.**

This is the cosmic experience that has been written about in all religions. It reveals itself in different names and descriptions, but the message is the same:

From the Christian Bible:

"The Kingdom of God is within you." — Luke 17:21
"Blessed are the pure in heart, for they will see God." — Matthew 5:8

From the Zohar, the literature of Kabbalah:

"God conceals himself from the mind of man, but reveals himself to his heart."

From the Bhagavad Gita:

"I am the self seated in the hearts of all creatures."

From the Buddha:

"The way is not in the sky. The way is in the heart."

When great beings, saints, and mystics characterize their most transcendental experiences, they're almost never simply descriptions of a void or nothingness. *"It was just all love,"* they report. People who have near-death experiences, or temporarily leave the body and return back, share that they entered a place where there was love beyond anything we can comprehend.

Perhaps the God in our story was right—*our hearts were a great hiding place for the ultimate truth, because most of us look everywhere else but there for love.*

**You can't really "find" love anywhere else but inside of you.
You can find a relationship, but you can't find love.
Feeling love, then, isn't about feeling emotions.
It's about cultivating your inner connection to the divine
and to the ultimate field of love.**

RELATIONSHIPS:
SOULS JOYFULLY SPLASHING TOGETHER

"All life is one. Differences are superficial.
They are only in the outer; they are only in the body.
But one great common Consciousness dwells as the Reality
within all names and forms, with all creatures,
not only all human beings, in all creatures."

— Ramanujan

Sometime today, you turned on a faucet in your home or apartment, and water emerged. You used that water to cook, to take a shower, to wash your dishes, and for many other purposes. You need that water. It allows you to experience more happiness, ease, and enjoyment in life.

How does water flow into your home? The water comes from an enormous original source and collects in a smaller reservoir assigned to your home. It's carried into your house by an intricate set of pipes that then connect you with the water. Are the pipes the same as the water? *"That's a silly question!"* you think. *"Of course they're not."* **The pipes create the relationship between you and the water—they supply the water, but they are not the water.**

This metaphor will help us answer our next important question:

If love is a vibrational field of divine energy, what's the difference between love and a relationship?

Love is like the water of life. It's a divine, limitless source that nourishes us and supports us in so many ways. We need it to survive. Each of us has our own personal reservoir of that love called "the heart." Our heart is the place where we collect and access that water from the source.

When two people have a relationship, they're each accessing that love from their own separate, individual heart reservoir. You have your own personal set of "pipes" that connects you to your love, and the other person has their pipes connecting them to their love.

All of the components of a relationship—affection, communication, shared activities, and so on—*serve as vehicles for your love to flow out and interact with someone else's love,* kind of like two streams of energy interacting together. (Visualize two streams of water dancing and splashing.) **But the source of that love is inside of you.**

A relationship is not the same as love.
Love is a vibrational field of sublime, life-enhancing energy.
A relationship is a vehicle through which you can experience love.
Another person is also a vehicle through which you can experience love.
But they're not the source of the love.
Love doesn't come from the outside of your life in.
Love comes from the inside out.

So what is it that we're feeling when we feel love?
What we call the "feeling" of love is the vibrational experience of the limitless field of cosmic energy as it moves into us and through us. That means any love we're feeling is divine love!

Why is it that you feel more love in one moment than you do in another? Here's the best way I know how to describe it:

Remember that you have your own individual reservoir of love—your heart. You can imagine your heart like your personal ocean filled with the energy of love.

1. Someone comes along—your mate, your child, your friend—and does something or says something that is sweet, kind, and caring.

2. Their loving energy is like the wind: it stirs your vibrational ocean of love energy to rise up in waves.

3. The stronger the wind of the other person's vibrational energy, the bigger the waves of your own love that you feel rising up in your heart.

Isn't this an illuminating way to understand what we mean by "love"? When you "feel" love, you're actually experiencing the movement of that life force rising up within you, like a quiet ocean suddenly rising up in waves. The same amount of water is always there in the ocean, but when it moves into waves, it seems like something greater has happened, as if the ocean itself has become bigger. **Love is always there within you, but sometimes it rises up in waves, and suddenly, you "feel" love.**

So perhaps some new, enlightened translations of the phrase "I love you" are:

"My love is rising up in waves."

or

"Your wind makes wonderful waves on the ocean of my heart!"

Once we gain this new, enlightened understanding of love and relationships, something else instantly becomes clear:

When we feel love, we're never falling in love.
We're always rising in love.

IT'S ALWAYS YOUR OWN LOVE

Have you ever wondered: *"How does someone else's love get into me?"* The answer is: "It doesn't!" No one gives you a transfusion of love, or provides bottles of love for you to drink every day. No one shoots a big stream of love at you with a special hose. *When you register that you're feeling love, nothing has been added to you that can be measured.* That's because nothing has been added at all. **It's always just your own love.**

Think back on the relationships you've ever had. Whether they turned out horribly or turned out wonderfully, *it was always your own love you were feeling.* Someone would do or say the right things that gave your love permission to rise up. **But the other person didn't actually put something substantial into your heart. Nothing they did added to the volume of your love. You simply decided to allow yourself to feel your love, opened the valve, and your own love began to flow out and rise up. But it was your love.**

Love isn't something we can actually "get" from anyone else.
No one can give you any love you don't already have.
No one can fill you with anything you don't already possess.
Sometimes you feel it, and sometimes you don't,
but all the love you ever feel is yours,
rising up from within you from the source of all love.
Love is its own source.

We usually assign our own experiences of love to another person, as if they're the source of what we're feeling—but they never truly are. Of course, relationships give you the experience of delight, enjoyment, comfort, camaraderie, and much more. The other person can be a great *"wave-maker."* But it's your love, and your ocean.

In the same way, your love doesn't leave your heart and flood into someone else's, filling them up and removing their emptiness. *Your love can call out to someone else's love, but it can't give them love they don't already have.* Each of us must learn how to move through the gateway of our own heart and access the treasure trove of love that is there before we can even experience love in anyone else's presence.

Here's a suggestion of how you can begin to notice these moments of your own love rising up the next time you're with someone you love:

Perhaps you're hugging your partner, or meeting a friend for lunch, or watching one of your children play, or observing your dog or cat do something adorable.

Simply become aware of the vibration of energy—that feeling you call love—rising up from your own heart. Allow yourself to feel it. Notice the waves of that love moving higher as you experience the energy of the other person.

Don't try to think anything to make yourself feel more loving.

In that moment, just recognize that what you're feeling is your own love. No one actually gave anything to you. Your own love is rising.

You can quietly acknowledge this and say to yourself:
Right now, I can feel my love rising.
In the presence of your heart, the waves of my ocean of love rise high.
My waves really love splashing against your waves.
But it is still my love.

WHAT IS THE CHOICE FOR LOVE?

"We are already one. But we imagine that we are not.
And what we have to recover is our original unity.
What we have to be is what we are."

— Thomas Merton

What if you could experience the fullness of your own love rising up in every moment of your life?

What if you could learn how to be "in love" all the time?

What if you could become a powerful field of overflowing love that uplifted and blessed everyone you met?
This is what awaits you when you make the choice for love.

The choice for love is a revolutionary and revelatory shift in your relationship with the energy of love itself. It invites you into a new, enlightened experience of love as a vibrational state of being.

It's the choice to allow yourself to feel the innate, limitless fullness of your heart.

It's the choice to invite love in its limitlessness to flow through you, work through you, express itself through you, and serve others through you.

It's the choice to have a totally conscious, committed, dynamic relationship with the field of love that dwells within you, as you.

As we'll see, the choice for love isn't a choice to simply be more loving toward others, perform more kind and loving acts, or remind yourself to think more loving thoughts. That book would be titled *The Choice to Love*. It's also not a manual to teach you how to look for love, or to figure out how to get other people to give you more love. Of course, that book would be *The Chase for Love*!

We all want love. However, we mistakenly believe that we need to wait until something happens from the outside to give us an experience of love.

We wait for someone to behave in a certain way so we can feel love.

We wait for something to happen that inspires us to feel loving.

We wait to see how we perform or what we accomplish so we can feel love for ourselves.

What this means is that *we're waiting for love to choose us.* We wait for love to reveal itself in some way that we recognize, and then we *give ourselves permission to feel our love.* The choice for love does just the opposite.

Love is a choice that *we* make from moment to moment.
Don't wait for Love to choose you.
In each moment, you can choose Love.

This is such a profound understanding. We don't have to wait to feel love, as if we hope it will be arriving at any moment. We know that love is the Prime Condition—in fact, *our* Prime Condition, and our true nature. *So there's nothing to wait for. There's simply a new kind of choice to make.* **Instead of looking for it, or waiting to receive it or to feel it, we learn how to choose it, to find that highest frequency of love and connect ourselves with it.**

So the choice for love means the choice to recognize, reconnect with, and swim in the unlimited and enormous field of love that is your most essential vibration.

> **The choice for love is the outward movement of the**
> **vibrational field of love that exists within you.**
> **You choose to bring that inner field of love out,**
> **giving it a direction and destination.**
> **When you feel that love moving from inside of you out,**
> **you're experiencing the movement of the life force itself.**

When we make the choice for love, we will be recalibrating ourselves to that most elevated vibration and allowing that energy to take form in our life. How does that unlimited energy of love express itself? It manifests as *delight, passion, compassion, connectedness, creativity, consciousness, wisdom, integrity, service, and the list goes on and on!*

> **You may or may not have the relationship you want.**
> **You may or may not feel good about yourself or your life.**
> **But you don't have to wait to feel love.**
> **You can make the choice for love.**

Expanding into this new understanding of love radically transforms and expands the possibilities for the way we experience love. It is a shift from *"I am loving"* to *"I love."*

Love usually means:
I AM LOVING (*fill in the blank*).
I am loving my husband, my daughter, my dog, my garden, my new car, etc.

When we make the choice for love, we begin to have a new experience:
I AM LOVE.
I am love, and love is rising up in me and expressing itself through me, flowing toward that person/object/experience.

Love becomes the way we relate to the entire world, and not just to a particular person or experience. We don't need a specific object of love for the energy of love to rise up.

I LOVE . . . and whatever is in my path will experience that love. I am a walking field of love.

We can take this one step further: It's not even that *your* love is rising up, or that *your* love is flowing out. **The truth is, it's THE love. There's only one love. THE love is rising up within you, and moving out through you.**

This is the journey we're taking together in these pages. As you'll learn in the upcoming chapters, making the choice for love requires learning how find your way back to the innermost part of yourself, your divine essence, beyond your personality and beyond your circumstances. You'll discover how to unblock the channels between yourself and that unlimited cosmic force, and increase your capacity to hold and transmit more of that source energy out to the world. Reuniting with your own immense field of love, you'll be free to make new, enlightened choices about how you relate to yourself and to others. Your shimmering, overflowing heart will bless the planet with love.

You Are Always in Love

"He who is filled with love is filled with God Himself."
— St. Augustine

As we begin to recognize what love truly is, it's easier to understand the overwhelming desire that can draw us to other human beings—*we are being pulled toward a mirror of our own formless self in another form.* We find delight in gazing at the heart-ocean of another human being in whom love is dancing and feeling our own love rise up and join in.

Love is the highest spiritual practice.
The boundaries between ourselves and others melt,
and we experience the true "We" and true Oneness.
Love is the way the Divine manifests and flows
in a tangible form from human to human.
That's how we get to experience heaven on earth—
through loving each other.

Haven't you experienced this looking into someone else's eyes? You know the two of you are different beings, and yet there is oneness flowing between you. The sense of boundaries melts, and something that is neither you nor them reveals itself. This is the sacred "we," which we'll talk more about.

When your ocean of love and someone else's ocean of love rise up together, love gets to dance with itself.

This is an enlightened relationship:
both of you agree to feel your own love at the same time.
That love resonates back and forth like a joyous bridge
connecting your two hearts.
Side by side, you celebrate the miracle of the love
that is dancing within each of you and between you.

All of us love the idea and experience of being "in love." *"I wish I was in love,"* we dream when we're single. Then later, when we have a *relationship,* we complain: *"I remember when we first fell in love, and wish we were more in love now."*

Here is the astounding truth: The highest part of you is that place that reverberates with love. The essence of you *is* that love. Therefore, you are always, already *in* love!

> **Right now, you *are* IN love.**
> **You have always been IN love.**
> **You can't *not* be IN love.**
> **You can cut yourself off from feeling it,**
> **or have a difficult time accessing it.**
> **But you will still be IN love.**
>
> **Love is all there is.**
> **It is everywhere. It's everything.**
> **It's limitless.**
>
> **Therefore, love is all you are.**
> **It's an unlimited ocean of divine energy**
> **You're already *in* it.**
> **In fact, you *are* it.**

As we'll see, we have to be in the state of love before we can have any kind of meaningful relationship. Learning how to be "in love" by ourselves, with ourselves, will allow us to experience true love for the first time.

THE ENLIGHTENED SOLUTION:
LEARNING HOW TO MAKE THE CHOICE FOR LOVE

"I will fill the world with love and create Heaven on Earth."
— Maharishi Mahesh Yogi

We are living in a vibrational Universe. Modern science tells us that everything in the Universe—all sound, light, and matter, including you—is simply pure energy vibrating at different frequencies. What we see as solid matter just appears to be solid, but when one looks at that matter on a sub-atomic level, it isn't matter at all, but pure energy. We are all vibrating consciousness.

Love is the supreme and highest vibration in the Universe. **When you're in the space and vibration of love, you spontaneously align with your highest. You're vibrating at your highest possible frequency. When you make the choice for love, you're choosing your highest.**

For this reason, learning how to make the choice for love is the ultimate solution and the ultimate vibrational remedy. There is no situation that will not benefit from being met with more Love:

No matter what you're faced with, the solution is Love.
More love, not less love.
More love for yourself.
More love for others.
More love for the Journey.
More love for your humanness.
More love for your challenges.
More love for your pain.
More love for your fear.
More love for your battles.
More love for the part of you
that doesn't want to give more Love.
Love is always the missing ingredient in every dilemma.

When it's dark and you bring in just a little bit of light, the darkness instantly disappears. There is no more darkness. **Love is like that, because the nature of that divine field of energy is light. If you bring love to something, the darkness will vanish.** That's why when someone is vibrating with a lot of love, we say, *"She's just glowing!"* They look as if they're illuminated from within—and they are. When you are feeling love, the world looks brighter, and it's easier to see the light in others because your own vision is infused with more light.

My telling of an old Sufi fable:

There was once a dark Cave who lived deep down in the ground where no one ever ventured. The Cave had never seen any light, and therefore never imagined that it existed.

One day, the great Sun decided to send an invitation to the Cave, beckoning it up into the sky to visit and see the light. The Cave didn't understand what the word "light" meant, but, not wanting to be rude to the Sun, who seemed very important, accepted the invitation. When the Cave arrived high up in the heavens, it was astonished at what it beheld. It had never seen light before, and it became overwhelmed by its magnificence, so much that it didn't want to leave.

The Cave decided that it was only fair to return the kindness, and so it invited the Sun to come down to where it lived deep in the earth so the Sun could experience the darkness. The Sun had never seen this "darkness," and actually had no idea what the word meant, but gladly accepted the Cave's invitation.

The next day came, and as promised, the Sun entered the Cave. It began searching for this "darkness" the Cave had described, but no matter where the Sun looked, all it saw was light. The Sun turned to the Cave and said, "Excuse me, Cave. I don't mean to be rude, but where is the darkness that you described that exists here with you? This looks just like where I live—all I see is Light."

Love carries its own light.
It illuminates any space it touches.

How do we begin making the choice for love?

We make the choice for loving ourselves no matter what we are going through, and no matter what we are facing.

We make the choice for loving ourselves no matter how many times we've fallen or faltered.

We make the choice for loving ourselves compassionately, even when we see so much else about us that is not love.

We make the choice for bringing love to our relationships, even when there is difficulty, discord, and so many reasons to shut down, shut off, turn away, and not love.

We make the choice for seeing the existence of the highest in others, even when they themselves have forgotten or forsaken it.

We make the choice for bringing love to the challenging and painful situations with which we're faced, even as our mind says, *"There's nothing to love there. There is no way to be loving."*

For me, making the choice for love has been the cornerstone of my own spiritual path, and love has been and still is my most essential spiritual practice. *Every time in my life I've been unsure of what to do, how to proceed; every time I've been weighed down by my own fears, anxieties, or concerns; every time someone else hurt me, disappointed me, wounded me, or betrayed me, I would call on love.* **I would decide that I was going to make** the choice for love, even if, at first, I didn't know what that meant, or how it would even be possible.

We have an exciting, powerful, and transformative journey ahead of us on these pages. Along with teachings and wisdom, I'll be offering you many Choice for Love Practices that are designed to help you align with your own highest vibration of love, and connect you with your most expanded heart, moment by moment.

To help you begin, here's the most basic and powerful Choice for Love Practice.

MAKING THE CHOICE FOR LOVE

To choose love in each moment,
simply ask yourself these two questions:

How can I bring more love to [_____*]?

What would that look like right now?

* Put in the name or description of the situation.

This is an essential practice that instantly raises your vibration, expands your consciousness, and moves the energy of love from inside of you out. I use this many times a day in my own life, and have taught this to thousands of students, who say that it has changed everything about how they live and love.

The power of these questions is **that you're not asking yourself:**

"How do I fix the other person in this situation?"
or
"What can I do to manage/control/manipulate/avoid the situation?"
or
"What could someone else do to bring more love to this situation?"

Rather, you're invoking your highest self, and by doing that, you've already made the choice for love.

The moment you ask: *"How can I bring love to this situation?"*
you've already shifted into the vibration of love.
You're already bringing more love to the situation.
The moment you ask: *"What would that look like right now?"*
you've already opened your vision to a new possibility,
and invited your higher consciousness to show you
some more enlightened options.

It's important to understand that these questions aren't meant to act like a token you put in a machine and out pops a prize. *They are vibrational questions, designed to recalibrate you by just your asking them.* You may ask: *"How can I bring the most love to this situation?"* and at first receive the answer *"I have absolutely no idea!"* Don't worry. It's normal for your intellect to answer first. Continue to ask until a choice or direction reveals itself, and it will. *Just by asking, you've called on love to show itself to you. The moment you start working with these questions, you've already made the choice for love.*

When you ask, it can be helpful to replace the word *situation* with the specifics. Here are some examples:

How can I bring more love to <u>the challenge I'm facing with my project at work?</u> What would that look like right now? *(Ask for more help. Celebrate the progress I've already made instead of beating myself up. Make a list of past challenges I've overcome. Stop gossiping about my project partner and undermining him by not including him in my research.)*

How can I bring more love to <u>this argument I'm having with my husband right now?</u> *(Tell him I appreciate the fact that he's willing to discuss this issue instead of making him wrong for not agreeing with me. Give him a hug. Suggest we take a break and go out for a walk. Remind myself of why I love him instead of focusing on how much I dislike this part of him.)*

How can I bring more love to: my impatience with my child/ this event I don't want to attend/the difficult conversation I'm about to have with my employee/anything? What would that look like right now?

You can also use this slightly adjusted version of the Choice for Love Questions that may help you go even deeper into the answers.

"How can I bring *the most* love to this situation?"

When you're in the space and vibration of Love, you spontaneously align with your highest. You're vibrating at your highest. *Choosing love, you can live in your highest. If you have nothing else to guide you, allow these questions to be your compass and your map. They will take you deep into the very center of your heart, and up to the very heights of your most enlightened consciousness.*

Opening Yourself to the Presence of Love

"We are more than just physical beings, we are whispers of love dancing in the breeze."

— Micheal Teal

We are all seeking the most exalted spiritual experiences, and I believe the most sacred of those is love. Love offers us an opportunity to have a living experience of the divine. It is the only activity in which we rise above our separateness and glimpse the indivisible unity that is the truth of who we each and all are.

**Love between yourself and another person is perhaps
the most intimate way you can participate in the great mystery.
You have the experience in which your boundaries
and the other person's boundaries melt.
For a moment, you transcend the illusion of separation,
and merge into oneness, not just with one another,
but with everything.
You become love.**

Over the course of my lifetime, I've spent many months on very long meditation retreats, initially in my younger days with my first teacher, and then, several decades after he went into seclusion, at the ashram of my second teacher. These were exquisite periods during which I could completely immerse myself in the depths of consciousness, practicing 12–15 hours of meditation a day, sometimes for six months or more, and living in almost total silence. I know that for most people, this probably sounds like a nightmare, but for me, it was bliss.

It was during one of these extended six-month retreats in the early 1970s that I experienced what I consider my spiritual initiation into love. This is a very personal story, one I've never shared publicly, but it belongs in this chapter about our return home to the heart.

One afternoon, I was meditating in my room, deep in a very silent and unbounded state. Suddenly I began to expand, and expand, and expand. All boundaries of time, space, and reality melted, and I completely left this body, this world, and this plane of existence.

Any sense of Barbara, any sense of individuality, any sense of anything but oneness did not exist. I (*although there was no "I" left*) was just in the great All. *It wasn't that "I" was feeling the Love. The "I" had melted into the Love. It was just Love. Love was everything.*

In that state, there was an awareness that everything in the Universe was created out of love, and everything that didn't look like love was still love. Everything that appeared separate from love was also love. There was nothing else, for how could there be? *It was all love.*

This was a knowingness, and even that knowingness was just love. It wasn't exciting. There were no thoughts like *"Wow, I'm having an outrageous spiritual experience,"* for there was no Barbara to think the thoughts. **I was love being aware of itself as love.**

I was in this state for what I later would come to realize was several hours, and at some point in that infinite Love, the tiniest fluctuation emerged, the glimmer of a consciousness of "I." *I am. I exist.* Slowly, that "I" began to become more conscious of itself: *"I am in a body living on the planet Earth. I need to return to that body now."* Even then, the experience was of love returning to a body, love breathing, love putting back on the costume of Barbara, love taking on a form.

Eventually, I found myself back inside of Barbara, in this body, sitting in my room.

When I emerged from that experience, I was permanently transformed. **For the first time in my life, I knew who I was. I had experienced my true lineage, and that changed everything—***I was love.* **And I knew that everyone else was also love.**

When I left my room later that evening to go to dinner, nothing looked the same or felt the same, and it hasn't ever since.

This experience changed my life. Now that I knew that love was the only and prime condition, and the source of everything, including me, I began looking for love everywhere, recognizing love everywhere, tuning into the vibration of love everywhere, and figuring out how to find my way back to love in all circumstances.

One of the other immeasurable gifts this experience offered me was the truly expansive and thrilling understanding that *when we tap into love even for a second, we tap into all of it*. When we plug into love for a brief moment, we plug into the wholeness and the source of love. This is why I've shared my story, because it reveals why our choice for love will be even more profound than we can imagine.

Love is love.
The full force of love is available in each drop of love.
Love you experience in one moment is love with everything.
Love you experience with one person is love with everyone.
Love with anything is love with God, Spirit, and the Great Source.

You've probably had a special moment similar to this, when your normal reality dropped away, and you suddenly felt an enormous wave of Love. Maybe you were holding your partner, or watching your sleeping child, or worshipping at church, or deep in prayer, or outside experiencing the mysterious beauty of nature. In that instant, you realized that everything you'd been telling yourself about being unloved or not good enough, and all of your stories and patterns were absolutely an illusion. In that instant, the limited ego, with all of its papers, affidavits, evidence, and reasons to prove that you're disconnected from spirit, looks like a foolish, annoying clown who's interrupting your bliss with stupidity! In that moment, you *know* love is real.

Making the choice for love is nothing less than a spiritual path that leads us back to wholeness. We learn first to feel our own love without limitation, to open to it, surrender to it, and bathe our wounds in its healing presence so we can become a pure vessel to receive and carry that love.

We emerge then from the temple of our heart to bring that love out to the world.

When you discover your own, inexhaustible love inside, you will begin to experience an intoxicating freedom. It's the freedom to be *in* love, no matter who is or who isn't loving you. It's the freedom to drink and fill up your own love, to celebrate the mysterious miracle of its presence in your heart.

> Love that no one can take away
> emerges from your own self.
> Invite others to enter into that state of your own love.
> You are the source of the love.
> Remember: someone may come to swim in your ocean,
> but it's your water!

OPENING TO THE PRESENCE OF LOVE

I want to offer you one more *wisdom souvenir* from this first part of our journey. It's the Choice for Love Recalibration Mantra:

CHOICE FOR LOVE
RECALIBRATION MANTRA

I open myself to the presence of Love within me.

Introduce this phrase into your awareness any time you like. You may want to gently hold it in your consciousness when sitting with your eyes closed, taking a walk, right before you go to sleep, or whenever you need to feel more centered and expanded. You can write the words down and place reminders on your refrigerator, on your computer, in your car, or on your bathroom mirror.

This is *not* the same as an affirmation. It's a vibrational gateway designed to create an opening in your heart, and not just an impression on your mind.

"Opening" means you are creating energetic space for something to happen. You're making the choice to experience love inside of you. You aren't waiting for love to do something—*you're choosing love.*

"Presence" means it is already there in you. It doesn't have to arrive from anywhere. It's waiting for you to experience it. You're not waiting for love, hoping it will show up. *Love is already, always waiting for you.*

"Within me" reminds you that you're not looking for the presence of love outside of yourself. It is the love inside of you, at the source of you.

Honor this presence of love as your own love, as *the love.*

Remember: you are that love . . .

I open myself to the presence of love that is within me.
May it reveal itself to me now.
May it rise up in magnificent, glorious waves.
May it welcome me home.

❀ 2 ❀

The Big Melt

Healing Your Relationship with Love

*"We waste time looking for the perfect lover,
instead of creating the perfect love."*
— Tom Robbins

You have a relationship you may have forgotten about. You might not be aware of its existence, even though it's the most important relationship you'll ever have. In fact, all of your other intimate connections— with your partner, your children, your parents, your friends, and your co-workers—are dependent on it. ***It's your relationship to love.***

Your relationship to love isn't the same as your relationship to *loving.* *It's about the way you relate to that source energy of love itself.* Just like your partnership or association with an individual is characterized by certain attitudes, behaviors, and choices on your part, so too you have an actual interactive relationship with the energy of love.

What kind of relationship do you have with love? It may be a co-operative relationship, or a contentious relationship, a harmonious relationship or an adversarial relationship. It may be a steady, consistent relationship, or an erratic, dramatic relationship. From moment to moment, consciously or unconsciously, you're choosing how to relate to that unlimited love energy that's available within you.

**When you're in a relationship with another person,
you're actually in a threesome!
You're having two relationships at once: one with other person,
and another with the energy of love inside of you.**

I like to say that *"love is always on the move."* We know from physics that the nature of all energy is to move, and as we've seen, love is the highest source of energy. So the nature of love is that it wants to move, flow, and express itself.

For a moment, picture an infant who's just a few months old. They reach out to be picked up. They grasp your finger with their tiny hand. They lean their head against your body. As soon as they get a little older, they begin to offer love to everybody: they touch the dog's face; they kiss their brother or sister; they embrace their teddy bear; they give a Cheerio to a stranger; they run to hug you when you enter the room. **They don't keep their Love in. They don't horde it. They can't contain it. It pours out.** *That's the nature of love on the move.*

It's not the nature of Love to be contained, controlled, or stagnant. It's the nature of Love to flow.

The experience we have of love moving through us and looking for an object of focus—our partner, our child, our friend —is the inherent longing of love to experience more of its own delight.

Most of us hear this and think, *"This sounds wonderful. Of course I want as much love in my life as possible—the more the better. There are no limits on how much love, joy, and expansion I'm willing to feel!"*

For many people, however, this isn't quite what happens. Instead of allowing ourselves to feel the full power of that essential love energy, **we interfere with the flow and movement of that life force.** *We attempt to control, manage, and modulate the flow of love.*

Instead of making the choice for love, we often make the choice for not feeling, and limiting the experience of our own heart.

When we're trying to manage our emotions and feelings of love, we end up pushing away the very love we long for.

PUTTING THE BRAKES ON INTENSITY

My wonderful, blessed mother was an unusual driver, as I believe were many women in her generation, since they learned to drive a bit later in life. Basically, her driving style consisted of having one foot on the gas and the other on the brake, practically at the same time. She liked driving fast, so she'd push down the accelerator, but then she would get nervous, so she'd pump the brake, which would jerk the car around as it slowed down. Then she'd speed up again, and pump the brake some more. Accelerate and brake, accelerate and brake.

My mother liked the intensity of going fast, but she didn't like the feeling of being out of control when the car would speed up. She had what I'd call a "conflicted relationship with intensity." I've shared this sweet story because one of the most important keys to understanding and transforming your relationship with love is to learn more about your own relationship to intensity.

Everything that most of us want—more love, more abundance, more success, more opportunities, more connection to Spirit—will inevitably bring more energy into our lives, and more energy coming in means more intensity. What do we mean when we say something is making us feel intense? *Intensity just means we're experiencing a lot of vibrational energy.* It's the life force moving through us in an accelerated and profound way.

"That honest conversation with my husband was intense." "Going to the hospital to visit my father was so intense." "It was really intense to find out my ex-partner is getting married." Each of these situations naturally stirs up a lot of strong emotions. **When we feel something is intense, it means there's an increase in the amount of vibrational energy moving through us.**

If we aren't comfortable handling strong vibrational surges of emotional energy, we will be "in tension." Why? There's a battle between the energy we're feeling and our discomfort in feeling it. **It is not the intensity that's the problem—*it's our resistance to it.***

> **If we have discomfort with intensity, it may create a battle between our desire for more love and intimacy on one hand, and our resistance to intensity on the other.**
> *We want to experience more love, but we're not so crazy about experiencing more intensity.*

Perhaps you can relate to this "vibrational battle": *I want to move, but I also want to be in control. I want to grow and expand, but I also want to manage everything that happens. I want to experience Spirit and divine love, but I don't want to feel overwhelmed by the energy. I want to be close, but I don't want to need you.*

Here's a new perspective: Contrary to what we tell ourselves, **emotional discomfort is *not* from feeling. It's from you *fighting the*** *feeling while you are having it.* When we feel things are too intense, we need to realize that it's not the experience that's causing the problem. It is our *discomfort with and resistance to the increase of energy* that is creating a feeling of tension within us.

If you let feeling flow, it's just like letting water out of an enclosed place—it moves, and the pressure subsides. *It's when you're feeling and trying to not feel that you get into trouble.*

The amount of energy it takes to hold back your Love is enormous. That's because Love is the life force—remember: it wants and needs to move outward into manifestation. **When you attempt to contain it, stockpile it, modulate it, block it, or ignore it, you make your feelings of Love the enemy, and this is a battle you will eventually lose.** The inevitable inner collisions that erupt will create a state of tremendous tension inside of you.

Love doesn't create discomfort.
It's your battle with Love that creates discomfort.
When you try to suppress love,
you've declared war on your own heart.
The choice for love is the choice to allow love to flow,
and learn to joyfully participate in the dance of the life force
as it moves through you, as you, and between you and another.

Your relationship to intensity doesn't just affect your intimate relationships. It can also have a significant impact on how successful or creative you allow yourself to be. I see examples of this all the time. *Someone wants to be more expansive and more successful, but they get to a certain threshold and stop.* There are many reasons for this, but one is that they unconsciously play small because some part of them knows they can't handle the increased intensity that will come with more responsibility, more exposure, and more accomplishment. They're afraid it will be too much and too uncomfortable, and so just when they begin to really expand, they suddenly contract and slow down.

Did you know that this is also how many of us who are seekers approach our process of growth and personal transformation? We start to move and feel our progress going faster and faster, and so much is changing, and we don't feel completely in control. Suddenly we think: *"Oh my gosh, this is too intense,"* and like my sweet mother, we start pumping the brake of our "car of consciousness" in order to try to slow it down a little bit, even while we feel like we should be speeding up. Then we wonder why we aren't further along.

How many times have you found yourself thinking, *"I can't handle any more* [fill in the blank]*"*: Love, responsibility, opportunities, revelations, decisions, demands for your time or advice. *But you can! It's an illusion that you're at your limit.* In the next chapter, I'll explain more about how to expand your capacity to hold enormous amounts of love, wisdom, and power—kind of like opening the overflow seating section in a restaurant, or adding new memory to your computer.

Hopefully you're beginning to understand more about your relationship to love. For now, begin to contemplate this important Choice for Love Recalibration Question:

"What is my relationship to intensity?"

THE INVISIBLE BATTLE: ARE YOU AFRAID OF LOVE?

*"Love takes off masks that we fear we cannot live without
and know we cannot live within."*
— James Arthur Baldwin

What is it about love that is so intense?

Why do we battle with the one thing we crave and long for the most?

When we finally have the intimate connection we've been seeking, why do we often do everything we can to disconnect?

What's so frightening about intimacy that we're often willing to risk losing it rather than surrender to it?

Have you ever wondered if you are afraid of emotional intimacy? Try imagining yourself with someone you really love. Perhaps you're talking and sharing the deepest parts of yourself. Perhaps you're lying quietly together, or holding hands watching the sunset, or gazing at your children safely asleep in their beds? Each moment pulls you closer and closer together, and you begin to feel something bigger than the two of you—it is a powerful energy of oneness. You have the sensation of falling into the other person, and you're both falling together into an intense swirl of love.

At first, you may love this feeling. You're so happy to be experiencing this kind of deep connection with another person. Then you might notice that you're *beginning to feel anxious and out of control*. Your usual boundaries are melting, and you aren't sure where you end and your lover begins. Your familiar protections have collapsed, and you suddenly feel vulnerable. It's as if you're being swallowed up by something and can't stop it.

If you're not able to hold that much vibrational intensity, you might pull back in this moment and turn away from the love for fear that you'll lose yourself in it. You may feel you need some space, or find ways to push the other person away in an attempt to avoid intimacy and prevent more moments of closeness. You might crave retreat from your partner, and in extreme cases, even from the relationship, and not understand why.

In moments like this, what are you afraid of? Drowning in your own vast ocean of love. Losing your separateness and being kidnapped into an experience of oneness that leaves no room for your individuality. Caring too much. Needing too much. Feeling too much. Loving too much.

If control and protection have been high up on your agenda,
you may find yourself terrified of true, deep love
and the intense moments of surrender it requires of you.
And you will find ways to flee from them.

The experience of oneness is always very powerful, whether with a lover, a friend, a child, or an animal companion. Sometimes, the intensity of that love and the sense of our boundaries melting can frighten us. One way we may try to manage that intensity and longing for love is to decide that *we don't really need it*. Our needs become our enemy, and we try to deny them, ignore them, and numb ourselves to them.

This is the invisible battle many of us have been waging inside of ourselves for most of our lives. *We become experts at modulating and managing the intensity of love and connection*, not only with intimate partners but with friends, family, and even our children.

Most of the time, we're unconscious that we're engaged in this tug-of-war. *"I love my husband. I cherish my best friend. Why would I ever push them away even for a minute?"* we wonder. And yet we secretly suspect that sometimes we do. Perhaps you're also recognizing someone you care about in this description, someone you love who seems to have a difficult time allowing themselves to fully feel.

**When we withhold love consciously or unconsciously,
we're not withholding from anybody else but ourselves.
No one misses the love as much as we do.
No one suffers as much as we do.
No one's ripped off as much we are.
When we decide to manage and modulate Love, we always lose.
When we truly love, no matter what the outcome,
we never lose.**

Why would you limit the amount of love you're willing to feel? Love is always a gift. Your love clears your own eyes. It washes the debris from your vision. When you're seeing through the eyes of love, everybody looks better. When you're not allowing your own Love to flow, everything looks empty and flat. Love makes the world beautiful.

How Big Is the Pool of Your Heart?

*"When you feel wretched, when you fall in your weakness,
have a dip in that pool of love."*
— Meher Baba

Imagine you and a friend are on vacation at a resort and want to go for a swim. The resort has two pools from which to choose. You walk over to the first pool and notice that the water level has drained down, and the pool has only a few feet of water at the bottom. *"Do they expect people to swim in this?"* you say to your friend in disbelief. You decide to check out the next pool, and once you find it, you're delighted to discover that it's filled to the brim with clear, sparkling water.

Which pool are you going to bathe in? Are you going to dive into the half-filled pool? No, you're going to swim in the pool that's overflowing with water.

Each of our hearts is like a pool of love. The question is: **What kind of pool of love are you?** Are you a pool that is filled up with love, one where people just want to "dive into" your energy? Are you a pool that's half-full, causing others to think: *"Do you expect me to dive into that? I could hurt myself"*?

What is it that fills up the pool of our heart? There's no limit to the amount of love that we can feel, or that's available to us. We just need to open the valve that controls how much of that cosmic life force we're willing to experience.

A few years ago, while I was visiting Hawaii, there was a tsunami warning. A large earthquake had erupted in New Zealand, and scientists were warning residents of the Hawaiian Islands that there was a possibility of tsunami waves. I remember thinking, *"This is amazing. Hawaii is 5,000 miles away from New Zealand, and yet energy from the waves there might travel all the way to these islands."* This movement of the wave energy is possible because of the size of the physical matter that's available to act as a conductor for that energy—in this case, the huge ocean.

When you throw a stone in a pool, it will create a ripple. If the pool has edges, the wave energy will stop expanding at some point when it hits a dead end. On the other hand, if you create a disturbance in a vast body of water, the wave will keep going and going because there's so much more space through which it can move.

In this same way, if the pool of your heart is tiny, and you transmit a wave of love, or wisdom, or intention, it can travel only so far and have a limited effect. What if your pool of the heart was even bigger, like the size of a lake? What if it was the size of an infinite ocean? **If your heart is expanded, the waves of love, inspiration, and upliftment you put out to others and the world can make ripple after ripple after ripple.**

Some people have what I call *"fear of the deep water of the heart."* They hang out in the shallow end of love, like the shallow end of a swimming pool, afraid of what will happen if they go into the depths. *"I'm afraid if I feel too much, I will drown. I don't know how to swim in deep feelings. I'm afraid I'll disappear or feel out of control."*

You don't drown with too much love and feeling.
You actually drown without them.

Have you ever been excited about going swimming in a pool or pond, only to discover with great disappointment that the surface is covered with slime, moss, or dead leaves? Is the pool of your heart clogged with emotional debris, and you invite people to jump in, but you haven't cleaned out what's been floating there for a long time? Perhaps you invite people to swim in the pool of your heart, but leave the "emotional pool cover" on. They know there's refreshing water underneath, and they long to dip in, but they can't get to it.

The choice for love is the choice to become a clear, irresistible pool of love. When you make choices that recalibrate you vibrationally, which we'll learn more about soon, it's like turning on a powerful filtering system that begins to circulate out all the old junk and clear the debris from your vibrational heart space. Once you unclog the system, more love can flood in, filling you up. **You want your pool of Love to be so pristine, so full, and so inviting that people can't wait to dive into it.**

The Big Freeze:
When Your Ocean of Love Turns to Ice

"The less you open your heart to others, the more your heart suffers."
— Deepak Chopra

We arrive in this world drenched in love and become messengers of that love to everyone around us. Hold an infant in your arms and you'll instantly feel the rivers of pure love pouring from their newly beating heart into yours. Their otherworldly magic is unmistakable. We recognize that they possess something we do not, something we once had but have since lost. We behold them in amazement, soaking up every beatific smile, delighting in every adorable gaze, and marveling at the unexpected and astounding miracle these tiny beings have somehow mysteriously performed—*they have cracked open our heart.*

The "they" I'm describing is *you.* It's the you before your openness and innocence were scarred by hurt and disappointment. It's the you before you learned that everyone wouldn't always see the radiance of your soul, or treat you with kindness. It's the you before the glow from your heart became overshadowed by life's tests and trials.

What happens to that love? Ultimately, nothing, because it's the essence of who we are, the divine energy that runs through us and *is* us.

However, our instinctual human nature instructs us to survive, and to protect ourselves from pain at all costs. **So each time we are hurt by someone, each time our trust is abused or our offerings rejected, it's as if we freeze a part of that love so that it cannot flow.**

Imagine that each of our unhealed emotions and unresolved issues from our past is like a huge block of ice. Slowly, block by block, we wall ourselves up, and wall that love in. At first, if we just have a few of these barriers, we can figure out a way to get past them, and others can find their way in. However, each time we say, *"I don't want to deal with this,"* and don't feel, face, and heal something we should, those ice blocks multiply.

Anything we do to "freeze" our feelings and numb ourselves to what is going on inside of us can also add to those walls: drugs, alcohol, overworking, overeating, and so on. *These will temporarily tranquilize our discomfort and sedate our unhappiness, but they will also end up disconnecting us from the very life force we need in order to heal and to love.*

Turning off never protects you from hurt.
Freezing up never insulates you from pain.
Instead, it creates a wall of icy numbness between you
and that which you long for—
love, intimacy, and true connection.

Eventually, we may find ourselves surrounded by and trapped inside of a fortress of frozen patterns and emotions. We want to be free to love, to live a totally fulfilled and joyous life, but we're stuck. *Our protections have become our prison.*

Can you recall a time when you tried to get close to someone, only to feel that, no matter what you did, you couldn't get in? It was as if you were throwing yourself against an impenetrable wall over and over again, to no avail—and you were. That was the ice wall they'd built to protect themselves.

Perhaps as you read this description you're realizing with regret, *This is how other people often experience me.* If we use the metaphor of your heart as a pool of love, consider what happens to that pool when a lot of you is "frozen." It becomes as hard as a rock. Imagine what it's like when someone who loves you wants to dive into your heart. They hurt themselves.

Freezing up is the enemy of life.
It is the enemy of love.
It stops the flow of love, and turns it into a river of ice.
How can we escape from the frozen dungeon of our own heart?
The ice needs to be melted, block by block, emotion by emotion,
wound by wound, truth by truth.
We need to make the choice to defrost.

THE BIG MELT: DEFROSTING YOUR HEART

If you live in a place where there is snow and ice during the winter, you know that when *the temperature rises and water starts to flow, it wears away at the ice and it begins to melt.* Soon what was frozen is gone, and in its place is a flowing river of melted snow.

In this same way, we defrost bit by bit. Each time we make the choice for love, the "heat" of that love helps us defrost old patterns, unconsciousness, and numbness. We learn new, enlightened ways in which to relate to ourselves, to others, and most of all, to that energy of love itself as it attempts to move into us and through us. Layer by layer, the icy walls around our heart begin to soften until they turn into slush and then vanish. **Now all of the power and energy we were using to keep our ice armor intact is available for us, and all the love that was trapped inside is free to flow.**

Have you ever been to a wedding or bar mitzvah, or on a cruise ship where there's an elaborate buffet overflowing with food? Chances are, if you have, you've seen an enormous decorative ice sculpture carved into one of many exotic shapes: a swan, a fish, a pair of love birds, a pyramid, a football, a unicorn—you name it. At first, the ice sculpture looks quite impressive, but a few hours into the evening, the surface starts to melt, the solidity of the artistic shape begins to disappear, and what once looked like a majestic eagle begins to resemble a sleepy, dripping chicken, and eventually, just an unidentified blob.

When H_2O is frozen, the water molecules move very slowly, sticking together to form ice. When the stuck molecules are exposed to warmth—in this case the air in a room—they start moving around more rapidly and can't stay together. What we see as melting is actually the water molecules moving farther and farther apart from one another, which allows them to change shape and direction. The puddle that forms on the banquet table is actually the H_2O molecules now free to move away from their formerly frozen identity.

This is exactly what happens when you begin to "emotionally defrost." *The rigid shape of your patterns slowly begins to melt. The hard edges of your protective habits start to blur. The sharpness of your judgments and limiting beliefs about yourself and your life soften.* The more you open to the powerful "heat" of love, the more everything will transform. Soon, just like the shrinking ice sculpture, your patterns become unrecognizable—and then they will just be gone.

The choice for love is the choice for the Big Melt.
It's the choice to defrost all of the places in your heart
that have become hard and frozen.
This Big Melt will allow you to experience Big Love!

When I explain this principle of what I call "The Big Melt" to my students, they always feel quite relieved. When those of us who are serious seekers accelerate our growth, we always go through periods when so much is changing and rearranging—melting—that we aren't sure what's happening, or as I put it, *"we don't recognize the new scenery yet."* Last month when a woman heard me talk about the mechanics of this process, she shared something I loved and had to pass on to you.

"I just had a huge revelation," she proclaimed: ***"I'm not falling apart—***
I'm defrosting!"

EMOTIONAL SWIMMING LESSONS:
THE DIFFERENCE BETWEEN THOUGHTS AND FEELINGS

"We're all fluent in the language of the heart.
We just don't speak it much."

— Dr. Barbara De Angelis

Last year, two of my students who are married to each other became parents of beautiful twins who are my spiritual godchildren. I have a special bond with little Aaron and Sofia, and during our most recent visit, I spent a lot of delightful time with them. They had just turned six months old, and naturally weren't speaking yet, but I could feel their love for me. Silently, we would gaze at one another, and the flow of energy between us was palpable, filling my heart with joy.

How was I able to experience the love of these special souls when they couldn't yet express themselves with words? **I could *feel* the vibration of that love traveling from their hearts to mine. They weren't thinking about how they felt toward me. They were feeling it.**

Do you know the difference between a thought and a feeling? You may believe you do, but many of us spend time thinking about our emotions *yet don't allow ourselves to actually feel them.* **Thoughts about feelings are descriptions from our mind. They're labels that identify emotions, but they have no energetic vibrational component.**

How do you know you're having a thought versus having a feeling? *Authentic emotions don't happen in your head.* Those are thoughts about feelings. Emotions are experienced in the emotional body, the energy body.

The difference between thoughts and feelings is the difference between sitting on the side of the swimming pool and eloquently describing what the water looks like, versus actually diving into the water and getting wet.

When someone experiences a feeling *while* they're feeling it, they're not just saying words. They're vibrating with a certain quality of energy. You can feel something happening to them. Does it matter if they're even expressing themselves out loud in that moment? Can you tell they're feeling without them letting you know? Yes, you can, just like I knew what Aaron and Sofia were feeling. **You're experiencing the vibration of their heart, not just words from their head.**

Are you someone who's normally very cerebral and logical, but tends to get very thrown off and unbalanced in certain emotional situations? **It could be that for most of your life, you assumed your thoughts about identifying feelings *were* your feelings.** This is why it can be very overwhelming when you suddenly experience very strong emotions. You're not used to the powerful vibrational intensity of a genuine feeling that hasn't been analyzed and distilled into intellectual information. In a sense, you have a low tolerance for full doses of authentic feeling—and, of course, that includes love.

Think back to a time when you were with a person who was speaking to you about an emotional topic, but you couldn't feel them. *"Of course I love you,"* they say, or *"I'm going to miss you too,"* but you can't feel any juice in what they're saying. It sounds dry and flat. **That's because they're telling you** *thoughts they have about feelings they're not actually allowing themselves to feel in the moment.* **They aren't feeling themselves, so you're unable to feel them. They're cut off from their "emotional body," and reporting on the emotions from their intellect. They're not in the love. They're in the idea of the love.**

Imagine a reporter standing at the dramatic scene of a tragedy. Somewhere inside of them, they're experiencing shock or sadness, but it wouldn't be professional to show their emotions. Instead, they report the facts, devoid of all feeling. This is what happens to those of us who get in the habit of intellectualizing emotions rather than experiencing them. We have a difficult time actually expressing feelings, and instead, we "report" on them. We tell ourselves we're communicating because we're sharing the content, but we're not allowing ourselves to feel, so we don't pass on the vibrational reality.

How does this impact our partner/friend/child/audience/listener? They can hear us. They can understand us. *But they can't feel us.*

You have to first fully feel yourself
in order for other people to fully feel you.
If you report on your emotions from your head
instead of experiencing them in your heart,
people will think:
"I hear you, but I cannot feel you,
because you're not feeling you."

The choice for love isn't the choice for new thoughts about love, new attitudes about love, or a new philosophy about love. It's the choice to vibrationally enter into the experience your own unlimited love, and open to the unfathomable and unlimited treasures that your heart holds.

FOLLOWING THE VIBRATIONAL BREAD CRUMBS OF YOUR EMOTIONS

Recently, the weather in California was unseasonably warm, and one morning I woke up to discover that, overnight, a fast-moving army of ants had come inside to cool off and were swarming all over my kitchen. I confess that, although I honor all creatures great and small, I really don't like it when my house is overrun by ants, and I knew that if they enjoyed their new habitat, they would telepathically send a message to thousands of their relatives, who would soon arrive in droves through every crack and crevice imaginable.

This wasn't the first time I've experienced an ant invasion, so I realized that getting rid of the ants I could physically see would only be a temporary fix. They were coming from a nest, and I needed to call my pest control company to find the source of the problem, or soon it would be totally out of control.

Sometimes when strong emotions rise up within us, it feels like an *"emotional invasion,"* and our initial response is the same as the one we'd have discovering trails of ants—we just want to get rid of them. I'm sure if someone invented an anti-emotion spray, it would become very popular!

Here's what is important to consider: your emotional discomfort isn't arbitrary. What does that mean? You don't suddenly get tense; you don't suddenly feel angry, or suddenly feel frightened. *Each of these emotions comes from somewhere, and believe it or not, they each have a benevolent purpose (other than to drive you crazy!).*

Your emotions are messages from your heart, hoping to get you to pay attention to something that needs your focus. For instance, if you have a lot of old, unresolved anger, it will eventually find its way through little cracks in the structure of your personality, seeming to appear out of the blue. Why? It wants to be resolved, healed, and transmuted back to compassion and love.

We'll talk more about your "emotional programming" later on. What's important here is to make the choice for love and, rather than avoiding or pushing down your feelings, pay attention to them. *I like to think of feelings as a vehicle attempting to transport you on a journey down a particular road. If you follow them, they will lead you to something significant—a revelation, a course correction, or an important decision.*

**Your emotions are like text messages from your heart.
Don't delete them.**

My experience is that once you pay attention to feelings that are rising up and see what there is to see about what they're trying to show you, the necessity for those strong emotions will be eliminated. The feelings will have done their job, and soon you'll notice that they've spontaneously vanished, leaving deeper healing and understanding in their place. *The more you heal the leftover emotional business in your heart, the more emotionally stable you'll actually become.*

Feelings aren't there to be fixed.
They're there to be felt.
Emotions are vibrational bread crumbs.
Follow them back to the source and see
what they're trying to help you notice or heal.
The feelings themselves are just messengers.
Don't eliminate them—listen to them.

Sometimes this guidance is challenging for very "spiritual" people to accept, especially if they have an aversion to their human side. They'll say something like: *"I don't feel my uncomfortable feelings. I just bless all of my feelings. For instance, right now, I'm upset, but I'm not going to think about why I'm angry. I'm just going to bless my anger."* My response is that the anger, or sadness, or grief is there *for a reason. It's not an enemy that needs our prayers—it's a part of you trying to tell you something.*

You don't just bless your anger. You unwrap it, you unravel it, you unpack it, you pull the threads of it apart until it reveals what's there for you to learn. The discomfort that comes with all unwanted, unpleasant emotions is energy that needs to be transmuted. We make the choice for love by paying attention to them.

Here's how the healing process works:
What's coming up is coming OUT.

When we try to stop having the feelings we're already having, we're actually interrupting our own healing process. This would be like stopping a woman who's in labor. She's trying to birth something. Your emotions are *energy in motion*—they are moving and flowing, and will eventually take you to places inside of yourself that you need to experience for your own freedom and authentic fulfillment.

If you're reading this, you are a more advanced being than most people on the planet. Your job as an advanced being is *not* to limit what you feel, but to heal your relationship with your heart so you can *feel more powerfully and deeply.*

As advanced beings, we have an obligation to keep ourselves clear.
Clear doesn't mean you are without problems, challenges, or worries.
Clear doesn't mean you don't have to battle with unpleasant emotions.
Clear doesn't mean that you understand or like everything
that is happening to you and within you.
Keeping yourself clear means that under all circumstances,
you do not cut off or shut off.

It takes courage to turn toward your heart and not turn away. It takes
fierce determination to decide that it's no longer acceptable to have any
parts of you that are walled off, shut off, or frozen.

Becoming a Perfect Container for Love

"My heart is my golden vessel
with which I serve my Creator all my days."
— from the Pesach Haggadah

Many years ago I read a short parable set in India about the spiritual
path. Inspired by its message, I've written you a story about the heart
called:

"The Pure Heart and the Humble Container"

In ancient times, the Gods were known to have discovered "Amrita,"
the elixir of immortality, which allowed them to have amazing powers, experience bliss, and live forever. The tales of this miraculous nectar
reached the earth realms, and the humans marveled at the thought that
just one drop of this drink of the Gods could make them immortal and
happy. But, of course, they were only human, and would never be able to
experience this divine beverage.

One day, the Gods made an astonishing announcement: In seven
months' time, as a great boon to humans, they would be bringing the
Amrita down to earth so that people could drink it. There was only one
stipulation: each person had to bring a container into which the nectar
would be poured. *If the container could sufficiently hold the liquid, the person
would be able to drink the Amrita and live forever.*

It so happened that there was a powerful King who owned lands for
as far as the eye could see, and treasuries piled high with gold and jewels.

This mighty ruler had all of the riches anyone could desire, except for one thing—he longed for enlightenment and immortality. The King was not unkind, but he was very proud, and it angered him that the Gods possessed something he did not. *"Behold how omnipotent I am!"* he would boast. *"Why can't the Gods see that I am worthy to share their nectar of immortality and allow me to take my place among them?"*

So when the King heard that the Gods had announced they were going to descend to earth for one day and distribute the Amrita, he was ecstatic. *"Finally,"* he boasted, *"I will be able to become immortal. Surely the Gods heard that I was displeased with them, and are coming just for me."*

The King ordered his servants to build the largest and most elaborate urn imaginable, which would serve as a container for the miraculous nectar. *"I don't care if you empty the treasury and people starve,"* he instructed his council. *"No expense is to be spared!"* He bought the strongest iron available from the most remote mines and had workers toiling around the clock to construct the gigantic urn. Once the urn was constructed, he had it covered with three inches of solid gold. He then had the entire urn decorated with the most rare and priceless jewels from his vault—grapefruit-sized sparkling diamonds, fire rubies, and deep green emeralds.

Indeed, the King's subjects did not have enough grain or supplies during the cold winter because he'd sold almost everything he had to pay for the magnificent urn, but he didn't even notice. He was too busy supervising the building of the gigantic container.

The finished urn was truly a sight to behold. ***"The Gods will be impressed, I am certain!"*** he exclaimed to his advisors. ***"No one else in the world is as great as I am, and therefore they could not possibly construct such a magnificent container. Only my vessel will be worthy of receiving the nectar of immortality. At last, I will triumph."***

Far away, in a small, poor, dusty village no one had ever heard of, there lived a humble devotee who worked as the caretaker for the local temple. He too had heard about the Amrita, and the announcement that the Gods were descending to earth to offer it to humans. This temple attendant was pious and prideless, and had prayed all of his life to be worthy just to have a vision of the Divine. So the thought that the Lords were actually coming in person filled him with ecstasy. *"I have nothing, and know there is no chance that I could create an appropriate container,"* he sadly concluded, *"but I will at least try as a way to honor this auspicious and sacred occasion."*

The devotee already worked long hours tending the temple, but now began to rise even earlier at 3:00 A.M. each morning so he could spend every spare minute fashioning his urn. Having no money to buy supplies, he gathered leaves and flowers from the forest and crushed them into a paste mixed with mud. He wrote prayers on scraps of paper, and layered them with the paste to form his container. He retrieved 11 tiny flecks of gold that had been swept up from the goldsmith's floor and thrown into the garbage with dirt and refuse, and reverently placed each on the outside of his vessel. As he worked, he chanted sacred mantras celebrating the glory of the divine.

At last, the devotee's work was complete, and as he looked at the finished product, his heart sank: *His urn was misshapen, lopsided, and not at all beautiful. In truth, it looked like something someone had tossed into a trash heap.* Still, he decided to attend the great gathering, if only to glimpse his beloved Gods.

Finally, the day of the cosmic visit arrived. The King had made the journey to the appointed spot one week earlier to ensure that he was near the beginning of the line, and brought 1,000 of his soldiers and dignitaries with him. Now the people began to gather from far and wide. Most of them were too frightened to participate, and just came to witness what they hoped would be a miracle.

Suddenly, in a flash of brilliant, supernatural light, the divine lords appeared. Their celestial radiance was dazzling, and the people fell to their knees in wonder. The Gods held up an enormous magical lotus flower, and everyone knew that within the petals of this flower was the famed elixir of immortality.

The first person to approach the Gods was a mighty warrior known throughout the land for his fierceness and bravery in battle. He rode up on his thundering stallion and gestured for his soldiers to bring up his container, a huge stone vat set on wheels, which was so heavy it took a hundred horses to pull it. Everyone watched in breathless anticipation as one of the Gods reached out and poured a single, tiny drop of the magic liquid into the cavernous vat. A loud rumbling sound emerged from the container, and it exploded into a thousand pieces, the huge stones tumbling everywhere as people ran for their lives.

The crowd gasped. *How could one drop of the nectar destroy such a massive stone urn?*

Next, a princess known for her ruthless cleverness approached. She had cut down an entire sacred forest of rare trees and taken only a small piece of the hardest wood from the center of each trunk to construct a special vessel woven from the impenetrable wood, sealing it with the honey from her pampered royal bees. One of the Gods stepped forward and dropped a bead of liquid into the center of the wooden container. Instantly, it burst into flames, and in seconds, the container was reduced to ashes, and the haughty and humiliated princess was reduced to tears.

Now it was the King's turn. He'd watched the first two royals fail to receive the elixir, but wasn't worried. He was certain that his superior container would dazzle the gods and withstand whatever magic was happening. He gestured for his bearers to bring up the bejeweled urn, which shone so brightly that people had to cover their eyes. He could hear the cries of delight as everyone witnessed the presentation of what was undoubtedly the most magnificent object they had ever seen.

"Welcome, great ones!" he shouted so all could hear. *"I have built you the most spectacular container made of three hundred layers of the hardest, most indestructible iron on earth, encased in solid gold, and covered inside and out with tens of thousands of priceless jewels. It is waiting to receive the nectar of immortality."*

One of the Gods tilted the lotus flower so that a small drop of liquid descended into the jeweled container. For a moment, nothing happened. Then, a malevolent, dark, noxious cloud of steam began to rise up from the urn, and within seconds, as if it had been acid, the nectar dissolved the King's container, jewels and all, until it completely disappeared and nothing was left but sizzling, black dust.

The King stumbled back, stupefied. How could this have happened? He had spent all the wealth in his kingdom to build this container. How could one drop of nectar have obliterated it?

The crowd froze in terror. No one wanted to come forward and offer their container, fearing there were supernatural forces at work, or that the Gods had come down only to trick them.

From the back of the masses, a man began making his way toward the Gods. Everyone strained to see who it was, and what kind of container he carried. *"Who is he?"* someone shouted. *"He is no one,"* another responded, *"just some lowly temple attendant from a poor village in my district. Look—he's not even dressed in any finery. And his container is ugly!"* People began to laugh at the sight of this poor, obviously ignorant fool approaching the Gods with his crude, pathetic vessel.

Overcome with devotion, the temple attendant knelt trembling before the Lords, tears streaming down his face and his head bowed in humility. *"Great Ones, I know I am not deserving of your elixir of immortality, and my poor container isn't worthy to even be presented to you. Still, I come before you in reverence."* With shaking hands, he held up his small, odd-looking bowl.

Just like they'd done with the others, one of the Gods tipped the lotus flower over the bowl, and everyone watched in total silence as a glistening drop of nectar made its way into the container. A few moments passed, and the Lord poured another drop in, and then another and another, until the man's container was completely full of the magical liquid. It was a miracle! His small, imperfect container had withstood the test, and he'd received the divine gift! Shocked, astonished, and confused, everyone in the crowd began to shout and call out all at once.

Now, one of the radiant lords stepped forward and spoke:

"Silence! Here is our message to you all: **None of the other containers could hold this powerful elixir of immortality because they were not pure. The strength of the container was not determined by the material, or the appearance, or the expense that went into it, but by what was in the heart of the person who created it.**

"It is clear that what was in this man's heart was love. *That love made his heart pure.* **It is only love that makes the heart pure enough and strong enough to truly cherish and hold anything, even the nectar of enlightenment and immortality."**

The Lord turned to the devotee. "From now on you will be known as Darshwana, which means 'pure of heart,'" he proclaimed. *"And you will live forever in bliss."*

I really enjoyed crafting this tale as it unfolded in my consciousness, and I received it as an important teaching for us all about the power of love. Of course, the container is a metaphor for our heart, and the nectar represents the divine energy, wisdom, and love that is at the source of everything.

Like the characters in the story, we all want full access to that powerful life force energy. Why don't we experience more of it? **The problem is *not* that it isn't available to us. It's not a supply issue—it's a container issue!**

When our hearts are not pure, when they're cluttered with old emotional debris and unhealed energies, they become like sieves, and no matter how much love we get, no matter how much wisdom, no matter how much of anything, we can't hold it.

Love wants to rise up in you, and to flow through you.
Your job is to become a magnificent container that can receive, hold, and transmit as much of that cosmic energy as possible.

How do we do this? **We defrost our frozen pain; we demolish our walls; we purify out all energies that are not of the highest vibration. Then we will be able to fully receive and contain that love and that divine energy, and allow it to flow through us without interference.** *This is how we become a walking, breathing delivery system of love!*

Imagine if the devotee's container had a hole in the bottom. Even if it received the divine elixir, the nectar of immortality would have dripped out onto the ground and been wasted. This is often what happens to us when we do receive love, or opportunity, or inner wisdom. If our container is in disrepair, or cracked, it's like a sieve. *No matter how valuable or precious what we receive is, we can't contain it.*

The journey of transformation is really one of repairing your container so that everything that wants to pour into you can, so that which flows through you doesn't get lost on its journey out to the world, and so no drop of love ever gets wasted.

Become a perfect container.
More than you can imagine is waiting
to be delivered to you,
and delivered through you.

From Me to We: Introducing the Field of Love

"When we try to pick out anything by itself,
we find that it is bound fast by a thousand invisible cords
that cannot be broken, to everything in the universe."

— John Muir

Your choice for love and the commitment to heal your heart is going to have a far greater impact on the planet than you can even imagine. That's because all of us are in a deep, mystical, very intimate relationship with each other. We are part of an infinite living vortex of energy, and thus, we are vibrationally connected in every moment of our lives.

You may be surprised to learn that every day, you are literally changing the world with your heart. **Your heart is a powerful electromagnetic field.** Even though we commonly assume that it's our brain/mind that possibly radiates out vibrations, the energy from your brain is nothing compared to the enormous force generated by your heart. Your heart's electromagnetic field is actually *5,000 times greater in strength than your brain's electrical field*, and is almost 60 times greater in amplitude.

The electromagnetic energy of your heart not only affects every cell in your own body including your brain cells, but it also extends out into the space around you. Scientists estimate that the actual electromagnetic energy radiating from your heart touches and interacts with everything and anyone within 8–10 feet of where you are in all directions, and beyond that in more subtle ways.

The quality of the vibration in your heart sends out electromagnetic signals that are always communicating with and changing the energy of everyone around you in profound ways. At the same time, you're receiving incoming electromagnetic waves of energy from other people's hearts. We register and associate these incoming waves of energy with the emotions we experience:

Someone you love comes into the room, and you "feel" yourself open and experience delight.

Someone you dislike enters, and you "feel" tense and agitated.

You walk into an office, and instantly "feel" it has "good vibes."

You arrive at a meeting, and immediately "feel" threatened and on the alert.

Your partner sounds calm and says nothing is wrong, but you can "feel" that he's angry.

These vibrational reactions are happening independent of your thoughts—*they're real electromagnetic changes in the field of your heart.* Your heart is actually interpreting electrical information that informs it of what's going on, and then it informs you.

Each of our hearts has its own electromagnetic field,
and when someone affects yours by sending out a wave of energy,
it registers as an emotion—you "feel" something.
That feeling isn't just in your head.
It's an actual vibrational experience happening
in your field of the heart.
A wave from their vibrational ocean creates
a wave in your vibrational ocean.

When your own heart waves are harmonious and coherent, they send vibrations of harmony and coherence out into the atmosphere. As you recalibrate your own vibrational field to the energy of love, all of the life-forms around you experience those vibrations electromagnetically, and are literally transformed by them. *They spontaneously begin to vibrate at the same higher frequency of love.*

Just like an antenna picks up signals and registers them,
the field of your heart picks up the electromagnetic energy fields
radiating from the hearts of people around you,
and the fields of other people's hearts pick up
your electromagnetic messages.
Your heart is *always communicating with every heart*.

This is a life-altering understanding: we are, indeed, changing the blueprint of other people's vibrational hearts all the time. We're sending out energies of peace, or energies of dissonance; energies of judgment, or energies of compassion. *Whatever is taking place in our heart is inevitably impacting and changing the frequency of the hearts of people around us.*

Remember: it's not that we're consciously *deciding* to send out electromagnetic waves that will wash up onto the shore of someone's heart. It happens automatically, because we're all living in an infinite vibrational vortex.

The choice for love is the choice to make a
powerful, uplifting, enlightening electromagnetic impact
on the world around you.

From the WE, Love Is Always the Right Choice

Questioner:	*How are we to treat others?*
Ramana Maharshi:	*There are no others.*

As we grow and evolve emotionally and spiritually, we must begin to shift from "ME" consciousness" to "WE" consciousness. WE consciousness is so much more than the intention to be kind to others, or to care about the world. It's the acknowledgment that you affect everyone and everything and they affect you.

On February 12, 1950, Albert Einstein, the brilliant theoretical physicist who developed the general theory of relativity, wrote the following in a private letter about the inevitable "we" that is who we are as humans.

"A human being is a part of the whole, called by us 'Universe,' a part limited in time and space. He experiences himself, his thoughts and feelings as something separate from the rest—a kind of optical delusion of his consciousness.

"The striving to free oneself from this delusion is the one issue of true religion. Not to nourish it but to try to overcome it is the way to reach the attainable measure of peace of mind."

WE consciousness is not a spiritual attitude.
WE consciousness is not about making a
conscious choice to feel part of the whole.
It means acknowledging the truth of the WE,
understanding you are already inevitably part of the great WE:
the WE of the planet; the WE of humanity;
the WE of love.
There are no others.

WE consciousness is called enlightenment. It's the consciousness of awakening. It's the truth of how things actually are.

ME consciousness is called delusion, as Einstein expressed: the premise that you're operating in some kind of vacuum, and that what goes on in your heart doesn't affect everybody in very concrete ways.

Our limited ego tries to convince us that it has a choice about whether or not to communicate the experiences taking place inside of us. *Do I want to show you my feelings? Should I push down my feelings? Do I want to acknowledge that I'm upset with you? Should I tell you I don't care, even though I do? Should I smile and act nice, even though I'm really angry? If I am good at covering it up, can I hide the truth?*

In the light of what we now know about our vibrational interconnectedness, can you see how absurd most of these emotional strategies are? These are irrelevant decisions, and they're actually delusional questions. **We may or may not act out these choices in real time and space, but what we're feeling *is* going to be vibrationally transmitted whether or not we consciously decide to communicate.** It's like a child playing hide-and-seek who covers its eyes, announcing: *"Now you can't see me!"*

The choice for love is the choice to acknowledge what is *already* happening: **You don't have the choice to NOT affect others or not be affected by others. It's a done deal.** The belief that it's okay for you to operate in any way but your highest (*at least to the best of your ability*), or that it's fine to deliberately indulge in any unloving emotions or behavior as long as no one knows about it, ignores the reality that your ME will always affect the WE.

Imagine yourself standing on the beach with your feet in the ocean. The waves that are breaking around you have been created by movement in the water thousands of miles away. You will never see those waves from that faraway harbor, or experience that storm which caused the sea to churn. Nonetheless, you're feeling movement against your body caused by something on the other side of the world.

We are each individual waves in this unfathomable ocean of consciousness, this vast vibrational sea. Yet our oneness is undeniable and irrefutable. Therefore, to make any choice but the highest choice for love is, by definition, self-destructive. *When we hurt others, we hurt ourselves.*

The choice for love, which is the choice for the recognition of the vibrational kinship we all share, transcends rules, ethics, and morals. It takes us to a new relationship with personal and social responsibility that isn't based on obligation, guilt, or political correctness, but instead originates from love.

Now we see even more clearly why it's so important to do the work of healing the heart—defrosting the frozen emotions that inhibit us from fully feeling, clearing out old patterns that interfere with our ability to love and connect, and keeping ourselves emotionally clear. *You're not just doing it for yourself. You're doing it for the world.*

Love brings illumination. It brings grace.
It reveals the door to your permanent freedom.
Don't try to resist it. Don't run away from it. Don't modulate it.
Don't pretend it hasn't arrived, or you will miss the gift.

Become aware of the Love.
Turn toward it.
Welcome it.
Receive it.
Open to it.
Surrender to it.
Bless it.

MORE LOVE! MORE LOVE! MORE LOVE!

MELTING BACK INTO YOUR OCEAN OF LOVE

"Lift the veil that obscures the heart,
and there you will find what you are looking for."
— Kabir

One of the most powerful ways we can recalibrate the electromagnetic field of our heart is to soften our boundaries, our walls, and our barriers. **Softening is a vibrational recalibration practice that invites the arbitrary and unnecessary divisions in our heart to melt, and teaches us how hold a more open, flexible energy space.** It removes the rigid barriers that have locked in old emotions from the past, allowing them to interact with our consciousness in the present, and to heal. It supports us to begin experiencing WE consciousness.

Softening creates instant expansion. Picture a hard stick of butter shaped in a rectangle. When you soften it, it immediately appears a lot bigger because the space it takes up has expanded. *So too, your softening instantly deepens and widens the pool of love available to you in your heart.*

Softening is not the same as being soft. As we'll see going forward, many of us have softness associated with old emotional programs of weakness, lack of power, danger, or being taken advantage of. The ability to soften is actually the opposite of powerlessness—**it empowers us to re-create ourselves.** ***When things are softened, they can be transmuted.* They can shift from one form to another.**

When you soften clay, you can mold it into something. When you soften metal, you can create a tool. The egg has to soften and open to receive the sperm and create life. Softening has to happen for all birth and change to take place.

It's an important contemplation to look at your life and see where there needs to be some softening. Is it the softening of an attitude? Is it the softening of a habit? Is it softening of blame or judgment, guilt or grief?

Whenever you're feeling stuck, upset, or off center, try asking yourself: **"Where do I need to soften right now?"**

A CHOICE FOR LOVE PRACTICE:
SOFTENING THE HEART

Here is a simple but powerful vibrational healing practice. I'll be offering you many other Choice for Love Practices and Meditations throughout these pages. This one is designed to help you learn how to transform your energy from the inside out, and create more expansion in your heart. That expansion will vibrate out in powerful, uplifting waves to the world.

The words of the Heart-Softening Practice invite your energy to recalibrate itself and shape-shift from what is rigid, stuck, or resistant to what is melting, flowing, and soft. You're asking what no longer serves you to dissolve.

This is a very useful and effective technique to practice whenever you're feeling upset, irritated, disappointed, judgmental, or angry, whether with someone else or yourself. You can also use this regularly as a way to begin to break down some of the emotional walls that may be keeping you from experiencing as much of your own expansion as you should, and to defrost the deeper layers of numbness that block your ability to enjoy swimming in that field of love.

～ THE CHOICE FOR LOVE ～
HEART-SOFTENING PRACTICE

When you do this on your own, you may want to close your eyes. For now, as you take in the instructions, just allow your energy to settle a little bit. Take some very deep breaths. Slow down your breathing, deeply breathing in, fully breathing out . . . allowing your shoulders to relax . . . allowing any tension in your body to unwind and let go.

Let your awareness expand out so that it reaches several feet around your entire body in all directions. Sit easily like that, without trying to do anything, feeling all of yourself and the space around you.

Now, have the subtle intention to soften your energy, and gently hold this phrase very quietly and subtly in your consciousness:

"May I soften."

Allow this phrase to float in your awareness. Don't mechanically repeat it. Don't try to understand what it means or think about it. Just allow it to be there. If you wish, you may also place your hand over your heart.

Visualize the melting of any hard places inside of you. You may want to add words to it that reflect issues you'd like to heal. For instance:

May I soften my resistance.

May I soften my confusion.

May I soften my stubbornness.

May I soften my pride.

May I soften my blame.

May I soften my anger.

May I soften my denial.

May I soften my grief.

May I soften my guilt.

May I soften my fear.

Just imagine everything softening. *Your heart is softening. Your mind is softening. Those things that have felt agitated are melting and softening.*

After you've expressed these things, or even if you haven't, you can offer a general intention:

"May all that needs to soften begin to melt."

Invite anything that needs to soften in your life right now to do so. Feel that at the deepest level of your being, you are softening. *Notice that as you soften, you begin to feel more expanded and more peaceful.*

You can also offer this intention:

"May all that is frozen in my heart begin to melt."

Feel that at the deepest level of your being, anything that has been blocking you is melting.

Then, when you're ready, lovingly offer these phrases into your consciousness:

"I am softening."
"I am melting."

Just sit *with the vibration of that thought for a moment.* As you think, *"I am softening; I am melting,"* feel the edges of your body melting into the air around it. Feel the awareness melting out beyond your head. Imagine any frozen energy or hardness in your heart melting. Imagine a rushing waterfall of love cascading in the center of your chest.

Float for as long as you wish in that expanded, delightful energy.

Whenever you're ready, you can complete this practice, and if your eyes have been closed you can open them. Notice right away how much more open, calm, and softened you feel.

May all the places that have been frozen in your heart
now soften and melt
so that the fullness of love can rise up
and flow freely out to yourself,
to others, and to the world.
May your pool of love expand and expand
until it becomes an unlimited ocean of joy and delight.

3

Untangling Your Heartstrings and Turning On Your Sacred Circuitry

"When your Source of supply, both spiritual and temporal,
is the Infinite Spirit,
your supply is unlimited and inexhaustible.
It can never fail."

— Henry T. Hamblin

There is a Supreme Power Source that exists in our Universe, operates our Universe, and allows everything else to exist. **That ultimate source energy and love *is* our true energy.** Human beings are brilliantly designed with an astounding capacity to experience that ultimate energy in the form of love, wisdom, and peace. **In essence, our own consciousness is like a home or building, already "pre-wired" for maximum voltage. The hub of that consciousness is in what we can call the spiritual or metaphysical heart.**

It's ironic that we try to become powerful by doing things, collecting things, controlling things, impressing others, seeking acknowledgment, and so much more. **The truth is that a source of infinite, unlimited power is *already available* to us, within us, offering us more than anything we could acquire or even experience on the outside.** We don't need to search for anything. We already have a VIP all-access pass!

Imagine that someone gave you a beautiful lamp unlike anything you'd ever seen, and told you it was very valuable. The shade was sewn in Paris from the finest rare silk. The lamp base was constructed of crystal and jewels. The bulb was a new invention that was designed to give off the most intoxicating and healing light. This amazing lamp sat on a table in your living room, but didn't seem to be living up to its potential.

"Something must be wrong with my lamp," you lament. *"It's not giving off any light. Perhaps it's defective."*

What do you need to make that lamp work? You need to plug it in. It wouldn't matter how exquisite the lamp was unless it could properly connect to the power source.

In this same way, each of us is like a lamp—an individual, unique vehicle through which that ultimate power source can be expressed. Just as a lamp or any appliance or machine is designed with circuitry that allows the electrical current to travel through it in order for the device to function, *so we too have been designed with a brilliant system of vibrational circuitry through which love and the life force flow.*

You are pre-wired
to be a magnificent and powerful emitter of Light.
However, your ability to be a clear conduit for the full transmission
of that divine Energy, Wisdom, and Love
needs to be restored to its full potential.

A friend of mine loves buying and renovating old country homes. One of the most common problems he faces is a house with very old and outdated wiring that can't properly and safely deliver the electrical power. Lights flicker, fuses blow, connections loosen, switch plates heat up, and there's no consistent and reliable electricity.

There's no shortage of power coming into these homes. *However, the wiring just won't support much electrical activity*—several appliances can't be on at the same time; lightbulbs don't radiate at their full wattage. As soon as my friend rewires everything, so much becomes possible. The house can now be beautifully lit and modernized.

Like these old homes, there is no shortage of power coming into you. You do, however, have a certain capacity for running that power based on your "emotional and mental wiring." If you have wiring or circuitry problems, you won't be able to experience and express the full potential of who you are capable of being. *You will be "lit" much more dimly that you should be, and you'll experience less love, power, wisdom, and passion than you can.*

How Much Emotional and Spiritual Voltage Can You Handle?

"The Universe is constructed of fundamental forces or fields,
resembling an invisible nervous system,
which stretches throughout space and is continuously vibrating,
becoming and transforming trillions of times per second."

— Joseph Rain

One way to describe this cosmic energy is to use the term *voltage*. It's another way of expressing the source energy, life force, love, Christ Consciousness, Light, Shakti, Chi—the Supreme. Here's the question for you:

"If that huge current of energy exists, why isn't it fully available to me personally, and what's blocking my connection to it?"

This same question began my own search for teachers, for wisdom and for awakening many years ago. I knew there was a "Big Outlet" somewhere, and I desperately wanted access to it. Somehow, I understood that I needed to plug in, stay plugged in, and increase my capacity to handle the maximum amount of "voltage" possible if I was to fulfill my dreams of serving the world.

Most of us long for more: *"I want more love. I want more creativity. I want more abundance. I want more connection to Spirit."* Remember, however, that everything is just energy vibrating at certain frequencies. So, as we've seen, asking for more of anything is asking for more *intensity*, which we now can understand as *voltage*.

When you ask for more energy to flow into you and through you,
in essence you're asking for more voltage.
When you ask for more love and intimacy in your life,
you're asking for more voltage.
When you ask for more creativity and insight,
you're asking for more voltage.
When you ask for exalted spiritual experiences and revelation,
you're asking for more voltage.

Even though at your full capacity, you're pre-wired to be able to receive maximum cosmic energy, power, wisdom, creativity, and love, *all of your circuits probably aren't currently operational, and therefore your ability to handle maximum voltage is limited. Your circuits can handle a certain amount of energy based on how clear or how blocked they are.* Earlier I described this principle as your relationship to the intensity of love. Now we're taking this one step further as we understand that what we call emotional intensity is actually "vibrational voltage" experienced in the heart.

What is your ability to handle that increased energy or voltage? What will happen to you if you can't handle too much voltage?

In 1969, when I was 18, I spent a summer in Grenoble, France, as an exchange student. This was my first trip alone to a foreign country, and I did my best to be completely prepared. I didn't know much then about traveling abroad, and one of my biggest concerns was how I was going to dry my very long hair. A friend loaned me an adapter for my hair dryer, reassuring me that she had used it on a trip abroad with no problems.

On the first morning staying with my host family, I showered and then proceeded to plug my hair dryer with its adapter in the wall socket. As soon as I turned it on, I noticed the hair dryer sounded twice as loud as it normally did, and seemed to be getting very hot, but I didn't make much of this—that is until a minute later when the dryer began to smell like it was on fire and I heard a popping sound! The hair dryer stopped, all of the power in the apartment went out, and I heard angry curses in French coming from the dining room, where my hosts were having breakfast.

I was mortified. What had I done? I discovered to my dismay, after a bit of research, that my friend had given me an *adapter* so my plug would fit into the French socket, but not a *converter*, which would convert the much higher 220 voltage to a usable 110 voltage. Twice as much voltage as its circuits could handle had poured into my dryer and fried it, tripping the circuit breakers in the apartment.

I used my eight years of French to apologize profusely to my host family, and later that day bought a French hair dryer. Of course, this isn't an anecdote about the misadventures of a teenage girl, but a lesson about power and voltage.

Electrical voltage is the flow of a certain kind of energy, and *all energy moves and interacts with whatever is in its path.* **When too much voltage** moves into a machine or appliance and meets resistance, it creates added "pressure" on the wires and circuits, and that friction causes heat that can create a fire or explosion. In order to prevent that heat from causing damage in appliances, homes, or buildings, a circuit breaker or a system of circuit breakers is installed. The circuit breaker detects too much intensity or energy, and breaks the connection to the power source in order to prevent a dangerous fire.

Hopefully you're beginning to see where this metaphor is taking us:

When our natural energetic circuitry isn't fully operational,
it can't handle the voltage and surges of power
trying to come into and flow through us in the form of
love voltage, wisdom voltage, creativity voltage, and abundance voltage.
Then, our system overloads, and we vibrationally short-circuit.

How to Tell If You're Vibrationally Short-Circuiting

You probably never realized that you have a Vibrational Circuit Breaker, but you do. Just as the circuit breaker in an appliance, in your house or apartment, or in a city's power grid will trip when it detects too much energy coming into the system, *so your own vibrational circuit breakers get activated when they detect that you're experiencing an overload of voltage or energy—more vibrational intensity than you're used to—either positive or negative.*

How can you tell that you're short-circuiting?

You shut off	**You become irritated and impatient**
You shut down	**You ignore responsibilities and tasks**
You go numb	**You indulge in distractions**
You fog out	**You isolate yourself and crave space**
You feel exhausted	**You feel agitated and restless**

You crave food, alcohol, and substances that will dull your consciousness

What's happening? Those behaviors or inner choices are your unconscious reaction to the overload of energy and *your attempt to "break" the connection to the energy* so you can become more comfortable.

Here are some very common examples:

*SHORT-CIRCUITING YOUR RELATIONSHIPS: You're in a new relationship, and starting to become closer and more intimate with your partner. If you don't have a large capacity to handle a high voltage of love, *the connection and closeness may begin to feel very uncomfortable to you, as we discussed earlier.* You could find yourself pulling away, shutting off, and becoming more critical of the other person. *These aren't actually feelings you are having, but behavioral circuit breakers—you're unconsciously trying to decrease and modulate the amount of love/energy/life force flowing into you.*

*SHORT-CIRCUITING YOUR CAREER: Your career has recently taken off and there's a substantial increase in the amount of energy pouring into your life in the form of attention, money, respect, responsibility, and pressure. All of this is what you've worked hard for and dreamed of. *If you don't have a large capacity to handle a high voltage of success energy, you may find yourself feeling overwhelmed and panicky, and actually doing things to sabotage yourself.*

We see stories about this in the news all the time. Someone suddenly becomes rich and famous, and soon becomes an addict and self-destructs. An athlete gains tremendous success and fame, and all of a sudden begins to behave badly and sabotage their reputation. A person wins millions of dollars in the lottery, and within a few years has lost it all and ruined their life. When we read about these incidents, we think, *"How could this happen? It doesn't make any sense. I'll take the fame/success/money! I wouldn't ruin everything like that."*

Often experts explain this as individuals who have deep issues with self-worth, and can't handle all of the good things that come their way. While some of that may be true, I also see it as a circuitry problem—a **huge increase in the voltage of energy pouring into the person's system, and they literally blow up, exploding their health, reputation, or life in the process.** The person's ability to process the energy of love or abundance is diminished or blocked to begin with, *so the sudden onslaught of so much—even good experiences—is too much.* The result is like plugging a small appliance into a nuclear generator. The appliance would incinerate.

This also helps us understand more about the mechanics of addictive behavior.

Addictions—drugs, alcohol, prescription medication, smoking, sex, gambling, eating, and so on—are all very powerful, temporarily effective, but highly dangerous circuit breakers. People frequently use them to shut off, numb out, dull down, or distract from their energy when it feels too intense, and when the voltage is too strong for their circuitry to handle.

When someone feels there's too much emotion, too much truth, or too much discomfort happening inside of them, they often decide to temporarily anesthetize themselves. "I feel so much better," they insist, *but what's really taking place is they've blocked or unplugged dozens of circuits so they don't have to feel what's actually going on.*

With all of these circuit-breaking behaviors, from the mildest form of emotional numbness to the most extreme addictions, the foundational problems aren't these behaviors themselves. These are just *symptoms* that a person's system isn't functioning properly, and therefore can't handle a lot of energy flowing through it. *Sadly, one of the many problems with addictions is that the very addictive substance or behavior creates even more vibrational interference, blockage, and damage, thus making it even harder for the person's circuitry to handle high-energy experiences like love, success, or spiritual awakening.*

I've worked with so many people who've spent their lives condemning themselves, thinking something's wrong with them because they appear to always sabotage their happiness and success. *"I must hate myself,"* they conclude. *"Every time I get in a relationship, I blow it and push the other person away,"* or *"Whenever I start making a lot of money, I do something to lose it all,"* or *"Just when I accomplish what I'd been working so hard to achieve, I manage to make bad choices and fail again."*

When I explain the concept of receiving good things as an increase of energy flowing into their system, and suggest that what they've been labeling self-sabotage is just an attempt of their system to not "overload" their circuitry, they feel like their brain has been rearranged. A few weeks ago, I was explaining this to one of my students who's a cardiologist and has been suffering from what he believed to be a habit of sabotaging his intimate relationships. His eyes lit up as I saw him shift his entire understanding.

"This makes so much sense!" he exclaimed. *"I was brought up with very little emotional 'capacity'—no affection between my parents, and a sparse amount to me. My tolerance for emotional energy has obviously been on the low end. From what you're saying, relationships just overloaded me. That's exactly how it always feels. I kept telling myself I needed space, and didn't want to settle down, but the truth is I crave intimacy. I get it now—It's like a patient whose heart is healthy, but his artery is clogged. If I unblock myself, I'll be able to handle the love voltage."*

I enjoyed watching this physician's face when he realized that his "emotional arteries" were clogged, not allowing for the smooth flow of love in and out, and that he wasn't deliberately sabotaging his love life.

Instead of feeling something is wrong with you, consider the understanding that *something isn't right about how you've been mentally and emotionally wired to handle large capacities of cosmic energy.* This helps you shift from thinking *you're* the problem to realizing that it's *your ability to process vibrational voltage that's been the problem.*

**Maybe you haven't been sabotaging yourself.
You've just been short-circuiting.**

Putting an End to Your Vibrational Traffic Jams

Why can't we handle huge amounts of everything—love, success, abundance, power, and spiritual energy? What's blocking us? In essence, anything that causes a disturbance in the flow and doesn't allow unlimited energy to travel through you will block the free and full transmission of energy: *old unhealed patterns, stuck emotional energy, or frozen feelings.*

One way to understand this is to think of it as a *Vibrational Traffic Jam.* There's a beautiful superhighway called your nervous system that's meant to handle a huge flow of traffic/energy, but if there's a block, it causes congestion and jams up the flow.

**Imagine love, power, and wisdom wanting to move through you,
but the road isn't clear.
It's been blocked by your emotional issues
and old, unprocessed vibrational debris
like one of those trucks that spills its produce all over the highway.**

I love this visual of our unhealed emotions and patterns scattered all over the highway to and from our heart like cabbages, onions, and potatoes that fell off of a produce truck, causing the cars behind it to slow down or stop. As we've seen, we all have some emotional spills that we never thoroughly cleaned up, and now they may be slowing down the flow of the source energy on our highway of consciousness.

Another way to understand your vibrational blocks or congestions is to think about them like knots in a wire that cut off the transference of energy. I use a wired earpiece for my cell phone, and I unravel the wire frequently so that it's nice and straight. Somehow, however, after a day or two going in and out of my purse, it mysteriously acquires dozens of knots. Naturally I don't deliberately tangle up my earpiece cord, but I swear it's as if a little gremlin lives in the bottom of my purse, and as soon as I unravel it, he mischievously knots it up again. These knots are like contractions in the channel through which energy is supposed to flow. They block the clear transmission of my voice unless I untie them.

Any emotional "knots" you have are slowing down or even blocking the maximum flow of power, love, and vibrational voltage into your life—knots of anger, knots of blame, knots of grief, knots of self-judgment. This is the transformational work we're doing—learning how to identify and unknot, unjam and melt your blocks so that you can receive all that the Universe has to offer rising up from inside of you and coming into you from the world outside.

Years ago, when I was in college, three friends and I lived for a while in a tiny house. It was old and run-down because it had been built in the 1940s, but it was all we could afford as poor students. The biggest problem in the house was the antiquated electrical wiring that wasn't up to code, and had been installed long before the invention of most modern electrical conveniences.

The wiring was so worn and insufficient that it could barely support any power coming into it without all of the fuses blowing. If someone was running the vacuum cleaner, we all had to stop doing anything else that required electricity. If someone turned on the heat, we had to have almost all of the lights out. If someone wanted to watch TV, they'd issue a warning that no one was allowed to use the toaster or blender.

We lived this way miserably for months. Frustrated and desperate, one of my wild and industrious roommates had enough. He informed us that our next-door neighbors, who both went to work all day, had modern electrical wiring and thus lots of power. *"I'm just going to 'borrow' some of it,"* he explained. The next day, as soon as they left for work, he snaked a long extension cord through our kitchen window, across the side yard, and into our neighbors' back patio outlet. For six hours, our circuitry was expanded, and we felt rich! Then, before they arrived home, he unplugged the extension cord, and the next morning, repeated the whole process.

Of course, a few weeks later we were busted when one of our neighbors came home early, and we had to revert back to living with far less power than we needed!

Many of us solve our faulty circuitry problems just like this. **We see where else we can plug in externally, rather than repairing our knotted or blocked wiring. We try to supplement our power from outside of ourselves so that we won't notice or feel our shortage.** My roommates and I adapted to living with less power than we needed. We sacrificed our comforts, lowered our expectations for what was normal, and got used to a long list of inconveniences. After a while, it was just the way things were.

Does this sound familiar? It should, because it's the way many of us adapt *to functioning in a dysfunctional way. We get used to living with less love, less power, less clarity, less wisdom, less energy, and less connection to the Source. Eventually, we forget that that isn't normal. Then we look for ways to get temporary hits of power from other people, interactions, and situations.*

Here are some examples you may recognize of ways you might try to plug into a feeling of power from outside of yourself when you're not fully connected to your own power source.

WAYS WE GET TEMPORARY HITS OF POWER AND LOVE ENERGY FROM OUTSIDE OF OURSELVES

We look for constant verbal approval or appreciation.

We seek attention and need the focus to be on us and not others.

We play helpless and get people to take care of us or do things for us.

We verbally diminish ourselves so that others are always giving us compliments and praise.

We insist that others reassure us all the time.

We keep score on how much people give us or do for us, or how much we do for others, and add these up as currency for the ego.

We need to feel in control of others, to always get what we want from them, or manipulate and manage them.

We compare ourselves to others and always need to feel better or superior.

We judge and criticize others, whether they're aware of it or not.

We get others to agree with us.

We make people work hard to get close to us and carefully manage their proximity.

We become contentious, always picking fights or arguments in an attempt to win at verbal sparring.

We feel we need to own certain things, do certain things, or look a certain way in order to feel good about ourselves.

These are just a few of the conscious or unconscious behaviors and patterns that emerge when we're disconnected from our power. The list is actually endless. Whether or not you can relate to anything here, it should be apparent that **all of these items are just tactics of the ego trying to plug into something on the outside in hopes of feeling more empowered on the inside.**

These choices will provide very transitory power hits that can feel like a temporary high. The problem is that, just like stealing power from the house next door, none of these experiences give us a true connection to our own power, self-esteem, and self-love, our own source of cosmic voltage, and when that momentary feeling wears off, we will need to repeat these behaviors again and again.

The choice for love is the choice to recognize ourselves as magnificent, miraculous beings designed with spectacular sacred circuitry, capable of receiving and transmitting unlimited amounts of energy in the form of love, wisdom, and creativity. Now we need to *locate and remove the blocks to that flow*.

Instead of believing that we aren't powerful, and that, in order to feel powerful, we need to do certain things or acquire certain things, we understand that Ultimate Power is *already* trying to move through us.

DON'T ASK YOURSELF: "WHAT CAN I DO TO *GET* POWER?"

ASK: "HOW CAN I RESTORE MY INNER CONNECTION IN ORDER TO ACCESS THE POWER AND LOVE I *ALREADY HAVE* AVAILABLE TO ME?"

WHY AND HOW WE UNPLUG OUR HEARTS: ARE YOU LIVING A LOW-VOLTAGE LIFE?

"There is no passion to be found playing small—in settling for a life that is less than the one you are capable of living."
— Nelson Mandela

I've lived in California for over 40 years, and been through several serious earthquakes. One of the first rules of safety we learn is to unplug all appliances, and turn off the electrical power to the house using what's called the "Main Disconnect." This is to prevent damage or even fire from a sudden electrical surge when the power is restored. These power surges are very dangerous and, as we've seen, can put too much pressure on the circuitry.

On our human journey, **many of us have experienced our own** *"emotional power surges"*—**times in our childhood or adult life when traumatic events, strong currents of pain, fear, sadness, or anxiety overloaded our system. These overloads of emotional energy created internal pressure just like an electrical surge of too much voltage.**

For instance, if you grew up with tension, discord, drama, anger, or unhappiness in your home, it's possible that it was too much emotional energy for your young circuitry to handle. In the same way, if you were faced with great loss or heartbreak as a grown-up, you may have performed a "disconnect" of some of your emotional circuits in order to not feel something painful, or not be overwhelmed by too much intensity— in a sense, to "protect" yourself from those surges of unpleasant energy.

When feeling is too painful,
we unconsciously disconnect some of our circuits in order to survive.
We become our own circuit breaker,
energetically and emotionally unplugging
circuits of our vulnerability, circuits of our knowingness,
circuits of our ability to love and be intimate.
Then we forget that we disconnected anything,
and conclude, *"This is just the way I am."*
We turn parts of ourselves off and forget to turn them back on.

When we disconnect our energetic circuits and don't reconnect, we end up living what I call a "low-voltage life." This is how many people function. They structure their entire personality and adapt their habits and relationships to accommodate the fact that they don't want a lot of vibrational energy coming in. *They've emotionally unplugged a lot of their capacity to hold energy, so they have to manage how much voltage they experience.*

I have a wonderful student who was a classic example of this when I first met her. Monica was bright, charming, and a very successful commercial photographer. However, she admitted to me that she felt very empty and depressed much of the time. *"I'm just not an emotional person,"* she insisted. *"I see everyone else with so many things they care about, people they care about, and I just feel like I can't relate. People actually annoy me."*

It didn't take long to figure out what was happening with Monica. She'd had a turbulent childhood with a cold, distant, overwhelmed mother and an alcoholic father. From a very young age, she felt and was treated as if she were invisible. The pain was so great that she simply retreated into her own world of her paints and drawings, and turned off.

It takes a lot of energy and maneuvering for a person to stay shut off when there's so much emotion inside. **Monica was a high-voltage person who decided to live a low-voltage life, and like everything she set her mind to, she succeeded at it.** She had no truly close friends, had never had a serious intimate relationship, pushed away anyone who got too close, and told herself she liked it that way—except that it wasn't true. She was deeply lonely.

Monica had unplugged so much of her ability to feel and hold energy that she could barely tolerate any emotional voltage moving through her. "You're operating on circuitry as if your circuitry is from a remote village in Uganda, but you're actually wired for the capacity of Tokyo," I told her. "No wonder you're depressed. You're missing all of the Love and the Light." Thankfully, she trusted me to help her turn her emotional circuits back on, and she is now happily married. She stopped making the choice for disconnection and made the choice for love.

> **If we experience a loss of power,**
> **or if we don't feel enough love, light, creativity,**
> **and wisdom coming through us,**
> **we can't blame it on the Power Source.**
> **The Cosmic Source *never* has blackouts!**
> **We have to turn ourselves back on.**

Making the choice for love means making the choice to see where, out of self-love and preservation, you've disconnected.

Here are some CHOICE FOR LOVE RECALIBRATION QUESTIONS to ask yourself:

When did I disconnect some of my circuits?

Did I experience painful power surges (traumatic incidents) that made me unplug?

What was it that I didn't want to feel?

How has my not being fully plugged into my own power source impacted my life and my relationships?

In what areas have I unconsciously decided to live a low-voltage life?

You were sent into this world and this body with a billion-watt capacity. Do you ever operate as if you're a 60-watt bulb? If you do, no wonder you sometimes feel depressed. No wonder you feel you're not living up to your potential. No wonder you feel like something's wrong with you.

You're pretending to be a tiny night-light,
when you're actually meant to be a fully lit
100,000-seat-capacity stadium
whose Light can be seen all the way from Space!
You need to find the circuits you've disconnected,
and turn them back on.

"All the powers in the universe are already ours.
It is we who have put our hands before our eyes and cry that it is dark."
— Swami Vivekananda

As an author, teacher, and speaker, I'm on the road a lot, traveling to different cities to offer seminars and give speeches. Like many of us, whenever I arrive at a hotel, one of the first things I do is look for the electrical outlets. Will there be enough of them to plug in all of my phones, tablets, computers, and other modern necessities? Will they be accessible, or hidden behind a heavy bed or armoire that I cannot move? When I find myself in a room with a multitude of outlets, I'm thrilled. "Now I can plug everything in and be connected!" I sigh with relief.

As we've seen, the moment people step into your energy field, they are experiencing the electromagnetic field of your heart. **Just as we feel comforted and reassured when we discover many electrical outlets in our hotel room, so people are always checking you for outlets, unconsciously feeling into your circuitry when they meet you, as if to ask:** *"Is there a place for me to plug in here?"* When they sense that you're operating on full power, when you look "lit up" and fully charged, they relax.

Do you want to be like a hotel room where there are no visible outlets, or a room with only one socket? Of course not.

Even worse, do you want people to plug into you and suddenly feel like their whole system just crashed because your circuitry was unstable and gave off destructive power surges? Of course you don't.

Aren't there people you know around whom you need a "surge protector," because their energy is so erratic? Do you want people to feel that way about you? That would be awful!

You want people to be able to plug into your vibrational circuitry, and say, *"Wow! I just want to stay plugged into this person forever. I never want to unplug. I feel so energized, so enlivened, so loved, as if I have the most wonderful energy running through me just from connecting my circuits to theirs."*

When your sacred circuitry is turned back on, so much more love will be able to come through you. You will begin to physically radiate love and light from within. This is what you experience when you meet a great Teacher, Holy Person, or Saint—*they are illuminated from within because they are fully plugged in and their inner radiance is turned on.*

As you work with the Choice for Love principles and wisdom, this *is* what will happen to you. You will look like a city glowing with millions of dazzling lights, instead of one small, blinking bulb.

**The more you do the work of unblocking your circuitry
and repairing your wiring,
the more the universal power can flow through you.
Then you expand from being just a single outlet
to becoming an enormous power grid with the ability
to transmit an unlimited amount of love, light, and energy
to everyone you know.**

How Juicy Are You?

It's peach season here in California, and I've been looking forward to being able to finally enjoy fresh peaches again. Last week I went to the store and was delighted to see a huge display of luscious-looking yellow peaches. I bought several that were already ripened, with perfect coloring, and could hardly wait to get back to my house and treat myself.

I drove home, quickly put away my groceries, and chose a peach to enjoy while I took a break and sat outside in one of my favorite chairs. Closing my eyes with anticipation, I slowly took a bite—and immediately knew something was terribly wrong. The peach was dry and mealy. I was so disappointed. Even though it looked wonderful on the outside, it was missing the one ingredient that would have made it a delicious peach: *it wasn't juicy.*

I'm sharing this little tale to make an important point. In a sense, life is like a big supermarket, with shoppers looking for what they want or need, and an enormous amount from which to choose. *You naturally want to be chosen—for love, for friendship, for business opportunities, and more.* You work hard to look good, sound good, and be someone that a partner, a potential client, or anyone would pick.

Do you want to be a dry peach? Do you want people to be drawn to you because you seem impressive and appealing on the outside, only to discover you're not juicy on the inside? I know you don't! You want to be vibrationally and emotionally juicy, so when people see you, speak with you, do business with you, or love you, they can say, "**Now, THAT'S a juicy peach!**"

What makes you juicy? You know the answer.

Love makes you vibrationally irresistible.

You'll be juicy when you're fully plugged in to the irresistible energy of Love that is your true nature.

**You've been designed with sacred circuitry.
You've been designed to be juicy!
Your sacred circuitry has been divinely structured in order for you
to experience the Unlimited—unlimited Love, unlimited Joy,
unlimited Wisdom, and unlimited Freedom.
That circuitry must be cleared out and fully turned on
for you to allow the highest voltage of love and spirit
to flow through you.**

You need to be as open as you can be and as big as you can be to hold all of that unimaginable, unfathomable Bigness. This is the work we are doing. You are beginning to restore yourself to your original factory settings so you can feel everything, receive everything, love everything, and know yourself as connected to everything.

This is what is so powerful about making the choice for love. *The practice of loving itself will instantly reward you by opening up more and more of your circuitry.* Your nervous system will be used to more powerful voltage/life force/cosmic energy. Higher levels of vibrational intensity can operate through you—more abundance, more energy, more everything. Then, your ability to transmit love, wisdom, creativity, and power naturally and spontaneously increases.

**Making the choice for love actually creates
more vibrational circuits in you.
The more you love, the more you literally get
emotionally and spiritually rewired.
Love enlightens and awakens you on the spot.**

Untangling Your Heartstrings

*"Why don't you make your whole body into a string
and play the music of the vibratory electromagnetic self,
which is your creativity,
and project to the heart of another person?"*
— Harbhajan Singh Yogi

For as long as I can remember, I've loved wind chimes. It's estimated that the first primitive wind chimes were created over 5,000 years ago in Southeast Asia from shells, bones, and stones and were used to ward off evil spirits. The ancient Egyptians were casting bronze wind chimes in 2000 B.C., and 1,000 years later, the Chinese began fashioning wind chimes and bells with musical tones that were often used in religious rituals, and as a feng shui cure to disperse stagnant or negative energy. In China, Japan, and Bali, wind chimes were hung from the eaves of sacred temples and shrines for protection and to attract benevolent spirits.

I have many different sets of wind chimes, from very large to very small, hanging outside of my home. Some dangle from tree branches, and some are attached to the eaves of the roof. The winds are abundant here, moving up the hill from the ocean or blowing down from the mountains, and my chimes are in a constant, delightful symphony of sound, each one offering a unique and different song as they joyfully sway with delight in the embrace of the Santa Barbara breeze.

One morning as I was lying in bed, I had the strangest sensation that something was different, but couldn't figure out what it was. Suddenly I realized it wasn't what *was* happening, but what *wasn't* happening—**it was totally silent outside. I couldn't hear any wind chimes.** I decided to investigate, and walked out into the yard off of the bedroom, where one of my favorite melodic chimes hung from a branch in an avocado tree. It was the one that always serenaded me each morning when I awoke, and offered me a tinkling lullaby each night as I fell asleep.

As soon as I saw the wind chimes, I realized what had taken place. The night before, the winds had been unusually strong, and *the strings that held the chimes had become totally twisted and tangled together in a mass of tight knots. Since the chimes couldn't move, they couldn't produce any sounds.*

For the next 15 minutes, I worked diligently to untangle and unknot the tight web of strings, one by one freeing the metal tubes so they were able to move and fill the air with exquisite mystical music. When I finished, a light breeze suddenly swept into the yard, and the wind chimes burst into a delicate choir of soothing sounds. I couldn't help feeling like they were thanking me for liberating them to serve their purpose.

As I closed my eyes and allowed the harmonious vibration of the tones to wash over me, my heart filled with understanding that those wind chimes had just offered me a new way to explain this important teaching:

> **Each of us has been created to be the living song of the divine.**
> **From your heart, the exquisite vibration of love can pour forth**
> **in uplifting and healing harmonies.**
> **Like a set of wind chimes, you are designed to dance,**
> **but you have to keep your strings untangled.**

All of us have had our strings snarled by the winds of disappointment, the winds of heartbreak, the winds of our wounds, and the winds of our pain and suffering. These things sweep through our lives like a relentless storm, *twisting and knotting us so that the source energy cannot flow freely through us.* We stop being able to share our most beautiful songs of wisdom, love, and joy with the world. We become too blocked and tangled to dance.

When I went outside to my chimes on the tree, I made the choice for love. I did not become angry at the wind. I did not curse the chimes for now being a tight, confusing mess. I lovingly unknotted each bunch of string and patiently untangled each metal tube. *"I'm sorry you got so violently blown around,"* I said. *"Soon you will be free to make music again."*

This is our path as seekers. We are wired for ecstasy, for wisdom, and for love. Holding firm to this vision, we steadfastly and courageously locate our knots, our tangles, and our disconnected circuits, and we unknot, untangle, and reconnect our way to awakening.

> **You are nothing less than Everything!**
> **You are connected to nothing less than Everything!**
> **You have been miraculously created to experience**
> **nothing less than Everything!**
> **Plug back into the Source.**
> **Turn your heart back on.**
> **Prepare to be dazzled.**

❧ 4 ❧

Loving Your Brain
into Awakening

"We don't see things as they are. We see things as we are."
— Anaïs Nin

Love. Intimacy. Happiness. Fulfillment. Joy. Delight. Peace. Brain. Wait—what's *brain* doing in this collection of words? What does the brain have to do with love and happiness? The answer is: *everything!* It's time to understand *the actual mechanics of how your brain gets programmed* to limit the amount of love you're capable of feeling, giving, or receiving.

What is your brain? It's an amazing and mysterious three-pound miracle. This wondrous organ is actually a brilliant, complicated computer that interfaces with what you think of as "you": that part of you that tells you that you're a separate entity from all you see around you, from other people, and the rest of the world—that you are David or Tiffany or Maria, or whomever you think you are. It's because of your brain that you can read these words and understand them, or that you know to put on a sweater when the brain sends you a signal that your body is cold. When you have to make a decision, it's your brain that gathers and produces "files" of information related to the problem from which you can choose.

Your brain contains many parts, each one being responsible for a different function to keep you alive. For our purpose, *let's look at the brain "circuitry," an intricate communication network called neurons—100 billion of them—like the wires in a computer.* The neurons gather and analyze information from within you as well as from the world around you, and communicate to each other through *a system of connectors called* synapses. There are trillions of synapses in your brain acting as the meeting point between neurons. A chemical substance called a neurotransmitter allows these cells to talk to one another.

Here's what is so astonishing:

**Everything that's ever happened to you, everything you've ever seen,
every word you've ever heard,
and every emotion you've ever experienced
is stored in your brain.**

For instance, your brain is what tells you not to walk out into traffic because you'll hurt yourself, not to put your hand in fire, not to eat dirt, and that it's not okay to hit someone, among millions of other commands. These directives may seem obvious now, but they weren't known to you when you were a baby. You learned that these activities were not okay from what your parents told you—and sometimes from painful experience—and your brain stored the information for future use.

Have you ever wondered how, once you do something enough times, even a difficult task that requires a lot of concentration and focus, at some point it becomes automatic? Remember your first experiences driving a car? It seemed so complicated to try and remember all the rules, when to accelerate, or where to look. Now when you get into your car, you don't even think about these details when you're driving. There are probably many skills that you use in your profession, in hobbies, or in sporting activities that, when you first learned them, were challenging to master, but now are just routine. You have the way your brain is designed to thank for this!

> *"In every human brain there are as many neurons
> as there are galaxies in the known universe—about 100 billion,
> drawn from 10,000 different cell types with threads of neural interconnections
> that number in the trillions. Memories are made of this gray matter.
> So are inspiration and imagination."*
> — Robert Lee Hotz

How do we learn things? In 1949, Donald Hebb, who's thought of as the father of neuropsychology, introduced a discovery that is now an integral part of the field of neuroscience. Simply put, it says that:

NEURONS THAT FIRE TOGETHER, WIRE TOGETHER

What researchers found is that when neurons in your brain are firing or actively communicating at the same time as other neurons, they eventually start to associate together. This communication process of your neurons passing information back and forth is known as "neuronal firing." **When brain cells communicate frequently, the connection between them improves. Messages that travel the same pathways in the brain over and over will, in time, begin to be transmitted more rapidly, and eventually with enough repetition, the transmission becomes automatic.**

This is what we mean when we say, *"I don't even think about what I'm doing when I am on the ski slopes—I'm on autopilot,"* or *"When I had my first child, I focused on every single thing I was doing to make sure it was correct, but now with three kids, I get them bathed, dressed, and ready for school without even noticing I'm doing it."*

Neural pathways that get used more often strengthen, kind of like roads that become cleared of obstacles and easier to travel on. The opposite is also true: neural pathways that are not used as much weaken. The fancy scientific term for this is **"experience-dependent neuroplasticity." What does this mean?**

**Even though you aren't aware of it,
how your brain thinks and experiences is actually
being reprogrammed every day.
That means that you're transforming into a different person
every day of your life.
So in order to transform yourself and your relationships,
you need to transform your brain.**

Being on mental "autopilot" doesn't seem like a problem when we think about driving somewhere familiar or doing routine tasks at work without having to focus on what we're doing. However, it's a lot more serious when it impacts our experience of ourselves, people we love, and the world around us, and, as we will see, takes us on emotional roller-coaster rides.

Why Your Brain's Emotional
Software Is Out-of-Date

"The past does not repeat itself, but sometimes it rhymes."
— Mark Twain

Recently I purchased a new Wi-Fi booster that takes the signal from my main modem and extends the internet network throughout the rest of my house. My modem was a few years old but had been working well, and the addition was going to serve as an extender. I attempted to set up the device, which I had done many times before, but this time no matter what I did, I couldn't get it to work. I contacted the technical support people for my device, and spent several exasperating hours on the phone with representatives who tried and failed to solve my problem. Finally, I insisted on speaking to the most senior, senior supervisor they could find. Within a few minutes, she'd figured it out: **My old, original router was using complicated programming that wasn't necessary anymore, but it didn't want to let go of it!**

"Here's the situation," she explained. *"The technology has changed and advanced tremendously since you got your first router. The new one we're attempting to set up is trying to talk to your old one, and tell it that it doesn't have to work so hard and go through so many steps to get the task done.* **But your old router isn't listening. It was programmed to do things a certain way, and it hasn't been updated. You could say it's stuck in the past, and that why you haven't been able to move forward with expanding your network."**

"What's the solution?" I asked.

"We're going to have to try and reboot and retrain your router until it cooperates," she answered.

Soon the system was operating perfectly, and my irritation turned into gratitude as I realized that my predicament was the ideal metaphor for why our brains need updating and rebooting so we can experience more love, more wisdom, and more freedom.

Your brain is just like a computer, or smartphone, or any device that has default settings and operating systems that can be programmed into them. You've probably downloaded a new version of a system for your laptop or phone in the last year, because you wouldn't consider running them using outdated software. Here's where this is leading:

When is the last time you updated the programs in your brain? Are you still using an operating system that's decades old?

Do you know that if your brain isn't "updated," it can keep you stuck in "old emotional settings" that prevent you from experiencing the love you deserve?

Every time you turn on your devices, their default settings go into action because you've programmed them that way. You chose the look of your desktop screen; you decided how often your computer automatically saves a document, how often files are backed up, and what type of font is used when you type. You chose what ringtone you hear when someone calls you, or if your phone will have a sound or not when you receive a text.

In the same way, your brain is programmed so that when you have certain experiences, they automatically wire with other experiences. These are your brain's default settings.

You experience these default settings and the wiring together of your neurons a thousand times a day:

You feel a little down, and suddenly find yourself craving ice cream even though it's ten o'clock in the morning.

You see someone who reminds you of your ex-boyfriend, and suddenly feel sad and as if your heart is aching, even though you're happily married.

You think about a barbecue you're going to over the weekend, and find yourself suddenly craving a hamburger, even though you just ate a big meal.

You start to walk down some stairs where you once slipped on some ice and, even though it is sunny and 80 degrees outside, you feel yourself clench up.

What's happening here? Your brain is "remembering" certain experiences associated with what you're doing, and presenting you with those emotions and reactions. *Your mom gave you ice cream to make you feel better when you were little, so when you're upset, your neurons pull up the information "ice cream," which is wired with sadness and comfort. I FEEL BAD. I NEED LOVE. LOVE = ICE CREAM. Therefore, I NEED ICE CREAM.*

Many, if not all, of our emotional experiences and reactions,
along with our thoughts, understandings, and beliefs,
are by-products of how our brain has been programmed
by our life experiences without our even realizing it.
When we haven't updated that information,
our brain will be stuck in the past, and so will our emotions.

EMOTIONAL FLASHBACKS: HOW YOUR BRAIN FOOLS YOU WITH OUTDATED INFORMATION

"The past is never where you think you left it."

— Katherine Ann Porter

The other day I was in a supermarket, and all of the sudden I heard a song playing over the sound system that stopped me in my tracks. It was the first song that I really loved as a teenager back in 1963: *"Sealed with a Kiss"* by Brian Hyland. Some of you who are older might remember it. The lyrics lamented having to say good-bye to your sweetheart over the summer until school resumed in the fall. Sigh . . . I was probably 13 years old when it was released, and I was obsessed with it. I would play it over and over on my little RCA 45 record player, sometimes for hours on end. This was a very painful time in my life. My parents had just gotten divorced; I felt very different from the other kids at school, and didn't have much confidence in myself.

That day in the market, it wasn't just that I heard the song and had memories of the past. *I felt emotionally transported back in time, as if I could experience everything as I had first experienced it 50 years ago: I could smell my boyfriend's cologne; I could see the details of my childhood bedroom; I felt waves of sadness and loneliness—exactly as I'd felt as the 13-year-old me.*

I'm sure you've had similar "flashbacks" triggered by various experiences—you discover an old love letter written by your former partner, and just seeing the handwriting, old emotions rise up as if you can remember how you felt when you fell in love; you get a whiff of a particular brand of suntan lotion that whisks you back in time to happy memories of the beach.

I had a very powerful flashback experience just yesterday. I opened a box I hadn't seen for years, and there sitting on top of an old blanket was a plastic dog comb that I'd used to comb the hair on my two precious dogs when they were alive. Tears poured down my face as I saw the soft white hairs still woven into the teeth of the comb. In that moment, I wasn't just remembering how much I loved and missed my babies—**I was having a vibrational flashback of actually touching them, smelling them, feeling their warm bodies beneath my hands.**

Why does the smell of French toast make you feel your grandmother is standing right next to you?

Why does hearing a song from your past seem to act like a Time Machine, transporting you years back so, for a few minutes, you can feel everything you used to feel?

Why did just touching my dogs' comb fill me with real sense experiences of smelling and holding them?

The answer is that your brain is offering you *outdated information.* **It "wired" these experiences together, and** *never "unwired" them.*

Of course, most of us don't mind, and in fact enjoy, these emotional flashbacks when they allow us to re-experience precious moments and cherished times. However, not all of our vibrational flashbacks are pleasant:

We drive past the hospital where a friend or relative died, and feel a wave of grief wash over us.

We hear the name of a person who hurt us, and our body clenches up in fear as if it is about to happen again.

Our partner says something critical, and we suddenly feel overcome with sadness as if we've reverted to being five years old back in our childhood facing our daddy's judgment and being afraid he doesn't love us.

Here are some examples of how our past experiences can create emotional challenges for us in the present:

When Suzanne was a little girl, her father was very hard to reach, spent most of his time watching sports on TV, and ignored his wife and children. Eventually, he left and they divorced. Now, 20 years later, whenever Suzanne's very loyal and caring husband wants to be quiet after work, watches TV, or isn't interested in a conversation she wants to have with him, she finds herself in a neurological, emotional flashback. She feels abandoned, alone, and full of despair, and accuses him of not caring about her.

Suzanne has **the experience of "lack of attention" wired together with "abandonment," and really feels frightened and rejected when someone doesn't pay attention to her even for a few minutes.**

❁

Robert grew up as a single child with a single mother. When he was little and attempted to be talkative or creative, his exhausted and stressed-out mom would become irritated and tell him to be quiet. Now, when Robert is about to give a presentation at work, or wants to talk to women at parties, he experiences terrible anxiety and fear of rejection.

Robert has the act of **"expressing himself" and the emotion of "fear of rejection" wired together** from these repeated incidents in childhood, so just the anticipation of having to communicate with anyone makes him a nervous wreck.

❁

Sarah's mother died she was very young, and her father soon remarried. Her stepmother had rigidly high expectations and standards, and Sarah never felt anything she did was good enough. Now Sarah goes into almost every situation feeling like she has to make everyone happy, do everything perfectly, sacrifice her needs for others, and never disagree with anyone.

Sarah has **the experience of "wanting to be loved" wired together with the emotion of "must perform perfectly,"** and consequently is obsessed with what people think of her, terrified of making mistakes and of anyone being unhappy with what she says or does.

Can you see the repeated neurological programming that created these emotional patterns?

*Suzanne's love neurons fired together so often with her abandonment neurons that they got wired together: **NOT GETTING ATTENTION = BEING ABANDONED. Whenever she doesn't get attention, even in the smallest way, she experiences loss and despair.**

*Robert's communication neurons fired together so often with his rejection neurons that they got wired together: **COMMUNICATION = FEAR. Whenever he has to communicate to anyone, he experiences profound fear of disapproval.**

*Sarah's love neurons fired together so often with her performance pressure neurons that they got wired together: **GETTING LOVE = PER-FORMING. Whenever she wants approval or acceptance, she feels she has to be perfect and do everything for everyone.**

The problem is that when we have these experiences, they don't feel like some kind of mental association or brain programming—**they feel like *real emotions happening now,* in real time.**

Remember my story about listening to a song from my early teenage years? Hearing the melody, I was instantly taken on a vibrational journey back to my childhood bedroom. I was flooded with the exact emotions of loneliness and insecurity I'd lived with as a child. I could smell the scent of freshly mown grass coming in the window, and the chicken my mother was cooking in the kitchen. I could see the details of my old record player. It was all so real. *I was having a neurological flashback!*

Here's the next really important point to understand: When your neurons start firing together and your brain is experiencing an old neurological association, it sends the information through your nervous system as thoughts and emotions, and you feel it in your heart. *You experience these messages as if the information is real, even though it's based on an outdated neurological pathway.* **You're watching an emotional rerun.**

Usually when we experience our emotional/neurological flashbacks, we don't know it's happening.
The reality that our thoughts and feelings create for us seems real, as if it's occurring now in present time.

Our brain is constantly playing "oldies but goodies" and we don't even realize it! This is why I always tell my students that:

WE SEE THE WORLD THROUGH THE EYES OF OUR ISSUES

Your brain's well-traveled neurological pathways are like the highways or streets of a big city at rush hour—bumper-to-bumper information bombarding you with mental and emotional messages that make it *difficult for you, in any given moment, to act, feel, or interpret reality in a way that is totally free of old information.* You're experiencing reality through the eyes—or neural pathways—of your issues and programming. **Therefore, as we've explained, a lot of what you're experiencing isn't REAL at all! In fact, it's actually what I call THE UNREAL.**

Breaking Out of Your Emotional Prison

"Your mind can be either your prison or your palace.
What you make it is yours to decide."
— Bernard Kelvin Clive

When I was in my 20s, I lived in the Bay Area, and used to see Alcatraz Island every day when I drove from my tiny apartment in Mill Valley into the city. The island is now a park, but for almost 30 years it was the site of the infamous federal prison that held some of the most notorious bank robbers and murderers in American history, including the gangster Al Capone. Alcatraz, or "The Rock," as it was called, had a reputation for being a penitentiary from which escape was impossible, and indeed during the 29 years it was in operation, no one successfully escaped, though many prisoners drowned trying.

Whenever I passed Alcatraz, I'd be overcome with an eerie sensation as I pondered the cruel irony of its location in what is one of the most exquisite places in the world. I'd imagine the prisoners, locked away for life and forced to gaze out at so much beauty. They could watch the birds flying freely, but knew they had no chance of escape. They could see the glistening water, the magical Northern California light, the picturesque sailboats passing by, but knew they would never have another moment of any kind of joy in their lives. They could see the magnificent bridges carrying the cars to so many wonderful places—but knew they would never go anywhere. **To be in hell and look out at something so heavenly had to be pure torture.**

In some sense, this is life when we live in our own emotional prisons. *We can see what's out there, but we're not free.* We can think, *"If I were free I could cross that bridge, I could swim in that ocean of love, I could be powerful and fly like that bird,"* but we don't know how to fully live it.

> To whatever extent we are not free
> to be our highest self in each moment,
> or are chained to reactions set in motion from our past,
> or are locked inside of painful emotions from which we cannot escape,
> we're living in an emotional prison.

This metaphor offers us both good news and bad news. The good news is that these aren't real prisons, just *neurological prisons*—our programming and our default settings that, as we've seen, don't allow us to act and react freely. The bad news is that, unlike Alcatraz, **emotional prisons aren't stationary—they're portable.** We drag them with us everywhere we go, like an "Emotional RV." We show up in our Emotional RVs at work; we park our Emotional RVs in the driveways of our relationships. *We know that they take up a lot of space, but we have a hard time letting go of them.*

In order to prevent other people from noticing our emotional prisons, and to keep even ourselves from acknowledging their existence, we can get very good at disguising them. These disguises are often mistaken for what we call *our personality.* For instance:

We may disguise our prison of anger with a very friendly, entertaining personality.

We may disguise our prison of fear of failure with a type A, hyperactive, superproductive personality.

We may disguise our prison of the fear of intimacy with a very cool, independent personality.

We may disguise our prison of the fear of abandonment with a super-helpful and self-sacrificing personality.

Of course, not all aspects of our personality are disguises, **but as we do more of this work, we will be amazed to discover how many parts of us are cover-up costumes we wear hoping no one sees the fear, vulnerability, insecurity, shame, anger, or despair that's underneath.**

We may say things like:

"This is just the way I am."

"I'm not distant—I just don't like depending on anyone."

"I don't have a temper, I'm just a very passionate person."

"I don't really think I'm a people pleaser—I just have a big heart and love helping everyone."

We even get people in our lives to move into our emotional prisons with us. And we get really adept at decorating our emotional prisons so they don't look like prisons at all, even to us.

Are you beginning to recognize and understand some of your own emotional wiring? Are you starting to identify some of the emotional prisons in which you've been living, and some of the "unreal" that you've made real? I hope so, because **recognition means you're already offering new information to your brain, information that is actually *changing* your brain.**

None of us wants to have these patterns, and often we don't even know they exist. We think it's just the way we are. But it's not—these are *unconscious default settings in our brain* that have determined how we think and feel for decades. Understanding this, we suddenly realize something very exciting:

> **Many of your emotions, behaviors, and habits are *not* personality traits intrinsic to your nature.**
> **They are simply old, emotional programs in your brain that you don't even realize are in operation.**
> **Just as your brain was originally programmed, it can be reprogrammed!**

Your New Operating System: Love

"Do not conform any longer to the pattern of this world, but be transformed by the renewing of your mind."

— Romans 12:2

Have you ever clicked the news icon on your phone or tablet, and been surprised to see an article about something you knew took place a few days earlier? Then it hits you—*you haven't refreshed your browser!* Your device was still stuck in the past. As soon as you hit the refresh button, it updates everything to present time.

Just like this, *we are all still getting "old news" about ourselves from our brain.* It's giving us stories that are 20, 30, 40 years old about who we are, how we need to function, and what is real: *"I can't trust love. It's not safe for me to express myself. I can't trust people to accept the real me. I have to control everything if I don't want to get hurt. I don't like intimacy. I need to make everyone happy so they won't be angry with me. I'm not smart and will never amount to anything. I'm an introvert. I shouldn't ask anyone for anything because then they will have power over me."*

These emotional headlines may have been accurate once, but today, they are your OLD NEWS.

This is why so many sincere seekers get stuck and frustrated. We begin to work on ourselves, and see patterns or behaviors we want to change. We truly are committed to changing; we have positive thoughts about changing and visualize changing. Somehow, however, we find ourselves falling back into the same patterns over and over again. Why? **In a sense, our brains are stuck. The neurons that fired together got wired together, and now they need to get unwired.** When we haven't pushed the reset button to refresh our consciousness, we get trapped in an emotional time warp.

Perhaps you're concluding: *"I knew it—it's my brain that's the problem. Why can't it stop feeding me all of this old information, and filling my head with thoughts that upset me? Why can't it be more helpful, creative, and brilliant?"* Before you blame your brain for many of your problems, I'd like to offer you a radical new way of thinking about it:

Your brain has really been doing the best job for you that it possibly can—*under the circumstances*!

What circumstances are those? Here are just a few:

The hundreds of thousands of hours of programming your brain has endured based on the millions upon millions of less-than-enlightened choices *you've* made, programming that you then blame on your brain when it doesn't work the way you want it to—even though *you're the one who took the actions.*

The habit you have of "hurting" your brain by overloading it with conflicting commands and contradictory messages that confuse it and "crash" its ability to find a solution, and then wondering

why it doesn't just give you all the answers you need as soon as you need them.

Your reluctance to live with consistent consciousness, so that you end up making unhealthy decisions and exposing yourself to emotional pain, which then floods your brain with a backlog of negative emotions it has to process—which you once again blame on your brain.

Your choice to numb, anesthetize, intoxicate, or fry your brain's neural networks by using substances that at the very least, inhibit it from functioning properly, and at the worst, shrink your brain, kill its cells, and create permanent damage so that it has to work even harder to function.

Need I go on?

My point is that *it's you who makes it difficult for your brain to operate as magnificently as it was designed to.* Your poor brain does the best it can considering the impossible burdens you've placed upon it, and then it has to cope with getting blamed for your problems!

The most miraculous thing about your brain is that *it's not hardwired.* It is designed to change, to learn, and to constantly improve. Everything you do, every experience, thought, or emotion you have, and every choice you make physically changes your brain. Therefore, when you complain that you wish your brain would *help you* be smarter, happier, and more successful, it's actually the opposite that's true:

You want your brain to be better,
but it's your brain that needs *your help* to be better!
You need to start loving your brain into awakening.

Remember my stuck computer and router? They needed my help so they could perform for me in the way they were designed to. I was the one who needed to change some settings, clean out "electronic debris" that was slowing things down, and refresh and reboot the operating system. As soon as I did, my devices began to work perfectly. I could almost imagine hearing them say, *"Thank you for your help, Barbara! We really do want to make you happy. We're geniuses, but we aren't the ones in control of what you do—you're in control of what we do."*

So how do we reboot our brain? Rebooting isn't something intellectual.

You can't change philosophically.
You have to change experientially and vibrationally.
So rewiring your brain happens by actually
doing things in a different way.
In each moment, we make the choice to love our brain
by *making the choice for love.*

HOW MAKING THE CHOICE FOR LOVE
REBOOTS YOUR BRAIN

Rebooting yourself and your brain means learning to recognize
habitual patterns of thinking, feeling, and behavior
when they're happening,
and making new choices for love that, minute by minute,
will reprogram you and help your brain create
new enlightened pathways.

The thing to understand about rebooting is that you have to do it everywhere, with everything. You can't simply say: *"I'm going to reboot my fear of expressing myself, so I'm now proclaiming that I want to express myself. I understand where it came from and I was afraid to speak as a child because I got humiliated and now I know it's safe. I tried this today at work, so now I've shifted."*

You *have* shifted—that one experience. You've created a new neurological association between expressing yourself and love, *a new "baby" pathway.* The next day, however, you're going to have another opportunity to do this when you are having a difficult conversation with your partner. The day after that, you're going to have another chance to practice this when your in-laws visit.

All of your old choices need to be rebooted, over and over again. Rebooting in this situation, rebooting in that situation, rebooting when you're tired, rebooting when you're not, rebooting when you're afraid to reboot, rebooting when you're courageous—until at a certain point, the new programming clicks in, and the new circuit finally gets established.

Your programming was not created by thoughts you had in your past, but by actual vibrational experiences.
Therefore, *you can't think your way out of your programming.*
You have to *vibrate* your way out of it.
To rewire your brain,
you need new, positive vibrational experiences.
You need to make the choice for love.

Remember Sarah earlier in this chapter, who felt in order to be loved, she had to please everyone? Imagine that Sarah decides to think positive thoughts about herself in order to change her compulsive pattern of performing for love. Over and over, she thinks: *"I am lovable and perfect just the way I am."* That positive thought will make her feel good in the moment, and it definitely will create a certain uplifting of her vibration and have a good effect on her overall.

However, the next time Sarah walks into a situation in which she is actually having the experience of wanting love, *her well-traveled neural pathway between LOVE and PERFORMANCE will get lit up in her brain like a freeway during rush hour!* She will be bombarded with neurological messages that she must perform for love. She'll start telling jokes; she'll compliment everyone she meets; she will feel nervous and anxious and not know why.

Sarah is responding to old commands from her brain. It starts sending her messages, like alerts that pop up on our smartphones: "URGENT: YOU ARE IN A SITUATION WHERE YOU WANT LOVE AND APPROVAL. YOU MUST PERFORM! YOU MUST MAKE EVERYONE HAPPY."

That old neurological habit overrides any positive thoughts she may try to overlay onto the situation, because that has been her programming. So how can Sarah rewire her emotional circuitry? The answer is:

She needs to not only have new, positive thoughts,
but she must make new, positive vibrational choices.

Each time she meets someone, chooses to be her authentic self, and receives approval for it, she creates a new neural pathway that says: "When I am myself, I am loved. AUTHENTICITY = LOVE." It's not that she's trying to believe this. She's experienced it, and so her brain will actually begin to change.

I hope you're getting excited about the opportunity you have to re-wire your brain. How do you do this? You use a fabulous new technology that is guaranteed to powerfully reprogram your neurological patterns and heal your heart: *it's called LOVE!*

*You make the choice to love yourself enough so that you start to do things differently, act differently, communicate differently, relate differently—by CHOOSING DIFFERENTLY.

*You begin to identify patterns that aren't serving you, and you make new, conscious, different choices in each moment.

For instance:

You've been afraid to speak up, so you begin expressing how you feel, and honoring yourself for your courage.

You've been afraid to let people see the real you, so you begin show-ing up authentically.

You've been afraid to stop self-sacrificing and people pleasing, so you begin to ask others for what you want, and say no when it feels right.

Before you know it, those old, carved, neurological grooves that de-termined how you behaved, how you spoke, how you thought about yourself and how you approached life begin to vanish. *You literally re-cre-ate yourself from the inside out—from the neural pathways in your brain out to your thinking and behavior!*

Throughout the rest of this book, I'll be sharing many more practical ways to reboot and rewire yourself, and create new, positive vibrational experiences that will give your brain and your consciousness new infor-mation about yourself and the world. **This updated information will literally change your brain, and free you from the prison of old be-haviors, old reactions, and old habits that aren't serving you.**

Before you know it, those neurological "oldies but goodies" will stop playing in your head. Stay committed to transforming, and be patient—**your brain needs time to catch up with reality!**

BUILDING A NEW, ENLIGHTENED BRAIN, CHOICE BY CHOICE

"Love is the great miracle cure."
— Louise Hay

Today, you ate something. You went somewhere. You experienced some things. You were affected by other people. These things are all events that happened to you. If I asked you: *"Are you the salad you ate for lunch? Are you the pharmacy you stopped at to buy some aspirin? Are you the weights you lifted at the gym? Are you the conversation you had with your friend?"* your answer would be, *"Of course not! What silly questions. I experienced these events. These things happened to me. But they are NOT me!"*

Naturally, you would be correct. We are not the events that happen to us. And yet, this is how many of us identify ourselves, and how it often feels.

All of us have had terrible things happen in our lives. This is the human school we are in. None of us has escaped heartbreak, loss, grief, or pain. These things *happened* to you. They probably caused some of the emotional and neurological programming we've been examining. *But they are not who you are.* We need to be careful that in acknowledging where we've been and what challenging events have taken place in our cosmic classroom, we are not defining ourselves by the past.

You are *not* the events that have happened to you.
You are *not* your emotional programming.
You are *not* the neurological pathways in your brain.
You are *not* your emotional prisons.
You are the consciousness that experiences these things.
You are the vastness of love expressed in your human form.

We allow ourselves to put aside old patterns and emotional costumes just as we put aside an item of clothing that we once loved wearing, but is totally out of style and no longer fits. We don't berate ourselves for how we looked in it—we admit that it is outdated, and that the time has come to let it go.

Don't forget:

> Your emotional patterns and programming
> are not good or bad.
> They are just *outdated and unnecessary.*
> Recognize and release them without blame or guilt.
> Let them go with love.

Each time you make a choice for love that is in alignment with your Highest, you will be creating a new, positive vibrational experience. New sets of neurons will start firing together and wiring together. This updated information will literally change your brain as you carve brand-new neurological pathways, and reprogram your experience of yourself and reality. *You will be transforming from the inside out.*

This is the beginning of true freedom: freedom from the prison of old behaviors, old reactions, and old habits that aren't serving you; freedom to move fully from the past into the present; and freedom to live with as much love and joy as possible.

> Who you think you are now is who you have been in the past.
> Who you really are is a treasure waiting to be discovered.
> Moment by moment, choice by choice,
> we love our brain into awakening
> and love ourselves to freedom.

PART TWO

ESSENTIAL
HEALING
FOR
YOUR HEART

5

Necessary Relinquishments

"When I let go of what I am, I become what I might be.
When I let go of what I have, I receive what I need."
— Tao Te Ching

There's a famous story about how, in remote parts of the world, monkey hunters trap monkeys. They place a banana in a glass jar and hide in the bushes, waiting for the monkey to come along. The monkey sees the banana and wants it, and proceeds to put his hand down into the jar. However, when he tries to withdraw his hand, it's impossible—because he is clutching the banana. The opening of the jar is too narrow for both the banana and his hand to fit through.

All the monkey has to do to get his hand out of the jar is to let go of the banana, but he stubbornly won't do it. He clings on to the banana. And this is how the hunter finds him and captures him.

Most of the time when we think of making the choice for love, we are called to reach out, to connect, to hold on. We all come to times in our lives, however, when the choice for love means the choice not to do something but to identify *what we need to stop doing*—the choice not to hold on, but to let go.

We need to make the choice for relinquishment.

All great teachers in all traditions have always talked about the road to freedom as a road of continual relinquishment. *Relinquishment is a high spiritual practice.* We come to what I often describe as a very narrow passageway on our path to emotional and spiritual freedom, and we want to move forward, but we're holding on to something very big—our ego, our story, our pride, our stubbornness, our blame, our resistance, or our regret. To get all the way through the opening into our own awakening and mastery, we're going to have to relinquish this big bundle of stuff, and we don't want to let go of it. Our mind complains: ***"I don't know how to keep moving and still hold onto this old part of me/pattern/***

emotion/relationship because I'm so attached to it"—and the answer is that you can't.

Undoubtedly you've faced times of necessary relinquishments—letting go of a relationship, a job, a friend, a home, or a dream you held close to your heart. As painful and difficult as these relinquishments can be, *I believe it's even more difficult to relinquish things about yourself that are no longer serving you.*

> **There are many moments on our soul journey that require
> a surrender and an offering up.**
> **You're asked to relinquish not something *outside* of yourself,
> but something *about* yourself:**
> **A way of thinking; an ego pattern; an emotional habit;
> A stubbornness or stance that has held you hostage;
> A limiting belief that's kept you stuck and small;
> An addiction that has enslaved you;
> An old story you've been telling yourself and others
> about your life that's not accurate.**
> **You're asked to relinquish these things
> because they are binding you.**
> **Like the monkey and the banana,
> you're gripping something so tightly,
> but in order to move forward, you will need to let go.**

At these times, it's easy to feel a sense of panic. Some conscious part of you whispers, *"You know you're going to have to let go of that, don't you? It's time. You're going to have to confront it. You're going to have to change. You can't avoid this any longer."*

The ego, the old, limited part of you, hears this, feels threatened and cries out, *"I don't want to let go of this,"* as if when you do, a cherished piece of you will disappear. ***"If I let go of this pattern, or this identity, or this way of behaving, or this way of trying to control everything, or this way of protecting myself, then who am I? Without this, I'll die!"*** The truth, of course, is exactly the opposite: *With* this, you will never pass through to freedom, and you will not fully live and love. **You need to let go of your banana.**

Relinquishment is a powerful word. We usually associate relinquish with the act of letting go and subsequent loss, such as "He relinquished his power," or "She was ordered to relinquish custody of the child." I love to research the origin of words to dig more deeply into the wisdom they offer, and *relinquishment* is derived from the Latin root *relinquere*, which means "to leave behind," "to abandon," or "to surrender." "To relinquish" implies some form of *conscious, deliberate giving up, or offering up*—not just a forced, simple, or inadvertent letting go.

For instance, if I let go of someone's hand after shaking it, I wouldn't say, "I relinquished his hand." If I let go of my money in order to pay for my groceries. I wouldn't say: "I relinquished my money to the cashier." These wouldn't be accurate descriptions of the simplicity of what took place.

Relinquishment is much more than merely letting go: It's a profound act of releasing something. There's an important element of surrender to it. We make an emotional choice to stop holding on.

Why is understanding relinquishment so important to us as seekers? Consider this for a moment: If you're like most people, your usual tendency is probably to try and figure out *what to do* and *how to be* so that you can become more successful, or be happier in a relationship, or transform yourself. *Your mind concludes that the more you want, the more you need to DO or GET.* Remember: There's nothing missing in you. If you're not missing anything, and you know you're not living as masterfully as you could, **it follows that PERHAPS it's not what *isn't* there that's the problem—it's what *is* there!**

This is a radical thought, but it's actually true:

It's not what you're missing that's limits and inhibits you.
It's the habits, programming, and patterns you haven't let go of and need to relinquish that are in the way of your freedom.
It's not about *getting* more. It's about *letting go* of more.
Instead of asking "What more can I do?"
ask yourself, *"What do I need to stop doing?"*

If you're running, and you want to stand still, you don't need to *do* anything—**you need to stop doing something.** You need to stop moving. If you're too busy, and you want to rest, you don't need to *do* anything, **you need to stop doing something.** You need to stop taking on tasks and saying yes to everyone.

Just like this, along with doing more things that are positive, expansive, and healing, we also need to *stop doing those things* that are blocking our Highest Self from emerging.

When we stop controlling, judging, hiding, resisting, manipulating, pretending, being dishonest, avoiding, indulging, distracting, competing, and all of the other behaviors and inner choices that contract our vibration, create dissonance, and disconnect us from our Highest, what we're left with is our true and magnificent Self!

> *"Love is the best school, but the tuition is high*
> *and the homework can be painful."*
>
> — Diane Ackerman

The first part of the title of this chapter contains the phrase Necessary Relinquishments. For many of us, this is where our difficulty begins: **What, after all, is so unnecessary to us that we must necessarily relinquish it? To our ego and limited self, every pattern, protection, and projection is completely necessary and essential.** *"I need ALL of this!"* it will insist to our Conscious Self. *"I need my anger to feel powerful. I need my walls to protect myself. I need my emotional caution so I don't get hurt again."* As we've seen in examining how your brain gets wired, your mind does believe that you need all of your walls, programs, and strategies in order to be loved. But the truth is precisely the opposite:

> **The very things our contracted and limited self believes**
> **are absolutely necessary for our emotional survival**
> **are actually the things that are not just unnecessary,**
> **but are holding us back from**
> **true happiness, true power, and true fulfillment.**

Perhaps you've had a glimpse of this. You've set an intention to not go along with your old patterns of behavior, and you're amazed to discover that if you don't play your usual games, or don't make your usual choices to shut off, or let go of your expectation of how things should be, a whole new you materializes! Stephanie, one of my students, described this perfectly in a recent e-mail:

"Last month when I visited my sister, I decided that, instead of trying to behave better, which I always attempt and fail miserably at, I was going to try practicing what you'd just taught us, and relinquish my need to control, my need to judge, my pattern of feeling I needed to fix her. I didn't try be more loving or enlightened. I just focused on not doing what I usually do, like you suggested. I refrained from giving her advice. I didn't make constant 'helpful' comments about what she could do better.

"I admit that I kept scaring myself by thinking, 'If I relinquish these habits or patterns, I won't even have a personality left! It's who I am. I'm a fixer. I won't know how to act with my sister or anyone else.' But I was wrong.

"When I stopped doing the things that weren't serving me, it was like a whole new me showed up, a me that was waiting for that other stuff to be cleared out so it could emerge. My sister actually asked me if I was on some kind of drugs or tranquilizers, because she'd never seen me so mellow! I told her I wasn't on anything, but I was off the drugs of my patterns. Who knew my real self was so loving and peaceful?"

You may not see the difference between trying to be better by doing certain things, and trying to not do something, but it's actually quite significant. There is an inner act of surrender that occurs when we relinquish the need to do something to which we've been attached. Stephanie was attached to fixing her sister, being right, and being in control. When she made the commitment to give those up, *her "not doing" created a powerful opening for her love and abundant heart to flow into her personality and out to the world.*

Learning to Unlearn: What Do You Need to Let Go of to Be Free?

"Truth, like gold, is to be obtained not by its growth,
but by washing away from it all that is not gold."
— Leo Tolstoy

I have always been a voracious learner. When I grew older and began my formal spiritual studies, it dawned on me that *as much as I still had to learn, I also had a lot I needed to* unlearn. The practice of unlearning is a necessary relinquishment, and an essential component of authentically transforming.

Unlearning is a powerful and important form of relinquishment.
So often we define ourselves by what we've learned
and how much we know.
The truth is that many times our greatest victories
and personal achievements
are in what we've "unlearned."

When you want to properly refinish a piece of furniture or paint a room whose walls are covered with old, peeling paint, you need to strip off the existing paint so that the new coat sticks. You scrape and sand off what you don't want there anymore so that the new paint will adhere to the surface and evenly cover every spot. **Unlearning is like stripping the old understandings from our consciousness so that our new revelations and awakenings can "stick."**

You can't just paste new understandings and wisdom on top of
your old, limited consciousness.
You can't just cover up old patterns with new behaviors
and expect them to stick.
They'll be undermined by what's been there before.
At the same time that you're learning new, expansive ways
of thinking and functioning, you have to be unlearning.

Later in this chapter, I offer you some Choice for Love Recalibration Questions that help you make your own list of what you might need to unlearn.

Here are just a few examples that many of us can relate to:

To unlearn how we keep ourselves in a constant state of anxiety by ignoring or avoiding unpleasant situations or feelings we need to face.

To unlearn the ways we push others away and keep love and intimacy out.

To unlearn all the ways we habitually judge ourselves and others.

To unlearn the "shoulds" we put on ourselves every day that set us up for failure.

To unlearn our old programming that keeps us having vibrational flashbacks.

To unlearn our fear of being authentic, so that our true self can emerge and come out from behind the mask.

To unlearn the habit of always trying to please everyone, even at the expense of our own self-respect.

To unlearn our pattern of hiding our true feelings from others.

To unlearn the way we shape-shift around people in order to try and control how they see us, and end up sacrificing our integrity.

Unlearning is a concept that many of us don't ever consider. Instead, we think, *"What did I learn? What did I get? What did I accomplish?"* **I'd like to suggest that perhaps some of your greatest accomplishments are in what you've already unlearned, what you've already stopped doing, and what you've already relinquished.**

True learning actually always involves some unlearning. The process of unlearning is not as visible or obvious as the experience of learning. *In the unlearning, however, you make space for more wisdom. You make space for more insights. You make space for more love.* **In this way, the choice for unlearning is the choice for love.**

We unlearn, and unlearn, and unlearn what is not true about ourselves, until we relearn and remember the magnificent and unique expression of Consciousness we are and always have been underneath our forgetfulness.

BREAKING THE MOLD OF YOUR PROTECTIONS

"One cannot shape the world without being reshaped in the process. Each gain of power requires its own sacrifice."

— Phil Hine

On my last trip to India, I had a very meaningful experience in a small village called Kumbakonam, situated in the southern state of Tamil Nadu. This town is known throughout the world for making beautiful bronze statues of the many Hindu and Buddhist deities. The artisans I met in the village were all descended from members of famous bronze-casting schools that existed in India between the 8th and 13th centuries. My home is filled with sacred objects, and I knew several that I'd purchased in California had been created right here in this ancient town, so I was excited to see their birthplace.

Bronze casting is a unique skill that is passed on from generation to generation. It was moving to watch these proud artists, whose fathers, grandfathers, great-grandfathers, and all the male line before them had lived in this same area and practiced this very same method. They were very enthusiastic to show us how the beautiful finished products were crafted, and delighted that we were so interested, as most tourists would stop in, purchase something, and leave without ever witnessing the superb skill of the villagers.

The first step in creating a bronze statue is to make a wax model. This requires great patience and precision, as the artisans sculpt the refined shapes and features of the Hindu and Buddhist deities using a special heated file, and fit together pieces such as arms and legs until the statue is complete. Layers of special clay are then painted onto the figure, forming a mold that completely encases the wax model. Next, the completed mold is heated in an open-ground oven, and as the clay bakes and hardens, the wax model melts and flows out a small hole at the bottom, leaving the empty clay mold, which is a perfect replica of the original.

Then it's time for the bronze alloy to be prepared and poured. Both the clay mold and the metal are heated to a minimum temperature of 1,800 degrees Fahrenheit until they're red hot. The hollowed-out mold is placed into a pit in the ground to stabilize it, and molten bronze is poured through the top into the waiting clay, filling up every part of it. Within the clay container, the exquisite metal statue is now hardening and cooling.

Now comes the fascinating part that I loved the most. **The artisans have to retrieve the finished statue from its protective clay covering by cracking and beating it off with hammers.** Breaking the mold so the icon can be removed is a very special act to these craftsmen, who consider the sculpture to be a sacred entity. They wait until the metal is sufficiently cooled and hardened, and only then do they initiate the hitting and cracking. When the bronze icon is completely free of its protective covering, it can be cleaned and polished.

I watched these dedicated artisans sitting cross-legged on the ground, just as the men in their generational lineage had done for centuries, intensely whacking the hard clay mold with metal hammers over and over again in order to free the sacred deity inside. **They explained how, on one hand, they had to be extremely forceful to crack off this very hard** covering, and on the other hand, they had to be careful not to break or scratch the beautiful bronze sculpture waiting to be unveiled.

In that moment, I realized that I was witnessing something profoundly symbolic, and being offered a precious wisdom gift: *This is precisely what each of us must do to ourselves to uncover our highest wisdom and love. Our protections have become our prisons, and we must remove them.*

> The mental and emotional walls, barricades, and barriers
> that we originally created to protect us
> eventually became the very things that imprison us.
>
> Now, to be free, we must relinquish them,
> taking apart and demolishing those same things we once
> carefully built, because we know they no longer serve us.
>
> We must crack the old mold of fear and unconsciousness
> that has been keeping our patterns in tact
> so the sacred gleaming form of our highest heart
> can finally be revealed.

At a certain point in our process of personal transformation, the hard-baked shell of our patterns that usually started out as our protections when we were young—to keep us safe or to make us feel powerful—now becomes no longer necessary. Something beautiful is waiting to be revealed, but first we need to relinquish the "mold" of habits and behaviors that have been covering it. **The sacred self we truly are has been consolidating and solidifying inside, just like the bronze statue, and the old, muddy covering needs to be broken into pieces and cracked off.**

The relinquishment of our old protections isn't fun. It requires hard work, just as the artisans demonstrated as they diligently pounded away on the hard clay mold. However, the removal is just preparation for what comes afterward, and the flow of more love, vision, creativity, and peace will be automatic as soon as we relinquish what's in the way.

> Just as water rushes in when the dam is removed,
> just as light rushes in when the window shade is raised,
> so the courageous efforts of our relinquishment
> will create space for the flooding in of love,
> the flooding in of wisdom, the flooding in of revelation,
> and the flooding in of unimaginable grace.

In nature we have so many examples of this paradigm of "removal preceding rebirth": the baby bird that hatches out of the egg by cracking it; the fruit that tears through the flower bud so it can grow; the butterfly that destroys the cocoon as it emerges. When you came into this world, you too had to break free from the womb. *Nature is often intense and even violent in its growth, and frequently the destruction, disintegration, or radical transformation of one thing occurs so something more magnificent can emerge.*

Perhaps as you've grown on your path of self-discovery, you're seeing so many things about how you function that are constricting you, imprisoning you, and need to be removed. Perhaps you feel an internal pressure, as the new consciousness within you presses against the old patterns, longing to break out and break free. *Do not fear something is wrong because there's that pressing, or because it feels uncomfortable.*

The pressing against the old is essential for rebirth to take place.
Your authentic, true self is expanding and expanding,
demanding birth and emergence,
insisting on being integrated into every aspect of your life.
This is the job of wisdom.
It pushes against ignorance,
fracturing its solidity with every new revelation.
Keep cracking. Don't stop.
Something exquisite is waiting to emerge.

Like the skilled artisans in India who carefully but firmly chip away at the clay mold so that the gleaming metal statue can be revealed, so we as seekers must diligently, painstakingly, patiently—*and always with love*—peel off those old, hardened protections that cover our original luster and sacred magnificence. We must free ourselves by relinquishing what is no longer necessary. And then we will shine.

Take a few moments now, or when you have time, and make a list of some of the things you need to relinquish and unlearn, and the patterns or situations that have been holding you back. These Choice for Love Recalibration Questions will help you focus your revelations. Just articulating these understandings *is* the beginning of the unlearning, and the first step in letting go!

Don't forget to make the list of some of the things you have already unlearned. Allow yourself to truly marvel at how long and profound that list is, and how much you've already attained as a soul in this lifetime.

CHOICE FOR LOVE RECALIBRATION QUESTIONS ABOUT RELINQUISHMENT

**What is it that I need to relinquish for this
next stage of my journey?**

**What is weighing me down and making it more difficult
for me to go forward?**

What are some things I need to unlearn?

What are some things I've already unlearned?

What do I need to let go of to be free?

Unburdening Yourself from Bitterness

*"We must empty ourselves to be filled with God.
Even God cannot fill what is full."*

— Mother Teresa

One of the most difficult challenges we face when healing our heart is to relinquish the anger for all of the ways we believe we have been harmed, and to unburden ourselves from the bitterness that keeps us from fully moving on from the past so that we can love fully in the present.

The burdens of blame and bitterness are heavy. They weigh our energy down. They make our heart and our energy field very rough and rocky and, at times, treacherous for other people to enter. They dilute the pure love that we have. They add agitation to the love or intimacy or caring that we try to give. They rob us of joy on a daily basis.

All of us have had innumerable experiences that created anger, blame, resentment, and bitterness. None of us have been able to avoid these cosmic lessons. None of us have been free of things that hurt our hearts or made us not trust the world, or filled us with despair.

We've talked earlier about how, because of past hurts, we build protective walls around our heart. Certain emotions are particularly sturdy bricks for these vibrational fortresses: *anger, blame, bitterness, and resentment. These feelings don't make us powerful, even though a part of ourselves tries to convince us that they do. They are seductive jailers that imprison us.*

What is the key to unlock those prison doors? It is a particular, elevated kind of relinquishment: *forgiveness.*

One of the most difficult but courageous acts of relinquishment you will ever be challenged to choose is forgiveness. When we contemplate forgiveness in light of our Choice for Love philosophy, we realize that *forgiveness is something that happens inside of you, and the first person it affects is you.* This is one of the most essential shifts in understanding to make when you want to heal.

We think of forgiveness as a gift you give to others,
but even more important, it is a gift you give yourself,
to release yourself from that prison of blame and bitterness.
You free yourself from the past.
You give it back for the purpose of your freedom.
You for-give.

Forgiveness does not mean that what happened to you was okay. Forgiveness does not mean you're saying it didn't hurt you terribly, or that it wasn't wrong. You will always recall the transgressions. **However, the higher understanding of forgiveness is that you are "giving for yourself—you are giving the past back."**

Of course, the ego vehemently protests against this idea. It reasons that by holding on to blame and anger we are powerful. *"I'm so furious at that person. I'm never forgiving them. I'm never going to even have one shred of compassion for them. I'm going to always be angry about what happened until the day I die!"* Obviously, there are people who've harmed you and who you want nothing to do with. However, continuing to recycle the blame and bitterness doesn't really hurt them, especially if they have no idea what you're feeling. It's only poisoning you.

When we hold on to blame and bitterness, we create *vibrational boulders* in our hearts that block the flow of love that wants to move out, and block the flow of love that wants to come in. Those boulders of anger, blame, and bitterness don't allow us to feel the joy we could feel. They don't allow us to be able to give or receive the way we deserve to. **They create energetic dams that sabotage our happiness.**

Another way to think about anger and blame is to use the metaphor of fire. When somebody does something that's hurtful or horrible, our anger and outrage *flare up*, don't they? It's almost like a fire that just explodes inside of you. However, all fires need fuel. When it runs out of fuel, a fire will begin to die down. This is why during dangerous fires, brave firefighters risk their lives clearing brush and chopping down trees so there's less fuel for the fire to consume.

Initially, when you're hurt or mistreated, it fuels your fire of anger. At some point, however, that incident or that relationship is over. Time passes. Yes—the scorched earth of your heart is still there, but there's nothing currently happening to fuel the fire.

Here is where many of us get stuck: **In order to keep that fire of bitterness burning, you have to keep fueling it and stoking the fire of blame. How?**

You relive what happened over and over again in your mind so you can stay angry.

You constantly talk about what happened, and how horrible it was.

You go on a campaign of negativity about the other person by gossiping, recounting your story, and attempting to enroll others in your own outrage.

I'm not suggesting that if something painful happened to you last week, you should forgive and be over it. On the other hand, many of us don't allow ourselves to heal, and let incidents from the past become memories of trauma, and not real trauma, because we become caught in a trap of re-traumatizing ourselves. **We're like emotional arsonists, resetting old fires again and again, instead of allowing the past to be in the past, and allowing our brain to rewire. And it takes a lot of energy and life force to keep the fires of anger burning.**

There is heartbreak and letting go from which we never recover. I've come to believe that we aren't supposed to recover, meaning to be as we were before, or to "cover over" the pain of what we experienced, but rather to understand that these lessons and losses do break something in us.

Necessary relinquishments aren't meant to break us down.
They are meant to break us open.

We will always remember the tests and the storms we have endured. However, we must not invest our energy in those things that would rob us of our ability to find joy in life. We rise up and understand that *the number one healer for anything that happened to us is making the choice for love*—love in *this* moment, love with the people who *are* in our lives, love for the lessons we are learning, love that is waiting to bless us *now*. **Love becomes a river of healing light that washes away those boulders, and extinguishes those old, smoldering embers of bitterness.**

There's no power in anger, blame, resentment, and bitterness. They disempower you. True power is proclaiming:
"Nothing that has happened to me
will rob me of my joy, of my ability to love and live with passion.
I will not let whatever you or anyone has done,
or whatever has occurred,
to steal one scrap of feeling from my heart.
I will defiantly live and love and go forward with an open heart.
This is my triumph."

"When another person makes you suffer,
it is because he suffers deeply within himself
and his suffering is spilling over."
— Thich Nhat Hanh

One of the ways we as human beings attempt to move forward in our lives is to create closure with our past. Why do we long for closure? Sometimes we want it because we are uncomfortable moving forward when things between ourselves and someone else are still emotionally messy and haven't been tidied up in the way we think they should. Sometimes, we've decided that, until we have closure, we cannot feel love for that person or ourselves again because of what we went through. Sometimes, we want closure because we desperately long to feel peace about the time we spent with someone or to forgive ourselves for what we endured rather than feeling it was all a waste.

We will all face painful moments when we realize that we're going to need to relinquish our expectation and hope of having closure with a particular person because it just doesn't seem possible. Do you have someone in your life with whom it's been impossible to create closure? Perhaps they're unwilling to heal. Perhaps they're incapable of rising up beyond what took place. Perhaps you know they're too stuck or stubborn to heal. Perhaps they've passed on and are no longer here for you to talk with.

It takes courage for people to face themselves, and to feel remorse for things they've said or done that were not coming from their most conscious, loving self. I hope on your journey that you are finding that courage, but sadly, many never will. *Most people will not wake up in this lifetime—until it is too late—and as Thich Nhat Hanh beautifully expresses, their suffering spills over onto the world.*

Making the choice for love sometimes means understanding that someone else is suffering so much on a soul level —even if they aren't aware of it—that their suffering has spilled over onto you in the form of selfishness, unkindness, abandonment, or cruelty.

This is particularly confusing to us when that someone is a person we loved—a parent, a lover, a child, or a friend. Our heart tells us we need to bring things back to a state of harmony and balance. We want to forgive or be forgiven. Yet we know it's just not possible, not now, and maybe never.

In these situations, we must create closure within ourselves through our own choice for forgiveness, compassion, and love. We cannot wait for the magical moment in which we imagine a beautiful healing could happen. We cannot tell ourselves that one day, we're sure they will see the light, and until then, we're going to be trapped in heartbreak. We cannot postpone forgiving ourselves until we are forgiven, or forgiving someone else until they have transformed.

Can you bless yourself, forgive yourself, release yourself, and not wait for someone else to give you redemption?

Can you have gratitude for the lessons you learned with them anyway?

Can you give yourself closure?

**Do not mourn the time you once spent with people
who are now gone, or time spent in situations that did not
become what you hoped for.
Time is wasted only when
we do not learn the lessons from our journey.**

TAKING THE DIAMONDS OF YOUR LOVE
OUT OF THE VAULT

*"Examine the lives of the best and most fruitful people and peoples
and ask yourselves whether a tree that is supposed to
grow to a proud height can dispense with bad weather and storms;
whether misfortune and external resistance,
some kinds of hatred, jealousy, stubbornness, mistrust, hardness,
avarice, and violence do not belong among the favorable conditions
without which any great growth even of virtue is scarcely possible."*
— Friedrich Nietzsche

Once I had a student who was passionately attached to her personal story of suffering. Courtney experienced some painful events in her past, as many of us have, but rather than use them to motivate herself and to cherish every minute of life, she clung to these past experiences as *evidence of why she couldn't love, wouldn't open up, and didn't want to feel.* No matter how many wonderful things happened to her, *she would use her unpleasant memories as weapons to overrule any evidence of goodness.*

One morning during the workshop she was attending, I decided to go around the room and ask people to name the tragedies and hardships they'd faced in their lives. As each person stood and shared, it became apparent that not one individual in the entire group had been spared from experiencing loss, challenge, and heartache. Here is a partial list of what we heard:

My brother was riding his bike and was killed by a drunk driver when he was only nine years old.

I lost most of my hearing to a rare virus when I was in college.

My daughter/father/mother/spouse died of cancer.

My husband cheated on me with my best friend and left me.

My father deserted my mom, and we were on welfare for years.

I was molested by my uncle when I was little, and when I told my mom she warned me not to talk about it.

My business partner stole my money, and I had to declare bankruptcy.

The new dream house we bought had undisclosed toxic mold, and I got sick and had to go on disability.

My father was an alcoholic who was verbally and physically abusive to my mom and us kids.

A jealous colleague spread false rumors about me in my industry, causing me to lose most of my business and involving me in a five-year lawsuit.

My son was an honor student and the perfect kid, but got into hard drugs and has been in rehab three times.

My parents never told me I was adopted until I was a teenager.

I developed fibromyalgia after the birth of my daughter, and live in chronic pain.

My ex-wife became addicted to painkillers, and I've had to fight her for custody of our children.

My mom has suffered from Alzheimer's for 15 years, and my dad and I had to put her in a special home when she stopped realizing who we are.

All of us shed tears of compassion listening to this litany of human suffering, including Courtney. I hadn't asked the group to share only for her sake, but for everyone's sake.

> **It heals the heart to know that**
> **our tests and trials are not singular,**
> **and that we do not walk alone**
> **even on the most devastating parts of our journey.**

Hearing what each person offered created an instant shift for Courtney. *"This just changed my life,"* she confessed. *"Your courage in sharing your* *own pain just lifted me up from this pit of self-absorption and anger I've lived in for so long. **It's shocking for me to see how I've been making my suffering special.***"

All of us, myself included, have our own horror stories, our own betrayals, and our own lists of what hasn't been fair, or how we feel the Universe surely must have singled us out for misery. Some of these tragedies are certainly more awful than others, and most of us know someone better off *and* someone worse off than we've been. I don't believe I've ever met anyone who hasn't faced serious adversity.

Many of us have been hurt, taken for granted, and betrayed like my student Courtney was. These kinds of wounds, the ones we're left with when someone appears to reject the gift of our Love, can often be the deepest and most difficult to heal. However, we must remember the truth: ***It's a mistake to use your pain as an excuse to wall yourself off, and keep your love locked away in a hidden vault inside the heart.*** It's one thing for people to rob you of your trust, your innocence, and your capacity for joy. But if you're still letting them do it and they're not even around anymore, they're still robbing you, and they win. *Instead of using your pain and disappointments as excuses for shutting off your heart and not loving, use them as the reason you insist on loving.*

We are all survivors.
Everyone has experienced loss in significant ways.
Some of us have lost children. Some of us have lost love.
Some of us have lost our health. Some of us have lost money.
Some of us have lost our dreams. Some of us have lost our hope.
We cannot hide behind the pile of our losses or what has happened to us
and proudly wave the flag of our suffering
as if *our* suffering is more special,
using it as an excuse for why we're not fully living and loving.
We must stack all of our losses into a big pile,
climb to the top in triumph,
and exclaim: *"Look how high up I am and how far I've come!"*

I vividly remember the first time my innocent heart was badly broken over 50 years ago! I was horrified that people could be so cruel and dishonest. **However, instead of driving me to conclude that I should love *less*, the pain made me determined to love *more*.** It was obvious to me that, as illustrated by the unkind behavior of the young man who had treated me terribly, *the world needed more Love, and it was all the more reason for me to dedicate myself to loving, no matter what.* This was the beginning of my understanding that, in each moment, I had a choice about what I contributed to the planet, and that those contributions would be changing it, even in the smallest way.

To look backward at who didn't appreciate your offering of love
is to not honor *your own* offering.
To look backward and remind yourself of who did not love you
is for *you* to not love you.
If your love wasn't received by someone,
that doesn't mean you should lock it away.
If what you gave wasn't fully appreciated,
that doesn't mean you should stop giving.

This is a profound choice for Love to contemplate and begin practicing. When you continue to look back with defeat at those who didn't appreciate your love, *you're the one not honoring your own offering.* When you continue to look back with resentment at those who did not see you, love you, or get you, *you're the one not getting you.* Instead, choose to be triumphant by not allowing these things to rob you of how you love today.

Just because somebody didn't appreciate that you're a diamond
doesn't mean that you've turned into a rhinestone.
You're still a diamond.
The right person will recognize that,
treasure that, and honor that.
Take your diamonds of love out of the vault in your heart.
Polish them until they shine.
Someone is waiting to receive them.

HAVE YOU BEEN ON A SPIRITUAL OR EMOTIONAL STRIKE?

Sometimes we make the mistake of feeling *we're entitled to not have to be loving* because of difficulties we've endured. It's as if we're saying to Spirit/God/Higher Power: *"Excuse me, God, Universe, Spirit (whatever you believe in). See this face? This is not a happy face. I am pissed off about the way things are going, so I am on strike. What? You want me to be loving? Forget it—you're not going to see any love, because I'm not happy with this situation, and I'm not happy with you!"*

I call this **"formally declaring your unhappiness,"** kind of like someone saying, "I'm formally declaring my candidacy for governor." I know many people who walk around formally declaring their unhappiness to everyone they meet, not necessarily with words, but with attitudes and vibrations. They make it clear that they are disappointed in life, in humanity, and in the cosmic scheme of things.

If you're walking around vibrating disappointment, that's what people are going to pick up when they walk into your energy field. It will feel like they've fallen into a big pool of festering disappointment. *"I'm disappointed in my mother, and I'm disappointed in my husband, and I'm disappointed in my business partner, and I'm probably about to be disappointed in you!"*

This stance of cutting off from Love will suffocate us. This stance of deciding to go on strike and declare our unhappiness will only take us down. Guess what else it will do? It will postpone the arrival of all the good things that we're waiting for, because we're vibrating so much disappointment that it will block our ability to receive.

*We cannot and should not abandon our choice to love just because we're not pleased with the way things are.

*We cannot abandon our choice to love just because our heart has been battered, our offerings unappreciated, and our devotion disregarded and discarded.

*We cannot abandon our choice to love even though we might be upset with what's happening at work, or with somebody in our life, or with the world in general, and decide we now have a free pass to be unloving.

> **Love does not punish, or withhold, or retaliate.**
> **It does not go on strike.**
> **It has no choice but to keep flowing,**
> **and keep finding places to humbly offer itself.**

Can you see people in your life as they really are, with eyes from the present and not eyes from the past? Can you love fresh and not punish those people in your life today for the failings of those who are no longer present? This is the choice for love.

Long ago, I decided to take the stance of choosing love. I decided to remain connected to the vibration of love no matter what, understanding that it is my lifeline to truth, to power, and to freedom. I formally declared my allegiance to Love, and it has never abandoned me.

YOU FREE ME AND I'LL FREE YOU: WHEN YOU HAVE NO CHOICE BUT TO LET GO

"There are always moments when one feels empty and estranged.
Such moments are most desirable, for it means the soul has cast its moorings
and is sailing for distant places.
This is detachment—when the old is over and the new has not yet come.
If you are afraid, the state may be distressing,
but there is really nothing to be afraid of.
*Remember the instruction: **Whatever you come across—go beyond**."*

— Sri Nisargadatta Maharaj

There are times in our life when in spite of our best and most sincere efforts, we are powerless to change what is happening to us. We are going through something we do not want to be experiencing. In that moment, we have two choices:

<u>Choice #1</u>: We can hate what we're going through, resist what we're going through, feel victimized by what we're going through, be frightened by what we're going through, and get overwhelmed by what we're going through. *Doing this, we will have declared war on our own reality.*

<u>Choice #2</u>: We can go through our passage with as much strength, dignity, perseverance, and consciousness as possible. *We can make the choice for love.*

Often the only way to move through these unwanted ordeals is to simply surrender, and the choice for love becomes the choice to let go.
Here is my story about letting go with love.

In 1991 for several months leading up to my 40th birthday, I had a recurring dream about a beautiful white dog who would be staring at me with intense brown eyes. I'd never had an animal companion, but as soon as the dreams began, I knew that this dog was calling to me, and that I was somehow supposed to find him. A few months later, I did. He was a bichon frise whom I named Bijou, and he became my first "child," my most treasured companion and my true love.

Bijou was a spectacular and unique being. I was told by many intuitives that he'd been a longtime spiritual teacher and healer but had recently become drained, and needed a "taking-care-of" life. However, he still wanted to serve. So he chose to come back in a dog's body, and he chose me, his old soul beloved, knowing that being with me, he could fulfill both needs.

Bijou was remarkable in that he simply didn't have dog energy at all. He would come to my seminars, walk up onto the stage, lie down, and quietly watch me for hours while I taught. The moment I asked people to close their eyes for a visualization, Bijou would also close his eyes. When I finished the visualization, he would open his eyes and walk around the room while people shared. If someone was very tearful, he would find that person and climb on their lap.

Each time I would set up a sacred altar at my home, Bijou would come into the room and bow down before it, and then recline in front of it for an hour or so after I left with his eyes closed. And no matter where I was in the house, when I sat down to pray, meditate, or chant, Bijou would come running in from wherever he'd been and leap up onto the chair or bed to participate.

From the moment Bijou came to me as an 11-week-old puppy, I recognized him deep in my soul as someone I had cherished for so long. This mystical love completely took me by surprise, as I'd never spent more than a few minutes with a dog in my life. That very first day, I remember thinking, *"I dread the inevitable time when I will have to say good-bye to him."* At some point during every single day for the next 17 years, I would find myself wondering: *"How will it happen? How will I know when he is ready to leave? Will he make it easy for me? Will I have to help? What will the circumstances be? How will I survive without him?"*

Many years of delight and devotion passed, but as Bijou began to age and became a "senior," my anxieties became more pronounced. Thankfully he had no diseases or conditions, but his eyesight and hearing faded, and his hips deteriorated so that eventually walking was very difficult. I was happy to push him in his doggie stroller and carry him almost everywhere, including up and down the stairs in my home. With the onset of each new infirmity, my heart grew heavier, but I thanked him for staying with me even in his discomfort. Even though his body was failing, his heart and spirit were just as radiant.

During one of his regular checkups, Bijou's vet told me that, in spite of his geriatric condition, he was otherwise so healthy that she didn't think he would just die a natural death, and would probably need me to help him leave his body. It was here—the moment I'd thought about and dreaded facing for almost two decades. I began praying that I would know when it was the right time, but was frightened that I would be so overwhelmed with grief that I would delay and Bijou would suffer. I was sure that he would want to leave before he lost his dignity, but not before he finished the work he had promised to do. *I knew the last piece of that work was about preparing me to let go.*

We had always had a profound psychic connection and communication, and now I began to ask: ***"Tell me when you want to leave, sweetheart. I don't know what I will do without you, but I don't want you to suffer."*** Bijou would just stare at me with so much love, delicately lick my hand once, and then put his little white head on top of my arm or on my shoulder as if to say, *"I will . . . but it's not quite time."*

Bijou's 17th birthday arrived, and although I was so grateful he was alive for us to celebrate it, I could feel something unmistakably different. He seemed further away, in a deep place, and I knew he was preparing himself to leave this world, and preparing me to live without him. Each time I had to travel to teach or give a speech, I was terrified about what would happen while I was gone.

A few months passed, and very reluctantly, I went out of town to give a seminar. I left Bijou with his "godmother" Alison, who he'd known since he was a baby, and I called every few hours, fearing that he would fail before I returned. Finally, I finished teaching, and just as I was about to drive away my phone rang.

"I'm glad you're on your way back," Alison said. *"Bijou seems very agitated: he's been crying off and on, and I have a funny feeling."*

I raced home as fast as I could, and rushed into the house to Bijou. I will never forget what happened next. As soon as he saw me, Bijou suddenly sat up and stared intensely into my eyes. Then, I heard a clear, calm voice say:

"You free me, and I'll free you. You free me, and I'll free you."

I knew Bijou wasn't actually speaking, and that I was hearing the voice in my heart, but it was so strong and deliberate that I began to shake. It was not an intuition of a message, or a subtle whisper of an instruction. It was loud, and it was him.

I didn't want to hear it, but I knew what I heard was the voice of truth. I knew what I heard wasn't my imagination. It didn't speak to me through my intellect, but directly in my heart, like a resounding pronouncement: *You free me, and I'll free you!* **He wanted to go. He was ready. And he was telling me that I was ready too.**

I lay down and held Bijou in my arms against my chest. He whimpered off and on, but I knew he wasn't in any physical pain. Bijou had always been very focused and deliberate, and now I could feel his urgency. He wanted to get out of his body. He was anxious to fly. Hours passed, and I finally asked the question I'd hoped I'd never have to ask: *"When?"* Once again, I immediately heard that same calm voice in my heart answer: *"Tomorrow."*

Tomorrow. June 24. Suddenly I realized what tomorrow was. It was a very sacred day for me, the birthday of one of my spiritual teachers. She had met Bijou several times, and blessed him, and I knew this was no coincidence. He was saying, *"Please do this tomorrow. I need to go on a day that has represented freedom to you."* Trembling and with tears pouring down my face, I made the call for the vet to come the next afternoon. As soon as I hung up the phone, Bijou totally relaxed and settled. I was following his instructions.

Through the night, we lay together with no space between us. I couldn't believe these were the last few hours during which I'd be able hold my sweet Bijou and feel his body breathing next to mine. I wanted these precious moments to last forever. I decided to tell him the story of his life from beginning to end. I reminded him of every place we'd seen, every game we'd ever played, every way he'd made me laugh when I was too serious, and every time he'd been the living pillow soaking up my tears. I recalled how he'd been a star in my TV infomercial viewed by over 200 million people, and how viewers all over the world had written that upon seeing him, their hearts had opened.

I thanked him for sitting next to me during the long months when I'd write each of my books, never getting up until I did, holding the space with such pure devotion and dedication that it gave me the strength to be a channel for wisdom to move through me. I spoke to him about his great deeds, his honorable life, and, most of all, how he had cultivated my heart in miraculous ways so that I had learned to experience profound, unconditional love. All the while, like an insistent mantra vibrating in my heart, I could still hear: *"You free me, and I'll free you."*

**The arrival and departure of beings onto this planet
are sacred passages, and when we honor them as such,
the souls who are coming or going
are ushered into their destination
with love and reverence.**

Bijou had brought me unimaginable peace for 17 years, and I wanted him to go forth on his journey in peace. The new day dawned. I chanted to him for hours, and read the highest wisdom to him from many spiritual texts. I created a special resting space surrounded by rose petals and crystals. It was not him but me who needed comfort then, and even as he prepared to leave his body, he offered me the most tender kisses of gratitude. *"Fly up, my darling one. Fly up,"* I whispered to him as he departed. *"Fly back to the Light."* And he did.

Letting go of Bijou was one of the two hardest things I've ever had to do in this lifetime. I was not wrong for those 17 years when I feared a part of me would be heartbroken living without him. Nine more years have passed since then, but I still cry a little at some point each day. I am weeping now.

Bijou has come to me in many mystical ways and forms. I had asked him to try and reveal himself to me as a hummingbird, and I cannot tell you how many hummingbirds I've had literally tapping on my windows with their tiny beaks, hovering a few inches in front of my eyes for minutes at a time, or sitting still on a ledge staring at me. He visits me in dreams, and guides me in ways I cannot put into words. I have seen his angelic soul body, which unsurprisingly was a breathtaking male being, and not a dog at all!

The mantra Bijou gave me continues to transform me. At the time, I helped to free him, and his passing did free me of my fear that I wouldn't know what to do; it freed me of the guilt I experienced every time I left him or saw him in distress; and it freed me of the complications his care had been causing in many areas of my life.

As time has passed, I've understood its profound, deeper meaning. **It represents the voice of our own great Self, our own great Love longing for us to create space for it to fully unfold in our conscious life.** *"You free me, and I'll free you. Free me from the places in which you've contained me,"* **it calls to us,** *"and I will free you of everything that is limiting you."*

The night I helped Bijou leave his body, I wrote this memorial for him:

My light, my love teacher, my wise one,
my ancient awakened yogi in a dogs body,
my comforter, my protector, my muse,
my most loyal companion and best friend,
my embodiment of dignity, courage, and grace,
my giver of delight,
my divine gift,
my ultimate blessing—

Fly joyously home now to the Great Brightness
and be free.

I will love you in this life and forever.

Like most of us, like you, I've faced countless necessary and often painful relinquishments in every aspect of my life as I've traveled on this mysterious human journey. I've had to relinquish people I loved who passed on from this world. I've had to relinquish people I loved whose paths diverged from mine, or whom I lost to jealousy and betrayal. I've had to relinquish Bijou and my two other beloved animal companions as they finished their work on earth and continued their journey in other realms. I've had to relinquish youth, perfect health, and the luxury of unlimited time. Even during the writing of this book, I faced some totally unexpected, heartbreaking, and dramatic relinquishments.

I do not pretend to enjoy these times of letting go. None of us do. But I've learned that, just as the bronze statue needs to be forged in the fire and then relinquish its unnecessary covering, just as the monkey needs to relinquish the banana to save himself from capture, so too I need to relinquish that which is holding me back from being free, again and again and again. This is the path to awakening.

I let go, and I wait, preparing myself to receive a wonderful new gift of grace that I trust and I know is already on its way to me, arriving to fill the empty space that's been created.

Love is always waiting to flow
into any place where there's not love.
Our job is to relinquish what's in the way
and create space to receive.
Unclutch what you've been holding on to,
and take your hand out of the jar.
There's nothing in there that you need.
Joyfully crack open the mold that encases your magnificence
so it can be unveiled for all to enjoy.
Trust, and then just let go.

❀ 6 ❀

Courageous Compassion
Choosing to Live with a Melted Heart

"The world is part of our own self and we are a part of its suffering wholeness.
Until we go to the root of our image of separateness,
there can be no healing."
— Llewellyn Vaughan-Lee

On our human journey, we will have many encounters with suffering. We will watch people we love suffer. We will be shocked when people we love make us suffer. We will face personal challenges and trials that cause us suffering. We will turn on the news and see unimaginable suffering of people we don't know. We will witness brutality, violence, disasters, terrorism, and tragedy that cause us suffering. We will suffer when we have to bear the burden of disappointment in ourselves, in people we love, in people we thought loved us, and in humanity.

These times of pain and suffering stop us in our tracks. We don't know what to think. We don't know how to proceed. We have no solutions. Our wisdom, our learning, and our process of transformation itself fall short. Our attempts to explain or understand excruciating events or personal crises seem like impotent weapons in a battle we wish was not happening, and one we're terrified that we cannot win. ***In these moments, even the highest truth doesn't soothe the heart.***

* It's just not enough to remind ourselves that we believe in the highest in someone we love when we're watching them self-destruct.

* It's just not enough to try and convince ourselves that we are a child of God when we realize we've made an irreparable mistake.

* It's just not enough to hear of a horrible tragedy, massacre, or injustice and to try to convince ourselves that surely, everything in life has a purpose.

And so we are left asking, "**What am I supposed to hold on to in order to get through this?**" The answer is **Compassion**.

There are moments in our life when nothing else will make any sense but just being in a state of compassion.

There are times of storms, turbulence, and trials when only compassion will allow us to stay afloat.

There are situations you must face that you can only face with compassion, survive with compassion, and understand with compassion.

This is one of the most important offerings of this book, and perhaps the most essential teaching about love—that for love to prevail, you will need compassion:

Compassion for this mysterious life journey.

Compassion for people you love, and people you don't love.

Compassion for people you know, and people you don't know.

Compassion for those who don't seem to have compassion for themselves.

Compassion for those who do not have compassion for you.

Compassion even for your adversaries and enemies.

Compassion for situations in which you feel utterly powerless.

Compassion for all suffering everywhere.

And, of course, compassion for yourself.

Perhaps you're thinking, *"This sounds wonderful, but I'm already a very compassionate person. I try to be kind to everyone. I help whenever I can. I donate money to charitable causes. I volunteer at my church. I'm always there for my friends if they want advice."* Caring about people, helping others, donating money, and volunteering are all good things, and, of course, kindness and service are laudable, but they are actions and vehicles to *do* something. Compassion goes beyond these, and is something different because it's not an outer action or choice. *It is an inner state of an opened heart.*

**Compassion is not a philosophy; it is not an attitude;
it's not even a set of kind or considerate behaviors.
It is *not* a doing. It is a *being*.
True compassion is an *inner* choice for
a certain kind of elevated love.
This courageous love extends beyond our own heart
to feel into the heart of another in an unconditional embrace.**

Compassion is not neutral. It's not just being there. *It's not a thought—it's an experience.* The word *compassion* originates from the Latin: *com* ("together") + *passio* ("to suffer")—to be in suffering together. We open ourselves to the experience of other people's pain and suffering. We don't turn away from it, but toward it. We don't avoid it because we're afraid it will hurt our heart. **We remember that, at the most essential level of existence, our heart is already connected to everyone's hearts. We make the choice to find a way to wrap the pain or suffering we see with love.**

Many of us are very kind people, but we still don't know how to be truly compassionate with ourselves, others, or the world, especially in situations when we feel out of control. When the mind says, *"I give up. I don't understand. I can't do anything,"* then the heart must take over with *compassion that does not do or fix, but fully feels.*

WHAT IS COMPASSION?

**Compassion is a willingness to be in the space of suffering
and bring your love to it.**

**You feel someone else's wound, your wound,
or even the wound of the world,
and just wash it with love, because that is all you can do.**

THE SPIRITUAL ROOTS OF COMPASSION

"Compassion is a far greater and nobler thing than pity.
Pity has its roots in fear; and a sense of arrogance and condescension,
sometimes even a smug feeling of 'I'm glad it's not me.' . . .
To train in compassion, then, is to know all beings are the same
and suffer in similar ways, to honor all those who suffer,
and to know you are neither separate form nor superior to anyone."

— Sogyal Rinpoche

For thousands of years, compassion has been written about and taught in the great scriptures and spiritual texts of all religions. Let's look at some of these ancient teachings about compassion.

In the Bible, *Romans 12:15*, it says, *"Rejoice with those who rejoice; weep with those who weep."* Have you ever just sat with someone you loved and witnessed their bleeding heart, their pain, and cried for them? Their pain becomes yours, and *somehow in your witnessing it and seeing it with compassion, they learn to see themselves more compassionately.*

From *1 Corinthians 12*: *". . . that there may be no division in the body, but that the members may have the same care for one another. If one member suffers, all suffer together; if one member is honored, all rejoice together."* Have you ever heard a tragic story about someone, or seen a report on TV about something horrible, and wept? You don't know the victims, but you feel as if you do, and your heart literally hurts for what they went through or are still going through.

In Buddhism, one of the most important teachings about compassion is represented by the divine being Avalokiteshvara Bodhisattva, known as the embodiment of compassion. The term *bodhisattva* means an enlightened one who vows to work for the enlightenment of all beings, not just their own, and help them be free of suffering. **The Sanskrit name Avalokiteshvara (also Guanyin or Quan Yin to the Chinese and Japanese) translates as *"he/she who observes the sounds of the world,"* or the *"regarder of the cries of the world."*** The vow of this Bodhisattva is to listen to the supplications, the cries for help, and the heartbreak of those in difficulty.

There is a beautiful phrase in Judaism that I feel also embodies an advanced understanding of compassion: "l'hishtatef b'tsa'ar," which translates as *"to participate in the sorrow of another."* What does it mean to participate in sorrow? It means to not resist it. It means to open to it. When coming to offer condolences to a family or a person who has lost a loved one, you come with the intention of just being with them, listening to them, holding them with love, and courageously sharing the space of grief with them.

All of these teachings on compassion share one thing in common. They point us toward compassion as a *choice to love*, and *not a choice to fix.*

* The Bible *doesn't* say, "Rejoice with those who rejoice, and calm down those who weep."

* The definition of *Avalokiteshvara* is the "regarder of the cries of the world," and *not* the "rescuer of those crying in the world."

* The translation of *l'hishtatef b'tsa'ar* is the participation in the sorrow of another, *not* the fixer of the sorrow of another.

From this, we deepen our understanding of what we might have considered compassion: *"I am helping you, feeling sorry for you, worrying about you, and doing things to fix you."* Instead, we realize that **compassion emerges out of our choice for the highest form of love, the love that is the same cosmic source energy dancing in me as me, and in you as you. It rises up from our recognition of our sameness, the divinity that is woven through all of our humanity as a singular cosmic thread.**

**Compassion is a melting of separation,
a transcendence of the "I" and a surrender into the "We."
It is a merging into the shared Heart of the World.
It is a willingness to hold others, and indeed the world,
in your own heart with love.**

From that recognition of sameness, we remember that we are sharing one universal heart. *In this way, moments of true compassion remind us of and renew our connection to the sacred.*

The Grace of Compassionate Witnessing

*"I do not ask the wounded person how he feels,
I myself become the wounded person."*

— Walt Whitman

Once I heard a fable about a mother who sent her young daughter out on an errand. The girl often went to the country store down the road, and her mother knew approximately how long it would take her child to walk there and return. But as time passed, and her daughter wasn't back yet, the mother began to get worried.

Finally, her daughter arrived at the farmhouse, carrying the sack of vegetables she'd been asked to purchase. "Thank goodness you're home. I've been so anxious. What took you so long?" her mother asked.

"I was on my way to the store," the girl began, "when I came across a little child whose doll was broken."

"Oh, now I understand," her mother said. "So you stopped to help her fix the doll."

Her daughter stared up at her mother with a puzzled look and replied, "No, Mommy. *I stopped to help her cry.*"

There's something very poignant and powerful about holding a space of compassion for people when they're in pain, and loving them anyway. I call this *"compassionate witnessing."* **We aren't just physically there. We are emotionally there.** We are participating in what another person is experiencing—*l'hishtatef b'tsa'ar*—and that compassionate witnessing says to them, *"You are not alone in your suffering, and therefore I am not alone in my suffering."*

**All of us want to be witnessed in our experience,
whatever that experience is.
The need to belong and to not be excluded is ancient and primal,
and significantly fundamental to who we are as a human species.**

Since the beginning of human existence, people have relied upon one another for survival. This interdependence goes beyond just the physical needs for food and shelter that caused your ancestors to hunt together, gather food together, or protect themselves together. It extends to our psychological survival and our deepest emotional needs—*to belong to a group, to connect, and to be seen by others.*

This longing to be "part of" is the foundation for so many of our societal rituals that revolve around rites of passage: births, christenings, bar and bat mitzvahs, weddings, graduations, birthdays, anniversaries, retirement parties, and, one day, memorial services. The occasion is important in itself, but it becomes so much more meaningful when we share it with people we care about. **The energetic field of their happiness, delight, and love radiates out from them, merging into ours and intensifying the emotional experience as our communal waves of joy can now rise higher and higher.**

Don't you get more excited seeing one of your favorite performers in a theater with 5,000 people than you would just listening to the songs alone in your bedroom? Isn't it more thrilling to watch a sport like basketball or football in a stadium with tens of thousands of other screaming fans than it is sitting by yourself in front of your TV? In these examples, you feel intimately connected to something bigger, something to which you belong.

This basic human need to be witnessed and not excluded becomes particularly important during difficult times. We need someone there to love us anyway when we are suffering, to witness our vulnerability, our chaos, and our courage—someone to *"help us cry."* Something profound takes place when we feel another person is there for us, just holding the space without judgment. We are able to stay in our feelings and the fire of our ordeal longer, and do the necessary healing.

Children intuitively understand this. *"Can you lie in bed with me until I go to sleep? I'm scared of the dark."* This is how they ask us to witness their fear. What they're really saying is *"I need you to help me feel safe, and I will feel safer if I do not have to experience this alone."* In this same way, when as an adult, you're going through a difficult time but know that you aren't alone, you become more courageous. Someone is compassionately witnessing your struggle, your heartbreak, or your grief.

The word *grief* has its origins in Latin: from *gravare*—"make heavy"—and from *gravis*, which means "weighty." Sadness is heavy. Grief is heavy. This is another, new way to think about compassion: **we help to hold the weight of someone's pain, sorrow, or grief, and make it easier for them to carry that heavy load of painful emotions.**

The witnessing of our heart by another is a sacred human experience. Especially when we are struggling, we want to be witnessed with compassion and with acceptance. We want to feel that we are not alone in our grief, our sorrows, or even our shame. When someone is willing to feel our pain with us, we feel loved, lifted up, and redeemed, and can begin to love ourselves again.

Being compassionate means that we make the choice to courageously be in a place of deep feeling with someone, to both be present in our own feelings *and* to feel what they are feeling. That heart space of compassion tells them: *"You're doing it right. You're going to be okay."*

"Trauma is not what happens to us, but what we hold inside in the absence of an empathetic witness."

— Peter A. Levine, Ph.D.

Stop for a moment and notice if, while reading these pages about compassion, you began to feel a bit melancholy or sad. *You may be experiencing an emotional flashback like I described in an earlier chapter.* Many of us carry emotional wounds and walls because we didn't get to experience this kind of compassionate witnessing from our families or loved ones. *When our parents or partners couldn't or wouldn't feel their own pain, they usually couldn't or didn't want to see ours either.*

The absence of safety and compassion leaves us stuck with a lot of unseen and unfelt emotions that we end up hiding from everyone or putting in our "emotional freezer." This is another reason why it becomes so meaningful and necessary for us to have new experiences of compassion.

Learning how to hold a space of compassion for others heals their old wounds of feeling emotionally invisible, and receiving that kind of compassion from others heals our own pain from the past.

One of the bravest and most compassionate things we can do is to look directly into the face of someone else's pain and not turn away.

COMPASSION BEYOND RIGHT AND WRONG

"Be kind to everyone you meet,
for each person is fighting a hard battle."
— Plato

Let me tell you a story from my own life about the profound awakening of my compassion.

Many years ago, I was with someone I loved very much, who did some terrible things that crushed my spirit and broke my heart. Once that horrific time ended, we began to work on healing our relationship and rebuilding the trust. I was relieved that the nightmare we'd gone through was over, but found myself unable to let go of the overpowering blame and judgment I felt for the choices he'd made. I loved him very much, and knew he loved me, but I couldn't stop thinking of him as flawed, messed up, and wrong. My mind was crowded with lists of his transgressions, and the only solution I could think of was to keep praying to feel more love.

One morning I sat down to meditate, and as soon as I closed my eyes, I was instantly flooded with pain. Familiar waves of sorrow, grief, and hopelessness washed over me, and I felt like I was drowning in despair from which I couldn't escape. I began to weep, and once again had the thought that I was in such horrible pain because of this person I loved. I imagined him in my mind's eye, felt how deeply I loved him, and began to cry even harder.

Suddenly I realized that *I wasn't just feeling my grief, but somehow I had tuned in to his grief.* My heart had opened, and instead of looking *at* him, I was allowing myself to fully *feel* him.

I could feel how hard it was for him to live with himself and the mistakes he'd made.

I could feel how impossible it was for him to love himself when he felt he had failed in so many ways.

I could feel his deep grief for all the time he felt he'd wasted.

I could feel how horrified he was to face how far he'd drifted from his highest self, and how terrified he was that he wouldn't ever be able to find his way back.

I could feel how heartbroken he was each time he looked into my eyes and saw the reflection of the pain he'd caused.

And I could feel that *he had absolutely no compassion for himself.*

In that moment, I experienced a life-changing revelation: *I wasn't weeping only for myself, but I was weeping for him. I hadn't been suffering only for myself, but I'd been suffering for him. My heartbreak was not only for myself, but I was also heartbroken for him.* **I was mourning the bend in his beautiful light.**

Now, along with the waves of pain and sadness I'd been experiencing, I felt towering waves of grace wash over me. It was the grace of compassion, flooding me with benevolence where before, there had only been bitterness, and filling my heart with light where before, there had only been darkness.

This grace of compassion also brought the grace of immediate understanding. I saw that as long as I didn't allow myself to feel compassion for this man, he would not learn how to feel it for himself. I realized that, because I had been imprisoned by my judgments of him, and because we were so vibrationally connected on a soul level, this wasn't allowing him to fully heal his condemnation of himself.

Most important of all, I knew that to make the choice for love, I had to make room next to my own suffering for his suffering. What had been missing in my healing journey hadn't been love—it had been *compassionate grief.*

**Can you feel the suffering of those who are making your suffer?
Can you weep for those who are unable to give you what you need?
Can you both feel your own heart and someone else's?
This is *compassionate grief.*
Compassionate grief requires that we make room
next to our own suffering for the suffering of someone else,
even if that person is causing our suffering.**

I know you have your own stories of heartbreak, disappointment, and grief. Perhaps they are in the past, or perhaps they are happening at this very moment. Think about someone who has caused you a lot of distress. They've hurt you. They've created difficulties for you. They've done something that has negatively impacted you and your life.

Your first instinct is usually not to feel compassion, but to judge. *They did it wrong. They didn't try hard enough. They made a big mistake. They blew it.* This is one of the most common ways we can cut off our ability to feel compassion—*we become stuck in intellectually determining what is right or wrong about what has taken place and stop there.* This leaves very little room for love or compassion.

Of course, the assessments you're making may be accurate. It may be true that someone is hurting themselves, hurting others, self-destructing, or making mistakes that are going to have very serious consequences. Nonetheless, seeing them *only* through the eyes of judgment instantly erects a vibrational wall of division and cuts off the flow of love.

What I call *"compassionate grief"* balances out the damaging effects of judgment, and protects us from becoming trapped in the unforgiving prison of "right and wrong." When we judge those we love without compassion, we're left with a feeling that something is wrong and it needs to be made right—by us, naturally. Rather than thinking, *"My gosh, that must be hard for them. I need to have more compassion. I should be a little more understanding,"* we conclude, **"It's wrong and I need to either reprimand it, punish it, point it out to the person, or fix it."** Then we become the judge, the punisher, or the rescuer rather than the lover, the friend, or the parent.

**It is hard to judge someone and fully love them
at the same time.**

Lack of compassion for others blinds us to the bigger truth, and binds us to rigidity and judgment. Your projections on people "freeze" them as being a certain way in your consciousness. Without compassion, you don't see them as multi-dimensional. You just feel that they're disappointing you, or hurting you, or not meeting your expectations, or frustrating you. You put them in the *"emotional doghouse."*

The irony, of course, is that our "helpful judgments" create a lot of reactivity in the very people we're trying to "fix," because we're seeing them as "bad" or "broken," even if that isn't our intention.

**For those of us who are helpers, healers, fixers, and caretakers
—and pride ourselves as being good at it—
our help can turn into an unconscious form of what I call
"spiritual tyranny," an insistence on making sure others improve,
even when they are unwilling or unable to.**

I love what my friend and fellow teacher Rashani Réa writes about in her inspiring book *Beyond Brokenness*:

"I decided to abandon the assumption that something is wrong if people are suffering."

For those of us who are called in this life to help, heal, uplift, and support others, this is a mind-boggling concept. **Our heart tells us that if someone is suffering, something is wrong. Thinking it's wrong or broken, we want to fix it, alleviate it, and offer a remedy.**

You probably have somebody in your life right now who you wish wasn't going through what they're going through, but there's really nothing you can do to make things better. This is especially excruciating when you see someone you love making terrible choices, succumbing to addictions, or sabotaging themselves. You feel, *"I'm supposed to do something. I must do something! I'm a failure if I can't fix it or make it better."*

It's heartbreaking to have a front-row seat at someone else's self-destruction. I've sat in that unfortunate seat, as I am sure you have. Often, however, in spite of our valiant efforts, the person's suffering continues. *Then, we either condemn them for not changing, or condemn ourselves for not being able to make things better.*

This particular lesson is one the Universe has been relentless in teaching me, over and over again. In my work and in my personal life, I've been forced to learn how to hold someone's suffering with love and compassion, and relinquish my projection of wrongness onto it. *After all, the vibration of Love and the vibration of wrongness cannot harmoniously co-exist.* **I've also had to learn that I can have love and compassion for someone and still *not like what they are doing.*** Don't forget that you can give yourself permission to feel compassion, *and* permission to feel your anger, disappointment, and sadness, all at the same time.

So how can you find your way to compassion beyond the trap of right and wrong? **Allow yourself to mourn for how someone you love has strayed off of the path, toppled into forgetfulness, and betrayed themselves, others, and perhaps even you. This kind of grief takes great courage to hold in your heart. *You must bypass the temptation to want to collapse into anger and blame, to rush forward into rescuing, or collapse into condemnation.* There is nothing to do but be in that space of grief, to weep not only for what you have lost, but for the person you loved who is temporarily struggling or lost.**

COMPASSION FOR YOUR BROKENHEARTEDNESS

"I call him religious who understands the suffering of others."
— Mahatma Gandhi

Having compassion for others means always remembering that suffering, failure, and imperfection are part of this shared human experience. Over and over again, we learn to find compassion for our humanity and the humanity of others, even in those moments when it seems impossible to locate any evidence of divinity. This is a high form of compassion—*to live with a kind of brokenheartedness for the world, for the suffering of people you love, and to still remain in that field of love even though you aren't able to do much else.*

**A person's suffering or struggle
doesn't make them broken.**

**Compassion helps you say to yourself:
"Somewhere beneath their darkness,
I know there's some light."**

Recently I was giving a seminar and we were exploring this topic of compassion. One of my advanced students was sharing her grief and heartache about her sister who, for a long time, had been in an emotional downward spiral. She was an alcoholic and a drug addict, and had lost custody of her children. Here is what my student said:

"For years, I told myself that I should be able to help my sister. I spent hundreds of hours talking to her, suggesting things she should do or where she could get support. I gave her money. I got her jobs. But nothing I did seemed to make things better.

"Just now, listening to you, I realized that I've been judging myself for failing. I thought I was broken because I couldn't fix it."

"I thought I was broken because I couldn't fix it"—that phrase resonated with everyone in the room, including me. Like so many of us, my student had used her inability to "fix" her sister as evidence that she too was somehow deficient, and had been depriving herself of her own love. *She had enormous compassion for her sister, but none for herself.*

As we learn how to live with compassion, we must remember to include ourselves:

**Sometimes making the choice for love means
remembering to have compassion for yourself
because you couldn't take away someone's pain.**

**Just because you can't fix what you see
as someone else's brokenness
doesn't mean that you are broken.**

LEARNING HOW TO BE A COMPASSIONATE PRESENCE

*"Each person you meet is an aspect of yourself,
clamoring for love."*
— Eric Micha'el Leventhal

One of my own most difficult spiritual lessons has been learning how to love people when I can't do anything to help them. **When you love someone and they're suffering, how can you love them and not suffer with them?** How do you stand in love and yet allow people to be on their own journey? This is, once again, when we take a deep dive into our own compassion, the form of compassion that calls upon *the presence of love* to just be there because that is all you can do.

When we offer our full, compassionate presence to someone, it will have nothing to do with words, wisdom, or advice. It will be the presence of the vibration of our most compassionate love.

What does it mean "to hold the presence of love" for someone?
*It means simply remaining in the highest vibrational space
of love and compassion, and holding the energy of
that vibrational space steady.*
**At that moment, love does not look like trying to fix them.
Love does not look like trying to make them feel better.
It looks like just loving them.**

I believe we forget that the presence of our love is an enormous gift. When I know someone's love is there for me even though I'm not with them, I can still feel them vibrationally wherever they are. I can plug into that presence when I need it. I feel calmer. I feel stronger.

When we find ourselves in circumstances in which our loved ones are fighting difficult battles, and we want to fix things that aren't readily fixable, we must remember that the presence of our love and compassion *will* bring them hope and peace.

**Never underestimate the impact you're having on someone
simply because they feel the presence of your love.
Even if you can't do anything for them,
loving someone always makes a difference,
whether you can see it right away or not.**

Recently I was giving a presentation about compassion to a group of health-care providers, and during my book-signing session, one of the participants approached me. *"I loved everything about your talk,"* she began, *"but I find that compassion is very unhealthy for me, and so I avoid it."*

I was totally taken aback by her comment, and thought that perhaps she was joking, but as I looked at her face I realized she was totally serious. Now I was curious about what she meant. "Tell me more about what you experience," I said.

"Well, you see, I've always been a very empathetic, intuitive person, which is why I became a therapist. Even as a child, my mother leaned on me for support and comfort. *The problem is that, whenever I open myself up to feel compassion for someone, whether it's with my clients or even with my family members, I end up feeling totally exhausted and drained.* If they're depressed, I feel depressed. If they're sad, I feel sad. It's so frustrating, because I'm really skilled at completely tuning in to people."

"My dear, here's the problem: **You're not tuning in;** *you're falling in!* **You're diving into a person's energy field and becoming engulfed by it. And once you're in there, you have a hard time climbing out.**"

The woman just stared at me, and for a moment I worried that maybe I'd gone too far in sharing the truth. Then, she proceeded to burst into tears and said, "You've just described my entire childhood. My mother was so needy and demanding that her emotions took over everything. I got lost in her for years, and really only felt free of it once she passed away. But I've always thought that made me more compassionate."

"That wasn't empathy you were feeling. It was enmeshment," I explained gently. **"It felt like you were tuned in, but you'd fallen into her energy."**

Many of us share the same aversion to compassion as the woman I met. In fact, it's one of the most common concerns that blocks our willingness to fully open to others—*we don't want to feel their pain.* We're frightened of diving into their emotional sea and getting swallowed up by it. **We warn ourselves that if we open our heart to someone, we'll**

have to either rescue that person so that they don't drown, or push the person away so we don't drown.

Falling into people is sometimes what a lot of us do who are afraid of abandonment, afraid of rejection, or, like the therapist, feel responsible for fixing others. We just merge into people and lose ourselves completely. We may have learned this from a childhood in which we experienced that "falling into" someone temporarily got us love. We may fall in because we don't trust the other person to love us on their own, so we try to become emotionally indispensable.

> **There's a difference between holding the presence
> of love and compassion for someone's process,
> versus diving headfirst into the pool of their emotions
> and then wondering how you got so wet!
> TUNE IN—DON'T FALL IN!**

The Gift of Your Compassionate Heart

*"Every act, every deed of justice and mercy and benevolence,
makes heavenly music in Heaven."*
— Ellen G. White

In my own life, I've found that the more I've expanded my ability to hold a vast presence of love and compassion, the more I am able to truly serve—not just people who attend my lectures and seminars, or come to study with me, but everyone I meet in even the most casual and transitory of circumstances.

This is a true story: Several days ago, I took a break from writing and drove to one of my favorite spots here in Santa Barbara to spend a few refreshing minutes sitting on a bench and gazing out at the ocean. I noticed a young woman standing nearby attempting to take some selfies of her face with the view in the background. Something inside prompted me to speak to her. "Would you like me to take a photo of you?" I asked. "That would be great," she replied. I posed her at the perfect location and snapped some photos I hoped she would like. "You're so nice to do this," she said.

Something about the way she thanked me pulled on my awareness, and I could feel that her heart was hurting. So instead of sitting back down on my bench and wishing her a nice day, I stood there next to her. I asked her where she was from, and she explained that she lived in Greece, and had come to California to visit her long-distance boyfriend, whom she'd met while he was vacationing in Europe last year. Before she even went further, I sensed that it had ended badly, that she was in town sightseeing alone instead of having the romantic reunion she'd dreamed of for so long, and that she was devastated.

In that moment, I felt the love in my heart rise up and reach out to wrap her in compassionate presence. I felt her feel it happening, even though she didn't understand what she was feeling. I experienced her melting into that unexpected field of love she'd been offered by me, a stranger. This all took place in 30 seconds, even though she hadn't said anything about what happened or what she was going through, and even though I hadn't asked. But I knew that she was feeling seen, and somehow mysteriously witnessed in her pain.

Suddenly the floodgates of her emotions opened. She confessed that when she'd arrived in the United States, her boyfriend was less than welcoming—unloving and cold. It turned out he'd met someone else and hadn't told her about it, and she had traveled all the way from Greece only to be rejected. This all happened in the first two days of her three-week trip. So here she was traveling around California by herself with only her broken heart as a companion.

With compassion, I listened. With compassion, I felt her pain—the pain all of us experience when the foundation on which we've been standing and believed was steady suddenly cracks. When her eyes filled up with tears, so did mine. I was offering the presence of my love in this devastating moment on her human journey. **I was participating in her sorrow, sharing her grief:** *l'hishtatef b'tsa'ar.*

"I'm so sorry for what you're going through," I said softly, taking her hands in mine.

"Can I tell you something?" she asked. "I can't believe I'm standing here sharing all of this with you, and I don't even know your name. I've been too embarrassed and ashamed to tell my mother and my friends back in Greece, but something about you just made it all pour out. I'm so sorry I bothered you with this."

"Please, don't apologize," I reassured her. "I think we must have had a cosmic appointment, because I wasn't planning to be here today, and I truly feel honored that you felt safe enough to share your heart with me."

"Thank you!" she said. "You have no idea how much I needed this moment. I feel like I've just broken out of something so dark. Please, now that I've poured my heart out to you, may I introduce myself? I'm Alexandra. Can I know your name?"

"It's Barbara."

The girl's eyes got very wide and she gasped. *"That's my mother's name!"* she exclaimed.

"So you did get to tell your mother everything after all." I smiled.

**The heart doesn't need information to be compassionate.
It just needs love.**

That day as I drove to the park, I had no idea that I was going to be in service to Alexandra. I wasn't looking for anyone to help or heal. But my heart lives in readiness to feel the pain of another heart, to share in the wounds of the world. *I didn't actually do anything. I allowed Love itself to do it. The miracle of that moment belongs to Love, which, when we allow it to, will always find a way to offer us exactly what we need, precisely when we need it.*

When you begin to live with more compassion, you will radiate compassion to others. Your vibrational field will feel like a safe haven of unconditional love. People will feel soothed just being in a room with you, or speaking to you even for one minute. It will allow them to begin to have compassion for themselves, wherever they are on their journey.

**We are all here to serve one another.
Each morning we wake up and have no idea
exactly how we will be called upon to serve.
Understanding this, we prepare ourselves ahead of time
to be a welcoming guest room of love and compassion
for our fellow travelers, who will cross our path
looking for the safe sanctuary of an open heart.**

AWAKENING YOUR COMPASSION

*"The most beautiful people that we have known are those that
have known defeat, known suffering, known struggle, known loss
and have found their way out of the depths.
These people have an appreciation, a sensitivity and
an understanding of life that fills them with compassion,
gentleness and a deep loving concern.
Beautiful people do not just happen."*

— Elisabeth Kübler-Ross

My beloved mother, Phyllis, was the embodiment of compassion. She bore so much and forgave so much in her life, including the act of forgiving me for my terrible behavior during my difficult teenage years, when I barely spoke to her. Although I didn't know it at the time, I was going through a heart-wrenching spiritual crisis as I tried to understand why this world into which I'd been born was so far from a place of Love that I somehow remembered.

I still cringe thinking back on how much pain I caused her by pushing her away. Thankfully, at the age of 18, I formally began my spiritual path and transformed from a frustrated seeker into a blissed-out meditator, and immediately fell back in love with my sweet and compassionate mommy. For the rest of my life, every time I'd buy her a gift, or send her on a vacation, I'd jokingly say, "And this is to make up for how awful I was when I was a teenager!" And we would laugh and laugh.

The years passed. I moved from the East Coast to California, and became busy and successful. My mother was my biggest fan and most devoted supporter, and I cherished her unconditional love. My mother got older, and so did I.

At some point when my mom was in her 60s, I noticed that the content of our phone conversations began to change. *"I just came back from my third cousin's funeral,"* she'd share. Or *"Do you remember my friend Sue from the swim club? She just was diagnosed with breast cancer."* Or *"I'm sorry if I sound a little down, sweetie—my next-door neighbor Dolores can't take care of her husband anymore, and it's just so sad, but she had to put him in a special facility."* Or *"I just saw in the obituaries that your high school math teacher died."*

The rhythm of her life's events also shifted, which changed the topics she wanted to discuss. Her fun trips to vacation spots became trips to the many doctors and hospitals she and my stepfather visited for his cancer treatments, and later, for hers. Her calendar, which used to be filled with exciting social activities, now was filled with medical appointments, nursing-home visits to her friends, and memorial services.

I called my mother every few days to see how she was and share my own news, but noticed to my guilt and dismay that I didn't completely look forward to these calls like I used to. I'd be in the middle of filming a TV series, or on tour for one of my books, and when I'd hear my mother's voice, I would feel tense and sad. Rather than lingering in the conversation for as long as I used to, I'd sometimes feel impatient to end it, and being my compassionate mother, she could tell, and would relieve me by saying, **"It's okay, darling. You can go. I know you're doing such important things. Just remember how proud I am of you, and how much I love you."**

Soon after my stepfather passed away, my mother, who completely adored him and had nursed him full-time for 11 years, was herself diagnosed with cancer, shocking us all to the core. During that time I visited her as often as possible, spoke with her three or four times every day, and immersed myself in every detail of her illness, treatment, and care. I prayed and prayed that she would recover. However, after only six months, she was gone, and I knew it was to unite with her sweetheart in heaven. And I became an orphaned adult.

I flew back to Philadelphia, to the tiny house I'd grown up in, and began the emotionally impossible task of going through all of my mother's possessions. Her love of life and of people was so pure and innocent, and she had saved everything: *every love letter from her husband; every card I ever gave her from the first time I could sign my name to what I didn't know would be the final one I'd sent her before she died; every news clipping of my interviews, articles, and bestseller lists; every one of my report cards from kindergarten on; every thank-you note she ever received from friends; every program from an event she attended, or show she saw on Broadway; every obituary of anyone she knew.*

It was time to clean out her night table, still covered with bottles of pills and painkillers. I'd been dreading going near her bed, because the pillows and covers were just as she'd left them the night she'd been rushed by ambulance to the hospital, and they still displayed the mold of her head and body. Sighing, I opened the first drawer and saw a prayer book carefully positioned near the front. As I picked it up, I noticed that there was a folded, frayed piece of paper that she'd placed between the pages.

With trembling hands, I unfolded the paper. On the top, she'd written "IN MEMORIAM." It was a long list, and **there written in her careful script were the names of all of her friends and relatives who had passed away.** The first name on the list was her high school sweetheart, Al, who had been killed in World War II and never returned home to marry her. I recognized the names of her parents, cousins, friends, acquaintances, neighbors, and members of her synagogue. Next to each name was the cause of death: heart attack, stroke, accident, pneumonia. As the years progressed, the handwriting became shakier, so when I came to the last name on the list, I could tell that she had taken extra care to write it as beautifully as possible. It was her beloved husband's: *"Daniel Garshman—Cancer."*

I clutched this frayed piece of paper against my heart and began to weep. I wept because I missed my mother, and could already feel the endless, unfillable vacuum her passing would leave in my world. I wept because I was so moved by her humble and carefully chronicled tribute to all of the loves of her life. **And I wept because, in that poignant moment, my heart was overcome with grief as I realized *how lacking in compassion I had been for the last 20 years as, one by one, she'd lost the people who had been traveling with her on this earth journey.***

I know that it's impossible for any of us to truly understand something until we ourselves go through it. I know that, as a 40-year-old building a demanding career, I couldn't possibly have been able to relate to what it was like to lose your father and mother, or have your best friend die, or see your beloved partner deteriorate, or experience your own health starting to fail. I know that, no matter how loving I'd been, I just couldn't fully get it. But in that moment reading the list, what I logically knew didn't matter. *All I felt was deep remorse for how much less compassionate I'd been with my mother than I should have been.*

Now, in my middle 60s, I know too well what my mother was going through at that same age. I have cherished friends and colleagues who are no longer on this earth. My high school boyfriend recently died. I have students who have passed away. I'm shocked when I read that an entertainer I grew up enjoying is gone. *"I didn't think he was that old,"* I think to myself. And then I look at my new Medicare card and realize that I am also that old.

What do I wish? I wish I had said to my mother:

Oh, Mommy, how heartbreaking it must be to not have Doris, your best friend since you were a little girl, to call every day.

How sad you must feel to see the names written in your phone book and know those people are gone.

How scary it must be to watch your body aging and your health becoming more frail.

I'm so sorry you had to drive to that funeral alone today.

I'm so sorry I bug you to wear your hearing aid, instead of understanding how frightened you must be of going completely deaf.

I'm so sorry I don't take more time to patiently listen to every single detail of what you are going through.

I'm so sorry I didn't cry more with you.

Tell me everything. I am here for you always.

This is a deeply personal story, but I felt it was important that I share it with you. It reveals a powerful moment in the unfolding of my own compassion. Since I was young, people have always complimented me on my loving and caring presence, and these have been personal values I've held even higher than success, wealth, or fame. I confess that I truly believed I understood what it meant to be compassionate. **My mother's death and the invaluable treasures of heart-opening revelations it produced taught me that, as compassionate as I already was, I could awaken into much more.** *There is always more.*

Perhaps as you've been reading this chapter, you've also begun to wonder:

"Is what I've been thinking is compassion only partial compassion?"

"Is my compassion secretly laced with judgment?"

"Have I mistaken my fixing, rescuing, and caretaking for compassion?"

"Do I resist feeling others because I don't just tune in, but 'fall in'?"

"Is my compassion conditional based on the efforts I think the other person is making?"

"Does my compassion extend only to people I know or love, but not to others who look different, choose differently, believe differently, or love differently?"

**Making the choice for love means having the courage
to look at where you don't have compassion,
and *still have compassion for your own lack of compassion.***

This is often not so easy to do because we think of ourselves as good, caring people. It is, however, essential for your growth as a soul, and your ascension from your humanity into a more full manifestation of your divinity. Of course, we begin to work on this compassionately, remembering that the full unfolding of our compassion doesn't happen in a day or a month or a year.

Here are some Compassion Contemplation Questions to help you start understanding, deepening, and enlightening your relationship with compassion.

**CHOICE FOR LOVE COMPASSION
CONTEMPLATION QUESTIONS**

What have I been calling compassion?

**What do I need to do in order to expand
my experience of compassion?**

**Where do I need to become more authentically
compassionate in my life?**

One easy way to work with these questions is to make a list of people in your life, both past and present. Contemplate each relationship through your new eyes of compassion. Ask yourself:

"Is there some way I could have been, or can now be, more compassionate?"

"How can I hold a space of more compassion for that person?"

"What do I see differently now that I have been missing because I didn't understand compassion?"

Imagine if everyone in the world took the time to ask themselves these questions and humbly listen for the answers. My eyes fill with tears just thinking about it . . .

SPIRITUAL COMPASSION: HOW YOUR LOVE HEALS THE WORLD

"Compassion is not religious business, it is human business;
it is not luxury, it is essential for our own peace and mental stability;
it is essential for human survival."

— His Holiness the Dalai Lama

Your path has not been perfect or easy. You have fallen, been knocked down, strayed from your highest, wandered away from the truth, lost love, and, at times, lost faith. Does this disqualify you from being capable of compassion? Absolutely not. In fact, it does the opposite. *Remember that it is your own imperfect but beautiful humanity that allows you to hold an authentic space of compassion for everyone you meet.*

Compassion is a great sign of spiritual and emotional maturity.
We come to a place beyond helping, fixing, managing, and judging,
and find we have arrived in an unending field of love,
beyond any doing, beyond any accomplishment.
From that love, our divine qualities of the highest love
reach out to embrace our own humanity and the humanity of others.

Now, more than ever, we can't *not* do this. Because the truth is, the condition of our world is that it *is* full of pain and suffering. For those of us who have such big hearts, who are idealists, who are old souls, we have two choices:

We can decide to shut it off. We can decide *not* to feel it because it's too unpleasant.

Or we can open to it, witness what we see with compassion, and hold it tenderly with our love, knowing that this very act of feeling that disappointment in humanity and weeping for it *is* part of the healing and transformation of it.

One of my students wrote a beautiful description about her understanding of this new choice to be compassionate without fear:

"I'm appreciating the pain of what it means to be human without adding the self-generated pain of hopelessness. The grief of not being able to 'fix' or 'do something' made me want to look away, to run away from all the pain on our planet. Now I know I am, we are, contributing to its healing, to the healing of humanity past, present, and future."

The more expanded and spiritually advanced you get, you begin to have the experience that, when you're feeling pain, you're feeling not just your pain but you've somehow tapped into *the* ocean of pain. You sense you're not just experiencing one person's grief but that you are experiencing that *river of grief that runs through all of us while we are in these human bodies.* When you allow yourself to feel those things, you bring love to them, and in the moment you're also healing a little bit of the global grief. Remember how you impact the WE:

Since we're all vibrationally connected, everything you offer into the collective ocean of consciousness affects everything else.

When you add drops of love, compassion, or understanding to one person, you're adding drops of compassion to that collective ocean.

When you sit with compassion for your own limitations, you're bringing compassion to the huge ocean of judgment in which so many people are currently drowning.

Of course, this brings us back to the importance of healing your relationship with your heart and expanding your capacity for love. *How comfortable you are with your own ocean of feeling will determine how comfortable you are with other people's feelings—i.e., the rest of the planet!*

Remember: Everyone is wandering around experiencing intense emotions all the time, whether they're conscious of it or not, and often feeling utterly lost and frightened on their journey. Our unwillingness to recognize and honor that creates separation and judgment, and doesn't make our world feel vibrationally safe.

**Living with compassion means being willing
to feel the wound of the world, to not be afraid of it,
and to know that when your love touches that wound,
it does create a healing that travels through
the mysterious vortex of our shared oneness.**

THE CHOICE FOR LOVE
"PRAYER OF COMPASSION"

I want to share a Prayer of Compassion I use at my events and with my students. There are many such prayers in different traditions, and I've adapted this one to make it feel more personal, and not just universal. *This prayer contains the highest intention you could have for the people you love, for the people who are suffering in the world, and for all of humanity—to pray for their inner spiritual freedom.* **No matter what else you are able to do, or unable to do, you can bring your highest prayer of love to others.**

THE CHOICE FOR LOVE COMPASSION BLESSING

MAY YOU BE FREE FROM SUFFERING.

MAY YOU BE AT PEACE.

∾ HOW TO PRACTICE ∾
THE CHOICE FOR LOVE COMPASSION BLESSING

Each morning or evening, or at any time you wish, take a quiet moment to think about our planet and all human beings everywhere. You don't need to be in a special place, but you may find it uplifting to create more of a sacred atmosphere by lighting a candle, standing outside under the sun or the stars, or whatever helps you feel expansive.

First: *Visualize our earth* and, if you wish, close your eyes. Take a deep, full breath and think to yourself or say out loud:

"May you be free from suffering. May you be at peace."

Next, *think about one or more people you wish to send blessings to.* They may be experiencing challenges or suffering, whether external or internal, or they may simply be people you love—your partner, your children, your family, your friends, your spiritual guides, your teachers, etc.

Visualize each person one at a time, or all together. Again, take a deep, full breath and think to yourself or say out loud: *"May you be free from suffering. May you be at peace."* You can say this once for each person if you wish, or if you're pressed for time, put them in a nice, cozy group in your mind.

Finally, think about yourself, your journey, your challenges, and your current pressures, worries, and concerns. Take a deep, full breath and think to yourself or out loud: *"May you be free from suffering. May you be at peace."*

You can make this blessing even more specific by *adding the name of a person at the beginning of the sentence, and adding the word* today *at the end,* especially for your loved ones and yourself. *"Barbara, may you be free from suffering today. Barbara, may you be at peace today."*

The Compassion Blessing may seem very simple, but it's actually quite powerful and moving. I chose each word very deliberately. Don't be surprised if offering it stirs up emotions. **The words and the message they contain come from the most elevated quality of love.** Thinking or saying them will help to melt the ice around your heart and wash it clean of whatever vibrational debris has accumulated.

If you'd like, stop for a moment and try this Compassion Blessing right now. You will feel the immediate vibrational shift as you recalibrate yourself to your highest intentions for yourself, your loved ones, and the world.

This is why we are here on the planet—to increasingly become more free of suffering, to increasingly find peace and actually be a source of upliftment and peace to others, whether it's with our family, our children, our employees, our clients, people we love, our friends, or strangers.

It takes great spiritual courage to live with an open heart in this world. As transforming beings, we do not fool ourselves: *living with deep compassion will often be living with heartbreak.*

And so the questions for each of us become:

Do I have enough courage to feel the heartbreak of the world?
Am I brave enough to feel the pain that is not mine?
If I don't do this, who will?

We compassionately remind ourselves that we are all in the process of being polished like stones turning into diamonds.

Compassion is a high spiritual practice,
a form of a living prayer.
When you can feel your own heart, you can feel everyone's heart—
the hearts that are joyful, the hearts that are hurting,
the hearts full of trust, and the hearts full of resistance,
the hearts full of hope, the hearts full of fear.
Feel it all. Feel everyone.
As you feel everyone, you'll feel yourself more,
and you will emerge sanctified by your own love.

❋ 7 ❋

Loving Yourself Forward

"The first ripple of love has to rise in your heart.
If it has not risen for yourself it cannot rise for anybody else,
because everybody else is farther away from you.
It is like throwing a stone in the silent lake—
the first ripples will arise around the stone
and then they will go on spreading to the further shores."

— Osho

If you asked me to name the one thing you need more than any other to move yourself forward on your path of personal growth, and bring more fulfillment and attainment to your relationships, your work, and your spiritual expansion, my answer would be simple: **You need more love.**

Have you ever asked yourself these questions?

How can I develop more self-confidence?
How can I heal emotional pain from my past?
How can I become a better parent and a better partner?
How can I stop being so hard on myself?
How can I find the courage to overcome my fears?
How can I stay more centered and steady, and not become so stressed out?
How can I learn to listen to and trust my intuition and inner voice?

The answer to all of these is the same: "LOVE." All of the wisdom, guidance, goals, motivational teachings, and to-do lists in the world can take you only so far unless you are *fueling yourself forward with love.* You may be thinking, *"I have people who love me."* However, the kind of love that's needed is not the love you receive from others, *but the love you need to give yourself.*

Love is the only motivating factor that will truly
help you heal, open, shift, awaken, and be liberated.
The secret for moving yourself forward
is learning how to love yourself forward.

I'm sure you're familiar with the conventional wisdom that encourages you to love yourself more by being nice to yourself: getting a pedicure, listening to music you enjoy, buying yourself a new outfit, treating yourself to a meal at your favorite restaurant, and so on. As we've seen, however, the experience of loving yourself isn't something that happens because of outside events or actions. *It can only occur from the inside out.* You can learn to *take care of yourself* by doing things on the outside, but *loving yourself has to emerge from within.*

Loving yourself is not just kind and caring actions.
It's the identification with your true self.
You experience yourself as an individual expression
of that Supreme love, and bring that into
your relationship with yourself every day.
The greatest act of self-love is the remembrance
that you *are* Love.

First Love Yourself = F.L.Y.

This is a true story about what happened to me while I was beginning to write this chapter on loving yourself:

A few weeks ago, I was astonished to walk into my living room and discover a tiny bird sitting on the floor. I stood very still and stared at the bird in amazed wonder. It didn't appear to be wounded. It wasn't frantically hopping around. It was just quietly and intently staring back at me.

"Where did the bird come from?" I wondered. I assumed it must have flown in when I'd opened the door to get the mail. Perhaps it had come in out of curiosity, but as much as I was delighted with this fluffy little visitor, I knew it needed to go back to its natural habitat.

I slowly bent down to try to gently pick the bird up, and it instantly became startled and flew up to the very high ceilings in the house. For a few seconds, it would land on something, and look out through the tall glass windows, as if it was contemplating whether or not it could get out.

Then, somehow realizing that it could see through to the outside but there was no opening, it would fly somewhere else, attempting to find another exit.

I ran around the house opening up all the doors and windows to make it easier for the bird to leave, and I tried to gently guide it toward them with my hands. Time after time, it would land right next to a door or on a chair near a window, but it wouldn't leave. For a few minutes, it even sat on the doorknob, but would not fly out to freedom.

Now the little bird began to flap its tiny wings, and I could see its small body quivering. *"It's okay, little one,"* I said in my most soothing voice. *"You're not imprisoned here—you can leave any time you want. Don't be frightened."* The bird would settle down when it heard me speak, but soon would fly away to another spot.

Finally, the bird flew into the center of a small straw basket that was sitting on a table, and just sat there. I knelt down nearby and allowed myself to totally open to this bird from my heart. I could feel the same life force flowing through both of us, the divine thread that connected us and all living things. For a moment, it was as if we were one. *Suddenly I realized what was happening. The bird needed to be helped out. Even though freedom was right there, it needed a ride.*

Very quietly and still in that space of love, I walked over to the basket. The bird did not move and, amazingly enough, allowed me to carefully carry it across the room and outside to the patio where I set the basket down on the table. I assumed that as soon as the bird felt the fresh air and the spaciousness of the outdoors, it would instantly fly away. However, to my amazement, it didn't. It calmly just sat there on the basket. I stared at the bird and it stared back at me.

From that mysterious place where we just know things, an understanding arose: **This young, little bird needs love; this little bird needs tenderness; it needs to be calmed and given confidence so that it can fly. You need to love it.** This seemed illogical, but I trusted my inner voice and decided to do something I'd never done in my life.

Slowly, I took my index finger, reached out toward the bird, and began to stroke it, starting at its tiny head, down its beautiful back and soft little brown wings. As I touched the bird, I allowed myself to feel all the tenderness in my heart, and imagined it pouring through my finger. *"You are so* beautiful, so magical," I whispered. *"You are so brave to come into my house, and to let me love you right now. It's safe for you to fly away whenever you want."*

For five minutes, I loved the little bird. I kept expecting it to leave, but it didn't. It closed its eyes, and fully received everything I was offering. It felt like time and space had disappeared, and the only thing in the world was me and the bird and the space of love.

Suddenly the bird opened its eyes to look at me one last time, and then it unfurled its wings and flew off over the trees, catching the warm morning breeze.

This story is about you, your own journey of awakening, and the choice for love. That day, the little bird was my teacher, **reminding me of how easily we each can become trapped and stuck in so many places inside of ourselves, even when we don't mean to, and that the only choice is to love ourselves up and out of wherever we've been hiding.**

The bird didn't fly into my house intending to become imprisoned there, but it did. Just like this, we don't always recognize when we are trapped in old patterns. We don't realize that, when we attempt to protect our heart, we can become stuck behind those emotional walls.

We settle into our emotional hiding places and tell ourselves that we can find our way out any time we want to. "I am going to shut off my feelings for a while, but if I meet someone special, I'm sure I'll be able to open up right away. I'm not going to care that much about anything for a while so that I don't get disappointed, but if I suddenly get an important new job or opportunity, I'm sure I'll be able to recover my passion and focus immediately."

Of course, this is not what happens. Like the bird, fear overtakes us. Our escape is right there, our doors to freedom and liberation are before us, our solutions are obvious, and yet we flap around bumping into our own walls, panicking, and not knowing how to find the way out to the light, and to freedom.

What do we need at these moments? Just like the little bird, *we need to be comforted, we need to be offered tenderness, and we need to love ourselves up and out of wherever we've been hiding back into flight.*

We need to F.L.Y. = First Love Yourself.

STOP SCARING YOURSELF FORWARD

"Power is of two kinds.
One is obtained by the fear of punishment and the other by acts of love.
Power based on love is a thousand times more effective and permanent
than the one derived from fear of punishment."

— Mahatma Gandhi

When I contemplate the visit from my bird teacher, I wonder how many people would have yelled at the bird and tried to scare it out of the house. This is often what many of us do to ourselves. We attempt to scare ourselves out of our patterns and insecurities. We attempt to strong-arm our love, wisdom, and courage to emerge. *This doesn't work.* Only love, compassion, and tenderness allowed me to help that bird so that it wouldn't become terrified, fly into the glass or a wall, knock itself senseless, and die.

You can't authentically shift from anything but love. You can't scare yourself into doing the right thing. You have to love yourself into doing the right thing.

Sometimes, if we weren't motivated or made safe with love growing up, we may think that being tough or harsh with ourselves is the only way to get ourselves to grow and succeed, and that empowering ourselves means kicking ourselves forward. Perhaps you've had parents or teachers who taught you this, but I disagree. *Intimidation and fear are crude tactics of the ego.* They're low vibrations. We usually learned to use them because that's what we saw or were exposed to.

Love is always the great motivator in life.
When you love yourself enough, you will grow and heal.
You can't scare yourself forward.
You have to love yourself forward.

As human beings, we have always grown through being loved. When you were a child learning to walk, you took your first wobbly step, and then fell to the ground. Your mother instinctively knew what to say: *"Good girl! You took a step! I'm so proud of you! You're so wonderful!"* Even though you fell down, and even though it hurt a little bit, you looked up at your mother's face gazing at you with so much love, and you found the confidence to pull yourself up and try again.

Can you imagine what would have happened if, when you took your first step and fell, she'd said, *"What a klutz! One step—is that all you can do? Let's see you go back and forth across the room three times . . . then maybe I'll be impressed"*? I always joke with my students that if we'd had this kind of feedback, none of us would ever have learned to walk. We'd all still be in strollers!

Scaring yourself forward will always backfire.
Fear can get us temporarily motivated,
but eventually, it will collapse us and deflate us.
Fear creates contraction,
and contraction leaves no room for
the life force to flow through us.

Remember our explanation of your emotional circuitry? *If you were intimidated forward as a child, you may unconsciously believe that the way to motivate yourself is through fear.* If you have love, achievement, and fear wired up in your brain, when you think, *"I want to be successful,"* your brain gives you the information that you'd better be hard on yourself. At these times, you really don't feel like you're scaring yourself. You insist, "I'm motivating myself," because that's what motivation feels like to you.

When you're in the habit of scaring yourself forward, you can only go so far before you inevitably rebel. Against whom? Yourself! You rebel against that critical part of you that's shaking its finger at you, saying, *"You'd better do this or else."* This is one of the reasons many people struggle with inconsistency—they're not loving themselves forward enough, and *at some point, an inner rebellion and uprising takes place.*

If you're overseeing your process of growth with a heavy hand,
you'll foster rebellion and revolt.
You're not revolting against anyone or anything on the outside,
but against your own self, your own goals,
your own transformation. You're the one who suffers.

I have never scared myself forward even once in my life. Every bit of success I've experienced has come from loving myself forward. Every inner attainment I've achieved has come from loving myself forward. Every obstacle I've faced has been vanquished because I loved myself forward.

Once when I was teaching this principle in a seminar, I noticed a very large, supermuscular guy wildly raising his hand to share. He was a well-known bodybuilder, and was working with me for the first time. "I get it, Dr. Barbara!" he announced as he leapt up. **"Fear is the Twinkie, and Love is the protein bar."**

"That's an interesting metaphor," I replied, not sure of what he meant.

"It's like this," he went on. *"Fear is like a sugar high. If you're at the gym, you can eat something that's going to help sustain you through a long workout, or you can eat something that will give you a temporary surge of energy, but only for ten minutes, and then you're going to collapse.* See? *Fear is the Twinkie, and Love is the protein bar!"*

The rest of the audience burst into delighted applause, and I joined in. I loved this metaphor, because it's true! **Fear is fast food for the ego. It temporarily pumps you up, but then lets you down. Love sustains you for the long term.**

"It is better to be loved than feared."
— Senegalese proverb

The dynamics in your relationship with yourself always create a blueprint for the dynamics for your relationship with others. Therefore, when we're in the habit of scaring or bullying ourselves forward, we will unintentionally treat other people the same way. Conventional wisdom often counsels us that, in order to be powerful, we need to make sure people are frightened of us. *This is not power—it's weakness.*

Authentic power will always create an environment in which people feel safe to be in our presence, rising to their highest vibration around us.

Fear is a low vibration.
It is not powerful to bring people down to their lowest vibration.
Using fear to control others has nothing to do with power
and everything to do with powerlessness,
manipulation, and control.
It means you don't have the ability to
raise people up to their highest, which is love.
When people fear you, you have lost all power.
When people love you because of how you love them,
the concept of whether or not you are powerful becomes irrelevant.

ARE YOU LOVING YOURSELF CONDITIONALLY?

"We are trampled most often by forces we ourselves create."
— William Shakespeare

When I teach about loving yourself, someone inevitably says, *"I agree with you, but I really do love myself."* When I ask them to list the moments in which they've experienced self-love, they're almost always **moments of outer achievement and external triumph**: *"I was promoted at work. I completed a project. I reached my running goal. I stuck to my diet."* These are all perfectly fine accomplishments, but they're very conditional expressions of self-love based on things going the way we want them to.

It's easy to feel good about ourselves when we do a good job, or when our relationship is going well, or when we achieve what we thought we should. However, when we're frightened, we don't always love ourselves.

When we're confused, we don't always love ourselves.

When we're needy, we don't always love ourselves.

When someone else doesn't love us, we don't always love ourselves.

When do we love ourselves? When we've performed properly, fulfilled our or others' expectations, not made mistakes, and gotten the results we desired. This sounds grim, doesn't it?

Most of us have a secret, unconscious list in our mind that starts out: *"I will love myself when . . ."* and it's filled with conditions we've decided we must fulfill to qualify for our own love. For instance:

I will love myself when I lose 20 pounds.

I will love myself when I finally start my business/write my book/achieve that goal.

I will love myself when I pay off all my debts.

I will love myself when I find the right person and get married.

I will love myself when my kids get good grades so I can feel I'm a successful parent.

I will love myself when I'm making enough money to buy my own home.

I will love myself when I am getting along with everyone and no one dislikes me.

I will love myself when I never feel insecure, depressed, or overwhelmed.

I will love myself when nothing upsets me or throws me off center.

I invite you to make a list of your secret conditions for loving yourself. You'll be shocked at how many there are, and how impossible it would be for you to meet them. No wonder you often find it difficult to get in touch with your own love every day.

When you love yourself conditionally, you cut yourself off from your own unlimited source of love inside:

> **The choice for love means the choice**
> **to love yourself for every step you're taking,**
> **for the times when you fall down**
> **and need to pick yourself back up,**
> **and for the times you take off and fly.**

Loving yourself means *loving yourself as you are, remembering that you are pure, divine consciousness and love.* It means accepting your humanity in all of its manifestations—your pleasure and your pain, your terror and your triumph. It means being tender toward yourself, and never punishing yourself for how you're feeling.

The choice to love yourself also means making the choice to honor yourself:

Honor yourself for your courage to wake up in this lifetime.

Honor yourself for all the things you've been doing to learn, grow, and heal.

Honor yourself for each moment of clarity and consciousness you've experienced.

Honor yourself for each frozen place in your heart that is melting.

Honor yourself for reading this book, and for all of the other steps you are taking to become a more enlightened human being.

One of the ways I love myself forward is by speaking to myself—out loud—with love, as if I am my most beloved. *"Sweetheart, you are doing such a wonderful job. You helped so many people at that seminar. I love you and I am so proud of you."*

Does this seem strange to you? Don't you wish someone else would say those things to you? So why not say them to yourself? **If you can't say them now to your own heart, you won't hear them, or even believe them, when someone else comes along.**

Sometimes we feel reticent to love ourselves this much, fearing that we will somehow be vain. Actually, the opposite is true. When you love yourself, you give other people permission to love themselves as well. I recall something someone once wrote about one of my revered spiritual teachers:

"She loves herself so much that it's hard not to like yourself in her presence."

This is true for all great beings. They vibrate with so much love that, in their presence, we start to feel good about ourselves. We spontaneously want to treat ourselves with more respect. We begin to get in touch with our own dignity, and our own love.

This is the real gift we can all give to the people we care about— our partners, our friends, our children, and our business associates. We model what it looks like to love and honor ourselves, and the highest in them will resonate with our highest, and rise up.

When you feel and celebrate your own love for yourself,
the expansive, uplifting waves of that love
will splash onto everyone around you.

Emptying Your Evidence Bag

*"Most of our faults are more pardonable than
the means we use to conceal them."*
— François, Duc de La Rochefoucauld

I have a confession to make—I love watching detective shows! I'm fascinated to see how the characters look for clues and collect the perfect evidence to make their case so they can catch the guilty culprit. There's always that crucial and dramatic moment when the detective confronts the villain with a list of irrefutable facts that say, *"It's over—you're going down."*

What does this have to do with loving ourselves? **Well, some of us are also "emotional evidence collectors," gathering lists of our mistakes, our failings, and our faults to use against ourselves.** If you're squirming reading this, you may recognize this pattern more than you'd like to admit: you scrutinize your conversations, activities, and interactions for evidence of your errors or wrongdoing, and at the end of each day, you unconsciously place what you collected into a mental file.

"I was late handing in that report. I cheated on my diet last week. I never wrote back to my college roommate and thanked him for the gift he sent. I skipped my morning meditation. I had negative thoughts about my best friend. I didn't finish three items on my to-do list." At the end of that week or month, we add up the evidence, and it now turns into judgment and condemnation: *"I failed. I blew it. I'm bad."*

Once you're in the evidence-collection business, you rarely stop with yourself, but impose this habit onto everyone. You walk around looking for the negative. You interact with others tuning in to what's wrong, and ignoring what's right. You stockpile emotional ammunition against people—sometimes even those closest to you. **This isn't love— it's warfare.**

Have you ever been on the receiving end of this? Out of the blue, someone with whom you've been close says to you, *"You know, three years ago when I moved, you didn't call me that first night to see how I was,"* or *"I was very hurt when our children graduated from elementary school, and you didn't ask me to put on a party with you, and instead asked Joanne,"* or *"You know, you've been working with that new firm for a year now, and you've never referred even one client to me."* **You're totally blindsided with a barrage** of evidence you didn't even realize they were collecting, and they've used that evidence to put up a wall between you, justifying it with a big pile of secret grievances.

Some time ago, I had a friend I'll call Katie whom I'd known for 15 years. She often leaned on me for advice during difficult times, and I had recently tried to support her new career by introducing her to one of my business associates. Unfortunately, I heard back that she hadn't acted professionally and had displayed a disrespectful attitude. Reluctantly, I called Katie and passed on the feedback about how she'd behaved, and suggested a way she might salvage the situation. She listened politely, thanked me profusely, shared that she'd received this same feedback before in her life, and appreciated my honesty and support.

A few weeks later, Katie, another friend, and I met for coffee. When I sat down at the table, I was immediately taken aback. Katie was glaring at me, and her greeting was cold and distant. When I asked her what was wrong, she proceeded to reiterate a list of petty grievances she had about me, evidence she'd obviously been collecting and saving up for years:

"Once on the way to an event, you asked me to pick up a few bottles of water for you, and you never paid me back. When I had my tooth surgery, you didn't call me when I arrived home that night, but waited until the next morning. Two years ago when we were at a party with one of your old friends and we were all laughing about our guilty TV pleasures, you teased me about how much I like watching reality shows."

Listening to this litany of festering resentments, I was simply astonished. I didn't even recall any of these events, but obviously they were in Katie's well-worn evidence bag. I could feel how, with each new accusation, she was fueling her own self-righteous anger. She sounded like a prosecutor in a court case, except I'd already been convicted over and over without knowing it, and now I was being sentenced. I had become an unsuspecting hostage in a war I hadn't even known was taking place.

This was such a sad event for me. Of course, Katie had always treated herself in this same way—with harshness, bitterness, and condemnation. It was a painful lesson, **because no matter how much I loved her, *her own lack of self-love didn't allow her to truly receive love*. The more loving I'd been, the more angry she'd become. The more I'd given her, the more resentful she'd felt, because *she didn't know how to give herself that same kindness and compassion*.**

Fear wants to convict. Love wants to pardon.
Love doesn't gather evidence of what's wrong.
In fact, it looks for evidence of what's possible.
You can't love and also look for evidence of
what's not lovable at the time.

I share this story because many of us act out these same dynamics with ourselves, and get in the very destructive habit of living with our own personal inquisition. We wake up each day to face continual tests, trials, and prosecutions from the relentless critic within, watching ourselves to see if we fail in some way. Then we imprison ourselves with recrimination, shame, and suffering.

You can't be happy if you're in an
adversarial relationship with your incarnation.
You can't love yourself if you're having
a hostile relationship with your humanity.
When you live like this, every minute is a battle.
Making the choice for love means
putting an end to your personal inquisition,
and liberating yourself from the tyranny of constant judgment.
Look at yourself and see what's right
instead of seeing what's wrong.

This doesn't mean you should ignore what you see about yourself that needs improvement, but you can begin to shift from the *habit of judgment to the habit of assessment.*

Instead of asking: *"Am I good? Am I bad? Am I doing it right? Am I doing it wrong?"* ask yourself:

"How am I doing? Do I need to make any adjustments?"

This moves you from *judging* something as good or bad to the more enlightened, neutral activity of *assessment.*

Judgment = Comes from the limited ego
Assessment = Comes from your higher mind

Assessment means that you're evaluating what and how you're doing. You're noticing whether your attitudes, choices, or beliefs are helping you or hurting you—if they are useful to you, or are not very useful. You're moving into self-reflection with less criticism, and more curiosity.

Making the choice for love means using your consciousness to course correct, rather than to condemn.

When you evaluate your behavior and habits on the basis of whether or not they are serving your highest, and on their usefulness to your intention of living the most awakened life possible, you are truly making a choice for loving yourself.

Choosing Perfect Love in Imperfect Moments

"We must embrace pain and burn it as fuel for our journey."
— Kenji Miyazaw

Many of us consider ourselves loving and compassionate toward others, but the way we deal with ourselves is with no compassion at all. We judge ourselves, criticize ourselves for our inadequacies or shortcomings, rather than having compassion and holding ourselves with love as we witness our most challenging moments. We ignore our pain, discomfort, or fear as if we need to push through them rather than embracing ourselves with love.

Compassion for yourself ultimately means honoring and accepting your human-ness. You are the divine living within human limitations. You are not perfect. You will make mistakes. You will do stupid things. You will be blind. You will not be able to always live up to your expectations. This is the human condition.

Cultivating compassion for yourself means learning to have compassion for your weaknesses, for your trials, for your failures, for your blindness, for your karma, and especially for your cosmic curriculum and all of its difficulties.

When we have compassion for ourselves, we can bring the expansive energy of consciousness to our challenges rather than the contractive energy of judgment. We can welcome understandably

disturbing feelings of despair, discouragement, embarrassment, and *understand them as indicators of great healing.* They're just signs that we've seen things we wish we hadn't seen about ourselves! The good news is that we *have* seen them, and because we've seen them, we're already shifting.

What do you need to bring to a situation that is challenging?
More love and compassion for yourself.
What do you need when you're feeling stuck?
More love and compassion for yourself.
Unless you meet yourself with compassion in the darkness,
you cannot move fully into the light.

Can you love yourself while you are in pain?
Can you love yourself while you're confused or frightened?
Can you love yourself even while you see the need to correct your behavior?
Sometimes, this is what loving yourself looks like—letting yourself be in your pain and confusion, not telling yourself you aren't supposed to feel it, and loving yourself enough to feel it.

Your patterns aren't walls to overcome.
They are doorways to tremendous wisdom.
Your issues are not your blocks—they are your cosmic curriculum.
When you treat them as if they're the enemy,
your journey of transformation will feel like a battle
instead of a redemption.
Open up your issues, knowing they contain keys to your liberation,
and you'll be flooded with freedom.

Whenever I teach about cultivating love and compassion for yourself, someone invariably asks me something like this:

"I have a friend who does exactly what you said. I think she has a lot of love and compassion for herself, because she's always thinking of what she can do to make herself feel good. But she complains about everything, and seems to feel very sorry for herself. I'm confused—is that what you mean by loving ourselves?"

"That's not self-love," I always answer. "That's self-pity."

There's a big difference between self-pity, self-indulgence, and self-love. **Self-pity is when somebody becomes so focused on their own problems that they forget that other people are having similar problems.** It's as if they're the only one in the world who's suffering, and being singled out for unhappiness by God or whatever force is controlling everything. They may even play the *my problems are worse than your problems* game, as if their suffering is bigger, better, or more deserving than others, especially if you're not giving them the sufficient amount of sympathy they feel they deserve.

Self-pity doesn't leave much room for empathy, understanding, or even love for others. Compassion for yourself is different.

Compassion is not the same as self-pity.
It allows you to feel that your own humanity is shared by others.
When you have compassion for both yourself and people around you,
you can see everything more clearly, and you realize
you're not alone on your human journey.

Self-indulgence is also not the same as self-compassion. *"I'm really stressed out. I'm worried about my deadline, and it's been a difficult month, so I'm just going to be compassionate with myself and spend the next week watching TV, not answering my e-mails, eating anything I want, and being loving to myself."* Is this self-love? Not really. **Compassion for yourself creates a space of love and understanding, but doesn't become an excuse to use your difficulties as a justification to indulge.**

THE CHOICE FOR PATIENCE

"There is nothing noble about being superior to some other man.
The true nobility is in being superior to your previous self."
— Hindu proverb

A few years ago I worked with a wonderful physical therapist who helped me deal with some physical challenges. He was moving places in my spine that had been stuck. These treatments were often really painful, because parts of me had been frozen in certain patterns, and now they were being manipulated in ways they weren't used to moving. If I'd judged the efficacy of his physical therapy based on how pleasant it was, or even how I felt immediately afterward, I would have stopped going after the first session. Luckily, I understand that transformation of any kind can be uncomfortable.

I remember at the end of my first treatment, my therapist gave me the speech that he obviously gives all of his patients: *"Now, remember, it's going to feel worse before it gets better. That's how you'll know the treatment is working."* In between my groans and moans of discomfort, I laughed and said, "I know—I give this same talk to my students all the time."

Often we have a hard time loving ourselves when we're uncomfortable. We misinterpret the discomfort as a sign that we're doing something wrong, and start loving ourselves less instead of more. When you're on an authentic path of transformation, there will be so many adjustments you'll have to make on the inside and on the outside. Just like in my physical therapy, you're moving parts of your emotional and spiritual self that have become stuck in the wrong position, loosening up places that have been contracted and causing you pain, and restoring yourself to balance.

Don't judge your process or your progress by your discomfort or how long it's taking, or you'll be misjudging it.
Don't stop loving yourself just because you're in pain.
Discomfort isn't always a sign that we're doing something wrong.
If we're not uncomfortable, we're usually not growing.

Transforming yourself and healing your heart is like working on one of those jumbo puzzles. At first you see so many mismatched pieces that you feel overwhelmed at the task before you. You don't even know where to begin. There doesn't seem to be any order or logic to it. Even when you do arrange a few pieces together, it doesn't make a difference to the big picture, which you still can't figure out. *The whole process isn't satisfying because you haven't made enough progress.*

At some point, however, you start to see some patterns in the pieces, and the result is that you become more enthusiastic about the puzzle. You see that it *is* something—a scene from nature, or a photograph of a city—and it does make sense. All of a sudden, your discomfort working with the puzzle turns into excited enthusiasm, and you can't wait to get home or finish your chores to sit down and make some more progress.

I know this feeling of overwhelm and frustration very intimately—I go through it each time I begin to write a book. I stare at the thousands of pieces of wisdom, anecdotes, experiences, and inspiration and at first can't clearly see the patterns. "There's so much material!" I say to myself. "But where's the book?" Slowly things move together, and I can see a vision of the whole. Loving myself forward with patience and compassion, I persevere. You're experiencing the finished product of that love right now!

"Do not judge yourself harshly.
Without mercy for ourselves we cannot love the world."
— The *Buddha*

I've never been a naturally patient person. I think it's because my vision of what's possible is so vast that human reality, including my own, just can't go as fast as my unfolding revelations. I can always feel 1,000 ideas longing to become manifested, 50 more books waiting to be written, and dozens of seminars calling to be designed. **I am so grateful that, at some point on my journey, I realized patience is one of the highest and most necessary forms of love.**

I love my readers, so I patiently take the time I need to write the best book I can.

I love my students, so I patiently study and learn all I can to continue to be the best teacher and produce the transformational maps to guide others to freedom.

This patience is the same quality each of us calls on whenever we care deeply about something. We love our garden, so we patiently take care of it, watering and nourishing the plants so they will bloom. We love our children, so we patiently help them with their homework, encourage their talents, teach them to tie their shoes and brush their hair, supporting them to grow into magnificent adults.

What if you became impatient with your garden when it didn't bloom as soon as you planted the seeds and stopped watering it?

What if you became impatient with your children because they couldn't talk, walk, read, or write as soon as they were born, and stopped nurturing them?

What if I became frustrated in the beginning stages of writing a new book, and decided that, since it wasn't emerging perfectly, I might as well not write it at all?

As absurd as this sounds, it's how you may be treating yourself when you aren't growing, succeeding, healing, or blooming as quickly as you think you should.

The choice for love means patiently seeing what is unfolding within you with loving eyes.
It requires us not to focus on what *hasn't* happened yet, but to see and celebrate what *is* happening.

The invisible is *always* growing within us. There's always something that is transforming and emerging. **Most of the time, however, we don't fully notice or appreciate our progress while it's happening, because it hasn't fully manifested.** And yet, it *is* there, just like your whole garden of radiantly colored flowers is miraculously contained within the tiny brown seeds.

Right now you have seeds growing within you—seeds of wisdom, seeds of creativity, seeds of confidence, seeds of healing, seeds of forgiveness, and seeds of love. They may be taking more time than you'd like expanding and fully blossoming into your life, but they are there.

So we make the choice for love. We water the seeds of awakening growing beneath the surface of our life with patience, consciousness, and compassionate recognition for each small sign of transformation that bursts through the crusty soil of our old patterns.

Later in this chapter, I'll offer you the Choice for Love Patience Prayer. I wrote it as a tool you can use to call forth your own self-love and patience whenever you need to.

LOVING YOURSELF FROM AWAKE TO AWAKENED

"Awakening is simply the direct perception of reality
without any filters getting in the way—
no projections, no beliefs, no interpretations. . . .
Awakening is the process of recognizing that reality,
over and over and over again.
So awakening is not a one-time discovery,
but rather an endless re-discovery—a continual deepening into
this radiant aliveness that we are, and always have been."

— Jon Bernie

India is my spiritual home, and I haven't had the opportunity to go there as much as I would like. My first visit was on my 60th birthday, and I arrived in the middle of night after traveling for almost 24 hours. I was exhausted but determined to set my alarm and wake up early so I could have a full day visiting ancient temples. The next morning, I set out with every intention of seeing everything on my list, but after a few hours, I was hallucinating from fatigue, and so I returned to the hotel and collapsed for 12 hours.

I woke again more refreshed the following day, and thought about the concept of jet lag. We get taken from where we are at an astonishing speed to find ourselves far, far away from home, where the cycles of light and dark are different, where everything is turned around. The mind tells us we are ready to proceed forward, but it takes the body some time to become accustomed to the new rhythms—in a sense, to catch up. And so for a while we feel strange, disoriented, and ungrounded.

Does this sound familiar? **It should, because on the spiritual path, we will invariably encounter what I call "spiritual or vibrational jet lag,"** times when our consciousness has radically shifted and we've vibrationally accelerated to a totally different way of being on the inside—and yet our personality, habits, and thought patterns are lagging behind, and haven't fully integrated into our transformations. *It's easy to misinterpret spiritual jet lag as many other things when we're experiencing it—depression, confusion, even failure. Often the old "you" is simply trying to catch up with the new, unfolding consciousness that's emerging.*

I'm going to tell you a secret: **Sometimes seekers on a path of personal growth are harder on themselves and more impatient about their progress than anyone else!** Do you know someone who you believe has lots of problems, but they don't seem to think so? Do you have a friend who seems blissfully oblivious to their unhealthy emotional habits, and yet you're constantly obsessed with your own patterns?

Those of us who are transformers have lofty goals, and frequently become frustrated when we don't achieve them. *We have peak experiences of revelation and breakthroughs, and then feel as if we've "crashed down," not because something bad happens, but because we stop loving ourselves when we can't permanently sustain these moments of awakening.*

For instance, you have an expansive weekend at a retreat, or an uplifting day by yourself hiking the nearby trails, or a sacred, moving morning at church. You're feeling very high, centered, and content. *"I'm in such a great place today,"* you conclude with satisfaction.

Then, something happens. Your mind suddenly remembers a challenge you're facing, and you're instantly overcome with fear and anxiety. One of your children does something to annoy you, and you lose your temper. You look in the mirror and notice some new wrinkles and get depressed. Your partner seems a bit distant, and you feel a wave of sadness.

Immediately you begin to judge yourself for having these reactions. *"I can't believe this—I was feeling so enlightened and loving for a few hours/ days/weeks, and now look at me! I'm a mess. I haven't changed or grown at all. So much for thinking I'm making any progress."*

Now, you're not only feeling despair about what originally upset you, but you're *invalidating every attainment or expanded experience you had earlier, or even that you've ever had, because of how contracted you're feeling in this moment.* **It's as if *you decide your moments of expansion and spiritual connection don't count because they aren't permanent.***

There are exquisite, grace-filled moments in which
we're able to *temporarily bypass all of the blocks
to our highest awareness*, and we're given a magnificent glimpse
of our most expanded and awakened self.
The meditation retreat, seminar, teacher, hike, church service,
or whatever uplifting influence we experience does just that—
it "lifts us up" and over our usual patterns and programming,
acting as a sort of cosmic helicopter,
and offering us a view from the heights of our consciousness.
In that moment, we *are* experiencing awakening.
We're just not *permanently awakened.*

Each time you make the choice for love, in that moment you're awakened.

Each time you hold a space of pure compassion for someone, in that moment you're awakened.

Each time you see clearly, or have truth come through you to others, in that moment you're awakened.

As long as you're in a body, you will always collide with your humanity. As the great master Ram Dass said, *"You are a spiritual being having a human experience,"* and that human experience is difficult. Yes, the divine lives within the human and cannot be tarnished, but the human *is human*, with its unique personality, physicality, and mystical journey of healing and remembrance.

Do not use your humanity to disqualify your recognition of your essential divinity. Whenever you come face-to-face with one of the more challenging parts of your humanness, make the choice for love and remind yourself:

My humanity does not invalidate my divinity.

If it's a cloudy day, and the sun peeks out from behind the clouds for a moment, is the sun less real or perfect because it's only appearing for five minutes? You would never say:

"You're not the sun. I just caught a brief glimpse of you, so I'm not going to acknowledge your existence until I see all of you and you never disappear. See? You just went behind the clouds again, so this appearance doesn't count."

Of course this sounds ridiculous. That moment of sunlight was real. When the sun emerges on a stormy or overcast day we think, *"I had five minutes of sun! It felt so good! I can't wait for more."*

Just because you collide with your humanity does not mean you're not growing in your divinity.

Just because you momentarily forget your wisdom does not mean you're not learning.

Just because you fall back into old pain doesn't mean you're not healing.

The sun *is* coming out for you right now—the sun of wisdom, the sun of revelation, the sun of remembrance and reunion with your highest self, and the sun of love. Slowly the clouds of your patterns and programming are disappearing. Every day there is more and more light. *You need to bask in that sunlight and let it count.* **You can't be constantly looking for the holes in your wakefulness. You have to see the wakefulness and celebrate it. It is a delightful glimpse of the sun of enlightenment peeking through the clouds of your forgetfulness.**

Wherever you are in your current journey, please be compassionate with yourself to allow the integration of this work. Remind yourself that in a way, *we are all "catching up" to the Truth*, to the Highest Self we are, and if you are patient, persistent, and wise, each day you'll find yourself more and more awake to who you really are.

I've written this Patience Prayer to help you recognize all of the transformation that is taking place in your life. My students find it really helps to read this to yourself out loud, especially when it's been difficult to feel good about your progress, or you need to nourish yourself with some more love. Feel free to add your own, more personal sentences to this list.

THE CHOICE FOR LOVE PATIENCE PRAYER

Each day, I'm a little more awake.
May I honor every moment of wakefulness.

Each day, I'm a little more conscious.
May I honor every moment of consciousness.

Each day, I'm a little more open.
May I honor every moment of openness.

Each day, I'm a little more aware
of what I'm doing and feeling.
May I honor every moment of awareness.

Each day, I'm a little more courageous.
May I honor every moment of courage.

Each day, I'm a little more compassionate
with myself and others.
May I honor every moment of compassion.

Each day, I'm choosing a little more love.
May I honor every moment of love.

You Are Proof of the Sacred

"At bottom every man knows well enough
that he is a unique being, only once on this earth;
and by no extraordinary chance will such a marvelously picturesque
piece of diversity in unity as he is, ever be put together a second time."
— Friedrich Nietzsche

The Hawaiian island of Kauai is my favorite magical place on the planet. I go there to rest, to deepen my connection to spirit, and sometimes to heal. Once during a particularly painful time in my life, I went on a pilgrimage to Kauai hoping to find a higher understanding of the turmoil I was experiencing, and longing for divine guidance that would allow me to move forward with more love for myself.

There's an enormous, water-filled cave on the island called Wai-a-Kanaloa that is said to contain powerful healing energies, and when one of my friends asked if I'd like to visit it, I eagerly agreed. We hiked up a rocky hill, then down again to the entrance of Wai-a-Kanoloa, and into its mysterious depths. I sat alone on the rock edge next to the dark water, and immediately felt embraced by the ancient, healing vibration of this hidden spot, which has existed for thousands of years.

It was still and peaceful, and I sighed as I recognized what a stark contrast this was to the storms of suffering that had been raging in my own heart. *"How many people before me had come here to pray, and to ask for blessings?"* I wondered. *"Who had sat in this exact spot on the rock and allowed their tears to drop into the waiting pool as mine were doing? Who had been healed by the invisible forces that resided here?"*

I closed my eyes and prayed for peace, for guidance, and for grace. I prayed for a miracle.

For a few moments, I felt myself pulled deep within, as if I were entering a cave just like this one deep inside of my heart. Suddenly I was surrounded by dazzling light and the most sublime, compassionate love, and these words revealed themselves:

"What if the miracle is the unchanging presence of the divine within you in spite of the harshness of your embodiment as a human being?

"What if the miracle is that, in spite of how much you have endured in this life, you have never abandoned the infinite ocean of love in your heart?

"What if the miracle is that, in spite of all the things you've faced—the losses, the pain, the suffering, and this current trial—you have never given up? You are still steadfastly seeking; you are still courageously ascending. You are still unconditionally loving.

"Remember, my daughter: Your light is stronger than any darkness. Your love is stronger than any pain.

"This is the proof of the sacred within you."

My whole body trembled, and I wept as I felt the truth of this message, and peace penetrated the places in me where fear and darkness had been swirling. I could physically sense and feel the invisible ones who served here embracing me, comforting me, and celebrating this sacred moment of seeing.

In hopes of receiving some guidance, I'd brought my phone into the cave, and as soon as I opened my eyes, I quietly recorded what I'd heard. In the weeks that followed, I contemplated the knowingness that had come with this message. It was so clear to me now that I'd had the truth reversed: My pain and human challenges weren't proof that something was **wrong** with me. Rather, my invincibility of spirit was ***proof of the sacred within me*** that would not and could not ever be destroyed.

Not: *I'm not perfect; therefore, I'm tarnished.*
Instead: *In spite of my imperfection, I am shining.*

This was and still is my miracle, and it is your miracle too. In spite of anything that has happened to you, you have not given up. You are reading these words. You are searching. You are learning. You are growing. You are healing. You are choosing love. You are unfolding like the most beautiful flower. It is impossible that you're not. Celebrate it. Delight in the mystery of your own rebirth.

Remind yourself:

In spite of my human experiences and my suffering, I am divine.
I've fallen, and yet I've had the courage to stand up again.
I've been wounded, and yet I've had the courage to love again.
This is the proof of the sacred alive in me—
In spite of my humanity, I prevail.

This is how to love yourself forward. Love yourself for every step you are taking. Love yourself when you fall down, and love yourself when you pick yourself back up again. Love yourself for where you've come from and how you've arrived here. Love yourself for where you are now. Love the journey forward that is already unfolding in this moment.

No matter what happens,
just love yourself while it is happening.
No matter what you're feeling,
just love yourself while you are feeling it.
This is the way to honor the truth of who you really are:
You are so very beautiful.
You are Love.

❧ 8 ❧

Digging for Gold in the Mud

Love for Navigating through Impossible Journeys

"Let me not pray to be sheltered from dangers,
but to be fearless in facing them.
Let me not beg for the stilling of my pain,
but for the heart to conquer it."

— Rabindranath Tagore

Sometimes we find ourselves on what can only be called impossible journeys. No matter how carefully we've planned, how sincerely we've tried, how deeply we've loved, or how respectfully we've lived, our road has inexplicably veered off in a horrifying direction in which we never intended to go, and we find ourselves traveling on what feels like a treacherous and painful pathway. Whether we're braving obstacles we never dreamed we'd encounter, battling circumstances we never imagined we'd have to bear, or facing shadowy places inside of ourselves we didn't know—or want to know—existed, it's clear that we're on a one-way highway, and must see the journey through.

These forced pilgrimages take us to hellish destinations we hoped we would never visit—*landscapes of devastation and loss, forests of grief and darkness, endless oceans of disappointment and betrayal, and barren deserts of despair.* This is why I call these journeys "impossible"—when we realize that we're so far from where we want to be, it seems it will be impossible for us to ever find our way back to peace and happiness.

What do we do when we find ourselves in impossible times on impossible journeys? How do we survive? How do we bring some kind of sanity and understanding to circumstances we wish didn't exist?

Impossible times are times of fire. *Fire is a force that transmutes what-ever it touches.* It is not matter, but a form of powerful energy—the life force itself. Fire added to wood transmutes it into fuel. Fire added to food makes it edible. The fire of the Sun transforms what would be a barren planet and literally keeps us alive. *So too the fire we face on these unplanned and unwanted spiritual and emotional itineraries is there to transmute us in some mysterious way that we won't understand until its job is done.*

I have known so many of these impossible journeys, and I have defi-nitely known fire. There have been unbearable times in my life during which I felt like I was surrounded by and living in an enormous field of flames stretching in every direction, as far as I could see. **I was func-tioning, teaching, and working, but all around me everything that was familiar was burning. What had been solid beneath my feet had turned molten, and my platform of stability, safety, and certainty had melted into an unending lake of loss.**

Impossible times are also times of light. There are many sources of Light in this Universe—the Sun and the Moon are the most obvious that come to our mind—and then there is the Light produced by fire. **There is an illuminating power in all Light, no matter what its source, and the fire of heartbreak, the fire of fear, and the fire of powerlessness we feel during our impossible journeys force us to see and face so much about ourselves and our lives.**

There is a cosmic fire available to us in impossible times.
Like all fire, it can be used for destruction,
or it can be used for rebirth.
The Light from the fire's flames may frighten us, but it is still Light.
We need to use it to see what there is to see.
It isn't meant to destroy us. It's meant to transmute us.

I don't know of any way that we can bypass our impossible journeys. I suspect that's the point—**we aren't supposed to bypass them, because we're being squeezed through a cosmic portal designed to move us closer to freedom.** And so we ask ourselves:

How can we use our impossible journeys to rise to our Highest?
How can we find a way to bring Love to the impossible?

FINDING THE GRACE OF GOLD
IN THE MUD OF IMPOSSIBILITY

*"Deep unspeakable suffering may well be called a baptism,
a regeneration, the initiation into a new state."*

— George Eliot

Here's a question to consider:

*"During which days do you learn more—the days when everything
is easy and you're in control, or the impossible days that you wish never
happened?"*

It is easy to be at your Highest, feel connected to your heart, and be loving when nothing is challenging you. What's there to learn when everything is fine? However, then there are those other days, those impossible days—days when your trust collides with your terror, when dreams collide with your disappointment, and when your faith collides with your fury.

On these days, when you feel like your heart is on fire, and your brain feels like you're walking around in a nightmare, you actually have the opportunity to learn more. You're forced to figure out how to find your way out of your own darkness.

These moments truly test our ability to hold firmly on to everything we know or believe to be true, and everything we've learned or studied. These are not comfortable times, but they are times of forced integration.

**Impossible times force us to put everything we've learned,
or tried to learn, into immediate practice,
to become not just a collector of wisdom
but a practitioner of wisdom.
The pain, fear, and frustration press on us,
squeezing out all of our saved-up learning and revelation
so that we can see it and find ways to use it.**

Looking back on my own life, the times of greatest mastery and triumph have always been the impossible, unbearable times when I've been in the fire of pain and suffering, and yet I had to and did rise to my Highest Consciousness. This is what is so terrible and wonderful about being a transformational teacher—*you don't get a vacation from being uplifting and inspirational just because you're experiencing personal trauma.*

I can recall many occasions during which I had to teach or lecture when horrible things were happening in my life. I've had to speak to thousands of people when my heart was freshly broken, or to address a conference when one of my dogs was 3,000 miles away dying, or go on-stage right after I was told my neighborhood was on fire and my house was in danger of being destroyed. I've had to appear on national television when all I wanted to do was hide in my house and cry.

One of the most impossible of these impossible experiences occurred some years ago while my mother was dying. Months before her diagnosis, I'd accepted an invitation to be honored with a very prestigious award that only a few women have ever received. The day to fly across the country arrived, and I knew in my heart that by the time I returned, my mother would probably be in hospice and getting ready to leave her body. When I told her I could cancel and stay with her, she insisted that I go.

I can still hear her gentle voice offering one of the last coherent things she ever said to me: *"It's okay, sweetheart. Please go. I want you to go. This is what you're meant to do and who you are, and it's why I'm so proud of you."* Two weeks later, she passed from this earth.

All of these were the worst days of my life from the point of view of my heart, *but the greatest days of my life from the point of view of my soul*:

They wove my wisdom deep into every fiber of my being. They pushed me to find and cling to my Highest Self when there was nothing else there for me to hold on to.

They forced me to dig into the mud of my circumstances and look for the nugget of gold I had to believe existed.

They compelled me to find Grace in the impossible.

What was that gold? It wasn't an external, positive outcome that emerged from each of these painful times. *It was the gold of my own consciousness and my own attainment,* which had been forged by the fire of impossibility and polished by the pain of surrender.

Your lessons are always leading you somewhere.
The bigger the lesson, the longer the path to clarity is going to be.
This impossible, challenging path between the lesson
and the ultimate revelation
is where the healing and growth actually take place.
Once you arrive at your destination, you're already done.

I Don't Remember Signing Up for This

"Suffering is the sandpaper of our incarnation.
It does its work of shaping us."

— Ram Dass

Here's a new fable I wrote for you:

A master jeweler decided it was time to prepare one of his most precious diamonds to be used in an exquisite and rare piece of jewelry. He placed the diamond into a special holder, turned on his tools, and began the procedure.

"Help! Wait! Please stop hurting me!" the diamond cried. *"I've tried to be good. I've just been lying there in the safe minding my own business. Ouch! Get that tool away from me. What have I done wrong? Why are you punishing me?"*

A recently finished sparkling emerald ring overheard the moans of the diamond and couldn't help but reply: **"You silly diamond, don't you understand what's happening? You're not being punished. *You're being polished!* You weren't singled out because something is wrong with you. *You were chosen because you're special."***

Diamonds in their rough state are very unimpressive, with no sparkle or luster. The innate brilliance and fire of a diamond is revealed only after a series of processes, including sawing, cutting, and polishing, which transforms the dull rock into a dazzling gem. So too we are all "polished" by our difficulties, challenges, and suffering. *We're often pushed against the impossible so that our hearts break open to levels of Love we wouldn't normally be able to experience.*

Many of the most transformational things that happen to us
in our life do not feel good.
They smash the apparent orderliness of our world.
They crack us open.
They force us out of the comforting rhythm of uneventful days
into the frantic groundlessness of emergency.
To correctly navigate through these times,
we need to try and not feel we're being punished,
which will only cause us to resist what's happening and create more pain.
Instead, we shift to seeing how we're being polished,
and offer up any rough edges of our ego to be made smooth and whole.

While these teachings about love sound uplifting, I understand that it's not easy to see our challenges from the highest perspective if we're in pain. When you're enduring impossible times, it's difficult not to think to yourself: *"Why is this happening to me? I don't remember signing up for this!"*

What if you *did* sign up for everything that has happened to you? As I always say, advanced souls—and that's you—have an advanced earth curriculum. What if you carefully chose your cosmic classes to help you progress to your next level of evolution and enlightenment? What if, before you came to this earth realm, you enrolled in Advanced Soul Classes, but you've since forgotten that they're the ones you chose?

Here are some "classes" I find are popular with awakening souls such as yourself. Perhaps you'll recognize some of them . . . !

What's Wrong with Everyone?: The Tolerance Symposium

You're Not God: God Is God! How to Stop Controlling Everything and Everyone

The Abandonment Immersion

Surrender: A Master Class

Curing Magical Thinking: How to See What's Real Instead of What You Wish Was Real

Pathways to Patience: Frustrations and Delays for the Impatient Seeker

Are You Sure This Is How It's Supposed to Be? Learning to Live with Imperfection

Survival Skills for Betrayal and Bitterness

Rising Above Rejection: Graduate Level

I'm sure you can add your own syllabus to this list, and I highly recommend that you do because it's a fun exercise. No matter what your personal curriculum, all of our cosmic classes have one thing in common—*they're designed to help us see how we respond when we feel out of control, and to help teach us how to find our truth and steadiness within.*

Our consciousness is tested NOT when we feel in control, but when we feel out of control.

Have you ever seen a car commercial on television in which the advertiser is attempting to demonstrate that their vehicle is incredibly powerful and durable? They don't picture the car sitting still in a nice field of flowers. They film it driving through several feet of water in the torrential rain, or navigating the twists and turns of a rough mountain road. The manufacturer is giving us the message that, even under these challenging conditions, their vehicle will perform with steadiness and reliability. You can count on it.

Let's be honest—we all look good when things are going well. We all sound incredibly enlightened in certain moments. The true test of our consciousness and our character, however, doesn't take place when our "vehicle" is moving along on the safe, smooth road, but when it/we are put through what can feel like tortuous conditions.

When impossible things happen, they are not happening to curse us, nor are they happening to torture us. I sincerely believe they are happening to force us to dig deeper and deeper into the core of who we are, to find our highest, our impenetrable strength, and our love.

Each time things are falling apart and you're forced to dig in the mud of your suffering for that which is immovable within your soul, you remember more and more of who you really are.

Impossible things free us in mysterious ways. They sculpt us into exquisite new shapes, just as billions of years ago catastrophic volcanoes, floods, earthquakes, and moving glaciers carved the earth's majestic mountains, canyons, lakes, and continents.

What looks like it will crush us is raising us up.
What feels like it will annihilate us is unearthing our magnificence.
When the ground is shifting violently beneath your feet,
and there's nothing steady upon which to stand,
don't panic or give in to despair.
Surrender and let go.

You're being taught how to fly.

THE GIFT OF GRIEF AND THE POWER OF ACCOUNTABILITY

"Your pain is the breaking of the shell that encloses your understanding."
— Kahlil Gibran

Sometimes our impossible journeys are invisible to everyone else, because they're not about things that have happened *to* us from the outside, but rather are about what's happening *within* us. Most often these internal revelations occur when we realize how far we've drifted from the person we want to be or from the life we intended to live. These kinds of impossible moments are not about losing something or someone else other than our own connection to our truest Self.

In these crucial moments on the path of awakening, it's no longer possible to *not* see something about yourself. The more you've been waking up, the more you realize you've been asleep. The more you realize you've been asleep, the more horrified you become, and the more despair you might feel.

Suddenly you understand how your habits of unconsciousness have affected everybody in your life—your family, your partner, your friends, and yourself. You recall feedback or criticisms you've defended against and, by the increased light of new wisdom, realize to your dismay that much of what's been said to you has been true. You see your walls, your masks, your costumes, and all the ways you forgot who you are at your Highest.

Your heart cries out:

"*I can't believe how unconscious I've been. I can't believe how unloving I've been. I can't believe how arrogant I've been. I can't believe how cold and insensitive I've been. I can't believe how shut down I've been. I can't believe how deluded I've been.*"

These are great moments and excruciating moments, great revelations and horrible revelations: You recognize how much time you've wasted. You recognize what you've stolen from yourself and others. Instinctively you want to turn away. **Yet the very thing that you don't want to do is exactly what you need to do to heal: You need to grieve.**

Sometimes the choice for love is the choice to allow yourself to grieve:

We grieve for how harsh we've been to ourselves.

We grieve for how unkind we've been to others.

We grieve for each time our heart was broken from childhood on, times when we had to be strong and were taught not to cry.

We grieve for the walls we've built that have kept love out, and for the frozen feelings that have been trapped in our heart.

We grieve for every time we chased love down the wrong street, only to end up in an emotional dark alley, being roughed up by that very person whom we were chasing.

We grieve for lost time—days, months, and years lost in delusion, indecision, or fear.

We grieve for all of the choices not made for love.

How you react in these moments of revelatory grief is crucial. You must react with courage and grace, and *not* shame or resistance. You cannot close your eyes to what you've seen or felt. You must stand steady, keep the door of your awareness open, and flood what you see about yourself with compassion and love.

Grieving is essential for the melting of the heart.
Frozen grief blocks our ability to receive and give love.
When we try to bypass grieving, parts of us go into deep freeze.
Grief and remorse serve us in essential ways.
They course correct us.
They melt our frozen consciousness, our frozen compassion,
and our frozen accountability.

Many of us have a real aversion to experiencing grief and remorse. We're afraid if we allow ourselves to feel these emotions, we'll somehow be condemning ourselves. Actually, as we began to discuss earlier, it's just the opposite: *when we don't feel our remorse or grief about something we've done to ourselves or others, we contract and freeze up.*

These powerful turning points on the path of transformation are what I call "**Moments of Accountability.**" I'm not referring here to being accountable to others, *but being accountable to yourself, within yourself.* It's easy to offer an apology or take responsibility for something you've done in order to get others to forgive you, but unless you learn from what happened and actually make a shift, your remorse will just be a form of managing or manipulation.

Facing your own Moments of Accountability can be one of the most humbling and difficult, impossible journeys you'll ever take. *"Why did I start working on myself?"* you groan. *"I just keep seeing more and more about my life that needs to change, and so much that I regret."*

These are perfectly normal reactions. However, don't mistake this appropriate grief and remorse for self-criticism, or conclude that you're being too hard on yourself. They are an important, and in fact essential, part of your process of becoming truly accountable.

Remember:

Moments of Accountability are always great Soul Moments.

I have a saying: *"Awareness is the beginning of redemption."* When you're really unconscious, you don't even know it. When you're really lost, you don't even realize there's anything for which you should be accountable. As soon as you become aware of how unconscious you've been, you're already moving through it.

Asking yourself, *"How did I get into such forgetfulness?"* is the beginning of remembering.

Asking yourself, *"How could I have acted out of fear for so long?"* is the beginning of courage.

Asking yourself, *"How could I have been so numb and shut off?"* is the beginning of finding your way back to love.

**When you dive into the center of what feels impossible,
you may feel like you're disintegrating and parts of you are dying.
Don't stop. Keep moving. Keep melting.
Soon you'll come out on the other side
to healing, wholeness, redemption, awakening, and peace.
Once we realize that we've been lost,
we are already on the way Home.**

CAN YOU DO THIS FOR JUST ONE MORE DAY?

"You can't fall off the floor."
— Author Unknown

One of the most frightening characteristics of a painful, challenging, or impossible journey is that *it seems like it will never end*. Time appears to slow down to a crawl. Whatever it is we have to endure—physical pain, emotional trauma, fear, heartbreak, or humiliation—we just want it to be over with. *"I don't know how I'm going to get through this,"* we cry out to anyone who will listen. The thought of living under these circumstances day after day fills us with dread, and we simply don't know what to do.

There was a time in my life, during the most impossible of all of my own impossible journeys, when I experienced this same dread. Whenever I'd imagine the possibility of being in what was then my current state of emotional agony for more weeks, months, or even years, I would become completely disheartened, and collapse into despair. **It was hard enough just to make it through one day, but the projection of my pain forward in time was too much for me to bear.**

One morning as I lay in bed grimacing at the thought of another day spent in what I knew would be emotional torture, I began to pray for guidance. *"Please tell me how to do this,"* I begged every Higher Power I could imagine. *"Please show me the way."*

From the silent space deep in the center of my heart, an answer arose in the form of a question:

"Can you do this for just one more day?"

I became very still as I contemplated the meaning of this question. It asked me not if I saw myself triumphing over the challenge of this situation, and not if I believed I would make it through no matter what it took or how long it took. Right now, those promises were too much to ask of me. **Instead, it asked only if I could do this for just one more day, endure this for just one more day, manage to make my way to the other end of just one more day.**

Suddenly my impossible journey wasn't one with no end. It had been reduced to a journey of just one day. Could I make an agreement with myself to go through this for just one more day? The answer was that *"Yes, I could."*

Of course, I didn't have control over how long my ordeal was going to last, or what outside circumstances would change, or even *if* they would change. It wasn't as if my agreement to do this for another day was going to magically transform anything in my external world, and that if I'd answered, *"No, I can't do this for another day,"* the Universe would have responded, *"Okay, I guess you've had enough. We'll fix everything up for you now."* **It wasn't going to make a difference to the facts of the situation I was facing, but it was going to make a difference** *to me.* My goal was to get through this next day, that was all.

As I began to move through my morning, each time I would experience some emotional pain or fear, I would ask myself the same question: *"Can I do this for just one more day?"* The answer was yes, and I'd keep going.

That afternoon I began to contemplate what would make getting through this one day easier and more bearable, and what I needed to avoid or watch out for so that I wouldn't make my day even more difficult. This produced two additional questions. This is how my Gateway Questions for Impossible Times were born.

GATEWAY QUESTIONS FOR IMPOSSIBLE TIMES

Can I do this for just one more day?

If so, how do I make this more bearable today?

**What do I need to avoid doing so that I experience
the least possible suffering today?**

I printed out many copies of these three questions and put them all over my house, where I could constantly see them. I carried a copy in my wallet and taped one to the dashboard of my car. Sometimes I would have to read and answer these questions once every few minutes. *"You don't have to this forever,"* I'd reassure myself. *"Just get through today. You can do this today."* On the worst days during this fiery and frightening time, I had to change the question to **"Can I do this for just one more hour?"**

Here's an example of how I would use these Gateway Questions:

STEP #1: I'd notice I was feeling emotional pain, fear, anxiety, etc.
I'd find my list and ask myself the first question:

"CAN I DO THIS FOR JUST ONE MORE DAY?"
I'd think about it, and tell myself, *"Yes, I can."*

STEP #2: HOW DO I MAKE THINGS MORE BEARABLE TODAY?

I would look at the list I'd already made of what would make things more bearable, and right then I would choose one.

For instance, items on the list might be:

* *Call your friend every few hours just to hear her voice.*

* *Take a 20-minute walk by the ocean, or in a park, no matter how you feel.*

* *Make a schedule of exactly what you're going to do, hour by hour.*

* *Choose from your list of prayers and meditations and practice one* (the list would be included here).

* *Do five minutes of deep breathing or chanting.*

* *Write or text someone you care about and express your love.*

STEP #3: WHAT DO I NEED TO AVOID DOING SO THAT I EXPERIENCE THE LEAST POSSIBLE SUFFERING?

This was a list of things I *should avoid doing* that would make me feel worse. I'd already made this list and would read it in that moment *to make sure I wasn't doing any of those things.*

For instance, items on the list might be:

* *Do not eat anything unhealthy that is going to throw your emotions off.*

* *Do not go back and rehearse the past and get stuck in "what ifs."*
Keep bringing yourself into this and only this moment.

* *Do not drift into the future that hasn't happened yet.*
Do not think beyond the next hour.
Keep bringing yourself into this and only this moment.

I'm sure you have your own methods for supporting yourself during painful emotional ordeals. Perhaps you've used the phrase *"One day at a time"* to motivate yourself to keep going. What I found, however, is that thinking, *"I'll get through this, one day at a time"* is more of a passive, hypothetical process that may not be enough to help you shift when situations are really dire. *It sounds good, but doesn't ask anything of you.*

These Gateway Questions are powerful precisely because they *are* questions that require answers from you, and thereby *actively involve you in your process.* They pull you out of "I can't," which is a very contractive vibration, and give you a tiny bit of empowerment. When you ask yourself, "Can I do this for just one more day?" you have to make a decision, and respond with a "YES." That *"Yes, I can"* may not seem like much, but it's an expansive vibration, and that strengthens and grounds you.

This practice was my anchor and saving grace. **During a time when there was so much I couldn't do, the questions gave me something I** *could* **do.** I couldn't know how I was going to deal with the challenges that were ahead of me. I couldn't know how I would handle upcoming situations. I couldn't predict how things were going to turn out. **But I could agree to do what I was doing for just one more day.**

I offer these to you to use on your own impossible journeys, or even during times that are stressful, challenging, or unpleasant. In passing them on, my hope is that they serve you as much as they served me.

LOVE, GRIEF, AND GRATITUDE

"When you learn to love hell, you will be in heaven."
— Thaddeus Golas

Is it really possible to find the love in impossible moments? *"When you learn to love hell, you will be in heaven,"* says writer and philosopher Thaddeus Golas. I remember reading these words many years ago, and being totally perplexed by them. Only decades later did I finally come to truly understand what he meant.

Hell, of course, can be defined in many ways. Most of us are really not living in hell. Hell is not having any food for you or your children to eat, and watching them slowly starve. Hell is living in a country where you can be killed for speaking out. Hell is being a refugee forced by war and terrorism to flee your home and having no place to go.

Even when, thankfully, we aren't experiencing these horrors, we still cannot and must not invalidate or diminish the excruciating visits into our own personal experiences of hell that have somehow been scheduled on our cosmic agenda. It's not fair for you to conclude, *"I know my problems don't mean anything because somebody else is being killed right now."* **You must have compassion for** *your own* **karma. You must walk every** step of *your own* path. And you must face and allow yourself to feel the pain of your own hells.

Facing and feeling our challenges is one thing. But love? How do we bring love to our impossible moments? This seems ironic and preposterous to consider. *How can we see a blessing in something that is causing us or those we love so much pain?*

Part of the problem is that our human nature is to label, limit, and compartmentalize, so once we decide something is terrible, it's very difficult to see anything good about it. The intellect does this in order to keep us mentally grounded and functional.

If we didn't have strong likes, dislikes, and preferences, life would be utterly chaotic. Imagine, for instance, staring at a restaurant menu and attempting to order if you hadn't determined your tastes. You'd sit there for hours, and have no idea what to choose, or even what basis on which to choose it. What if you had absolutely no strong preferences about the type of clothing you enjoyed wearing? It would take you forever to get dressed each morning, and perhaps your dilemma would end in your wearing nothing at all!

Some of us actually remember this inability to choose from our own pre-teen years, a time before we really knew what we liked or disliked, and some of us have experienced this more recently with our own very young children attempting to make decisions before they have many set predilections about color, style, food, and so on. "Just pick *something!*" we tell them, not fully appreciating that their brain isn't actually fully programmed yet, so they're more spacious and enlightened—and less judgmental—than we are!

As we grow older, we all become increasingly trapped in *black or white, either/or* thinking. This manifests in the simplest circumstances, such as how we feel about a movie we see, or our opinion of a political speech we see on television. We form an opinion, make a decision, and take a stance: *It's good/It's bad. I hate it/I love it. I want to keep it/I want to get rid of it. He's right/He's wrong. It succeeded/It failed.*

Unfortunately reality is not this simple and compartmentalized. It's woven with countless layers and nuances, complexities and mysteries. There's no time in which this is more painfully obvious than when we attempt to navigate through the unfathomable experiences of our impossible journeys. **At these moments, we don't have any difficulty** deciding how to label what we're going through—*we know it's not heaven, and it sure feels like hell.*

I've witnessed something fascinating that often happens when we begin to proceed forward on a spiritual or religious path. **We may find ourselves feeling compelled to swing to the other extreme—never seeing anything as negative and insisting on only seeing and feeling the positive:** *"This [impossible situation] is a blessing. It's perfect, and I am certain it will have a perfect outcome. I am accepting this with peace, and surrendering to divine order."*

This sounds delightful and inspiring, but it's still a stance that we've overlaid onto what are usually very complicated problems and difficulties. Of course it's important to try and see things from the highest perspective possible. The problem with using only this approach, however, is that *it's asking us to bypass our humanity and immediately leap into our divinity, frequently leaving our unpleasant emotions behind to writhe around on the floor of our heart.*

The choice for love isn't a choice for *only* seeing the heavenly aspect of a situation, nor is it a choice for only seeing the hellish component. *It's a choice that makes room for both, because that's what is real.* It asks us:

Can you allow yourself to experience both suffering and love at the same time?

Can you wish something hadn't happened, or weren't happening, and yet still find moments of love in it?

Can you hate something, and wish it would end, and still love the blessing it has inadvertently brought you?

Can you learn to search for tiny moments of heaven that are hidden within your hells?

Can they live in your heart side by side?

How do we do this? Perhaps it means to be able to sit quietly with compassion next to our hellish circumstances or emotions. Perhaps it means to love ourselves in impossible times by working hard to not feel our trials are cursing us or stalking us, or that we've somehow been condemned. Perhaps we find the courage to look deeply at our dark passages and notice some little glimmers of light in them.

This is a tall order—I know—*but it's an invitation to make the choice for love so that your impossible times don't become devoid of love.*

"Find a place inside where there's joy, and the joy will burn out the pain."
— Joseph Campbell

Can we wish something hadn't happened and yet feel undeniably that it's cracking our heart open? For me the answer is yes. Think back over the past few years of your life and recall something that took place (or is taking place now) that was hellish and impossible, something you desperately wished would change. *Can you see any blessing that occurred or is occurring? Can you glimpse any little bits of love shining in the dark sky of what you experienced as impossible?*

I've had a long list of circumstances in my life that, at the time, I would have given anything to eradicate. However, even as they were taking place, I couldn't deny that they were cracking my heart open to levels of love and surrender that, without these unwanted events, wouldn't have been possible.

Many of you have had a relative that was ill or elderly and eventually passed. There's always tremendous grief when you lose someone you love, and yet you often feel surprising, undeniable, new and deepened connections and love in those final days of transition and beyond. There may be blessings because the person is no longer in pain, blessings because you had an opportunity to heal and forgive, blessings because there were ways your life was limited, and now those limitations have been freed up.

Do we need to feel guilty about these contrasting emotions? No. *Can we grieve and also be grateful? Yes.*

You can be heartbroken one minute, and peaceful the next. In one moment you can utterly hate something and wish it would end. In the next, you can admit to yourself that it is, unmistakably, helping you grow.

Stop feeling you need to choose one emotional stance
or one attitude, and instead, be willing to sit
in the crowded living room of your heart
with all the feelings that have gathered there.
Welcome each one. Love each one. Honor each one.
They are all precious parts of you.

I remember when my dogs Bijou and Shanti had both finally passed. They lived long lives and were very old at the end, requiring what amounted to full-time supervision and care from me. I can so clearly recall the first time I realized I could now go away for two days and not have to arrange a babysitter to stay with them. It suddenly dawned on me that I could leave the house and not have to worry about carrying them both into every store so they wouldn't be frightened and alone. *I felt terrible grief—and I also felt relief to not have to worry about them anymore.*

I knew enough to understand that the emotion of relief did not contradict the grief, and that even though being without my animal companions for the first time in 18 years was devastating, it also carried blessings. I loved my freedom. I hated their passing. I didn't need to choose hell or heaven. *They were both true.*

Once when I was going through an impossibly difficult time, one of my dearest guides in the world said the following to me:

"You are unique because most people crash or soar. Right now, you're doing both."

These words impacted me to my core. I realized that I had, indeed, learned how to do both—to still choose love while going through hellish times, to compassionately allow myself to fully feel the tragedy of my circumstances *and* to collect every scrap of blessing and revelation the impossible was offering me. This is your path and possibility as well.

Part of us can be crashing and part of us can be soaring.
Part of us can be grieving and part of us can be growing.
Part of us can be praying for mercy
and part of us can be seeing the Grace in something.
The choice for love makes space
for everything that is living in your heart.

DILUTING THE DIFFICULT WITH LOVE

"Where there is great Love there are always miracles."
— Willa Cather

Many years ago, at a time when I was going through what seemed a truly impossible journey, I decided to travel by myself to a tropical island, hoping to experience some peace and healing. I've always found the ocean to be powerfully transformative, and I felt drawn to it now as I sought some kind of comfort from the painful ordeal that had shown up in my life.

On my first morning there, I walked out into the calm, turquoise sea, and stood very still immersed in the warm water up to my shoulders. It was early, and no one else was around. Suddenly I began to weep, which was nothing unusual for me in those days. But what happened next was different.

Somehow I could sense the ocean fully receiving my tears, my grief, my human pain with unbounded compassion. It was as if I could feel Mother Ocean calling out to me: *"These tears are not too much for me as they have been for others. Behold how vast I am! Give them all to me, my dear one. Don't hold back anything. They are sacred because they are born of pure love."*

I let all of the hurt in my heart out, and felt my salty tears pouring into the salty sea. Instead of dropping onto my tissues, my pajamas, my sheets, or my friend's shoulder, where their damp presence was impossible to ignore, they merged with the waves, the tides, and the huge ocean. *In that moment, I felt my grief being diluted by something far greater than itself—in the unending sea, my tears vanished, and were swallowed up by ancient waters that had swirled and danced for millions and millions of years.*

As I offered my tears into the waves, I could feel the ocean offering something back. *I was being rocked and embraced with love.* My wounds were being washed with the mysterious, timeless gifts that pulsated in the water: the wisdom of the whales and dolphins and all sea creatures who had ever lived; the courage of every ship that had ever sailed from far-off lands to discover places they hadn't known existed, ships whose captains and crew were long gone, but whose discoveries had created pathways for new worlds; the prayers of every other human who had stood in these waters and wept over some tragedy or heartbreak, their pain now forgotten as they'd since merged back into Spirit, or perhaps even returned again to live another, new life.

In that moment, I understood something profound. *My impossible journey and my pain and my tears were all part of something that transcended my own life and were inextricably joined with every impossible journey and every tear from the beginning of time.* **I bowed my head in reverent awe and gratitude to the sea for the presence of love she had revealed to me.**

Later that day as I sat on the sand contemplating my experience, I was aware of two things. First, my pain hadn't miraculously vanished. I still hurt and would still have to travel on this difficult road for a while, but something profound *had* taken place. *The loving energy of the ocean somehow diluted the intensity of my pain.*

Often when we are having a difficult time, we wish we could just remove the unpleasant emotions we're experiencing. *"I want this sadness/ anger/fear out of me!"* we cry. As we've seen, these efforts to cut off from or cut out feelings don't ultimately work. They disconnect us from our source, and from the very power that can heal us.

What would you do if you had a very concentrated, dark liquid, and you wanted to get rid of the intensity? You can't remove the color, but you can *dilute* it by adding water. What if you were making a soup, realized you'd put in too much salt, and wanted to get rid of the salty flavor? You can't remove the salt, but you can add something else that will transform the soup—you *dilute* the broth with more liquid.

This is known as **the principle of the second element: When you're in a dark room, you don't try and get rid of the darkness—you bring in the light.** The moment you introduce the second element—the light— the darkness gets eradicated. You don't have to *do* anything to the darkness. *In a sense, the second element—the light itself—transforms the darkness.*

We've seen that love is an infinite vibrational field of the highest, most expansive energy.

Love is the ultimate diluter!
When we add love to any situation, any other emotion,
or any interaction, it *dilutes* the less enlightened,
more contracted energy, transmuting it into
a higher, more enlightened form.

Whether you realize it or not, you experience this principle of dilution all the time:

You're feeling upset, and call your best friend to confess your fears and sadness. *She listens with love, and somehow the loving space she holds for you seems to dilute the intensity of your upset.* Your friend was the second element you added to dilute your anxiety.

Your child is scared about doing something new. You hold him close, ask him to tell you all about it, and listen carefully to every word he says. *Your energy of love dilutes the intensity of his fear, and he suddenly feels much better.*

The healing energy of love is our greatest offering to ourselves and others. **Love will alchemically transmute the negativity in any situation by diluting the contracted energy with love's own most elevated vibration.** More and more, we understand why it is essential to fully heal and reconnect to our heart, and to expand our capacity to experience and share our love: The more vast the ocean of our love, the more it can transform whatever it touches.

The bigger the ocean of your heart,
the more things can dissolve in it.

That day on the island during my impossible journey, I experienced the blessing of the compassionate ocean diluting my pain and heartbreak, and teaching me how I, too, could embrace myself with love. It inspired this very personal poem, written that evening. I share this so you can know that we all must take these pilgrimages into the painful parts of our heart, and I dedicate it to everyone who has ever wondered what happens to our tears when we offer them into the sea.

When the Sea Swallowed My Tears

Today I stood in the Sea and prayed for Grace.
The double river of my salty tears flowed down my face
   as liquid offerings into the ocean.
I watched my tears disappear into the Water,
   who received each one as if welcoming home a long-lost beloved,
   merging them into the great blue vastness.

The Sea was kind to me today.
She did not expect me to be strong
   or serene or selfless.
She had room for all of my grief,
   all of my pain,
   all of my heartbreak,
   embracing me with her warm, gentle waves as I wept.

I wonder what happened to all those tears
   and the sad story they carry.
Maybe somewhere in the ocean tonight,
   a dolphin or a turtle or a whale
   will swallow one of my tears,
   and suddenly, inexplicably
   find itself calling out your name . . .

Author, teacher, and Franciscan priest Friar Richard Rohr, whose writings are wise and compassionate reflections on our spiritual journey, reiterates all I've been offering in his own words:

"Your heart has to be prepared ahead of time through faith and prayer and grace and mercy and love and forgiveness so you can keep your heart open in hell, when hell happens."

Here are some Recalibration Questions you can use to help you make the choice for love during your own impossible journeys and moments. These are designed for your contemplation, journaling, and discussion. Remember everything you've learned about compassion and patience, *and don't pressure yourself to feel rushed to receive instant answers.* The questions are designed to open your awareness to new wisdom and guidance that are already waiting within you.

Pose the questions with love, and give the answers time to reveal themselves not only in your conscious mind but in the silence of your heart. Be on the lookout for events or experiences that may also act as messages from the Universe to you, living answers to your questions.

RECALIBRATION QUESTIONS:
TRANSMUTING THE IMPOSSIBLE INTO LOVE

How do I bring love to this impossible journey/situation?

How do I use this impossible journey/situation for my expansion, and not for my contraction—for my freedom, and not for my imprisonment?

What inner actions do I need to take in order to navigate through this impossible journey/situation with grace?

How do I allow the fire of this impossible journey/situation to transmute me into something greater?

What gold can I find in what only looks like mud?

MAKING YOUR WAY SAFELY HOME

"Sometimes I go about pitying myself
And all the time
I am being carried on great winds across the sky."
— Ojibway saying

Several years ago I made a pilgrimage to a very isolated spot where my friend the renowned poet Rashani Réa lives on the big island of Hawaii. This simple but sacred sanctuary is off the electrical power grid, far away from everything, and is bordered only by open pasture, endless lava fields, and thousands of acres of undeveloped forests. I was in the midst of a powerful spiritual rebirth, and wanted to spend undistracted time embraced only by nature, in an environment with no modern conveniences. Although Rashani was the only other human being there, I was delighted to find myself sharing the land with many beautiful animal companions, including dogs, newborn puppies, cats, peacocks, goats, horses, and every variety of tropical bird imaginable.

When I arrived, Rashani told me that something very unusual had just taken place, something she felt was mysteriously connected to my visit. Just a few days before, a tiny white kitten had shown up trembling with fear in front of the main house. This little kitty, who couldn't have been more than five or six weeks old, was weak, frail, completely dehydrated, and could barely stand.

The kitten weighed only eight ounces, and yet somehow with no food, no water, and no shelter from the scorching Hawaiian sun, she had trekked across miles and miles of sharp, hard lava fields to find her way to the sanctuary. It was a miracle that she was alive and hadn't starved to death or been killed by the many wild animals roaming the area. In spite of the insurmountable dangers, the hostile, unforgiving conditions, and the terror this vulnerable baby kitten must have felt, she'd found the courage to survive her impossible journey.

Rashani named her *Pu'uwai*, which means "Heart" in Hawaiian.

Rashani set out to save Pu'uwai's life. She fed her with an eyedropper, applied medicinal ointments to her infections and wounds, and loved her. Even in her delicate state, this indomitable kitten had an unmistakable healing presence, and I honored her as a teacher who had shown up to be a part of my own healing pilgrimage. As I write these words, I can vividly remember how miraculous it felt to hold little Pu'uwai in a curled-up bundle against my chest, such a precious, tiny container of life and Divine Intelligence. *It was as if she was purring and pouring love into my heart.*

Just like Pu'uwai, in the course of our lifetime we will courageously set out on many challenging and improbable pilgrimages, and have to traverse across interminable fields of our own desolation that cut us and test us. Like her, we may feel utterly alone and be tempted to give up. But if we listen closely, we will hear a voice calling to us from our heart, whispering: *"Somewhere there is shelter. Somewhere there is safety. Somewhere there is Love."*

So we keep moving as we must, finding strength from an invisible source, clinging with all of our might to the belief that surely beyond the flames, beyond this desolate landscape, **there will be redemption, there will be peace, and Love will be waiting for us. Our impossible journey will become a triumphant journey.**

The last I heard from Rashani, Pu'uwai was healthy and thriving. I've thought about her so many times as I've encountered challenges large and small, and taken many more journeys that require determination, spiritual stamina, and faith. Sometimes I visualize her as she must have been then, a tiny speck of white crossing the vast expanse of frozen black lava, and I can almost hear her Spirit Voice whispering, *"Don't stop. If I can do it, you can do it."*

**In joyful times, we can meet our delightful experiences
with our full and overflowing heart.
We bring love to love.
In hellish, impossible times,
our infinite ocean of love receives our pain with tenderness,
surrounds our pain with light,
and dilutes our pain with compassion.**

Love is the ladder of Light we must climb to move us out of the darkness.

No matter how difficult it is to find our way to it, no matter how much a situation looks like it's devoid of Love, no matter how dark it is, we must make the choice for love, to find just the tiniest filament of Love, and follow it.

When we do, it will lead us forward, and lead us Home.

PART THREE

LIVING IN LOVE, NOW MORE THAN EVER

9

The Whispered Wisdom of the Heart

*"Divinity has one ultimate secret, which it will also whisper in your ear
if your mind becomes quieter than the fog at sunset:
the God of this world is found within."*
— Ken Wilber

One of my favorite flowers is the peony. They bloom during the late spring and early summer in a variety of colors, and often have a spicy, exotic fragrance. The peony is frequently used in Asian culture and art, particularly in China, where the symbol of the peony is very auspicious. I'm looking at a dazzling bunch of peonies on my desk right now, and marveling at their glory.

Last week, I was in the flower section of a market selecting some peonies. I was delighted to find several bunches of closed peony buds, and was putting them in my cart when the woman next to me spoke up. "You know, there's another bucket over here with much nicer flowers, like roses," she explained. "I'm not familiar with that particular flower you're holding, but they don't look very good—so closed and brown."

"Thank you," I replied politely. "Did you say you've never seen peonies before?"

"No, I haven't. They look very strange."

"Well, I'll give you a little lesson. Peony buds look like small, squashed tight balls, but they just haven't opened yet. When they do, they'll magically explode to about 10 times their original size with layers and layers of petals."

"That's amazing," she said in disbelief. "Because right now, they just look like nothing."

"That's how they start out," I explained. "**But when they open, what looks like nothing now will blossom into the most miraculous mass of something.**" I reached into the bucket, pulled out a new bunch, and handed them to the woman. "Here, please take these as a gift, and just be patient. Soon you'll experience some magic."

As seekers of truth and freedom, we have many moments when we can sense the buds of wisdom and revelation within us, but that, just like the peony, still seem tight and inaccessible. We long to feel more expanded, more radiant, and to tap into the guidance and direction we know is there inside of us, but our mind seems unable to grasp the answers we long for. Perhaps we're desperately seeking inspiration on a project, but it's just not coming. Perhaps we're trying to get some definitive direction for an important decision, but feel lost in a swirl of conflicting thoughts. *"If only I could figure things out!"* we lament.

You have an infinite source of truth, light, and wisdom within you. It has never been closed like a peony. It has always been there, perfect, ready to offer you an abundance of truth. However, it can't be accessed by the mind and the intellect, any more than we could will a flower bud to open. **That's because it's not information—it's wisdom.**

What is the difference between information and wisdom? Information is a collection of facts gathered by the intellect from external sources. We use these facts to educate ourselves and learn about the world. Wisdom is different. It can't be achieved by sorting through the information collected in our mind, no matter how much there is. *That's because information is sourced from outside, but wisdom emerges from within.*

**We can locate information with our mind,
but in order to experience wisdom, we must go within.
Wisdom blossoms in the heart.**

The root of the word *wisdom* actually comes from two old Latin words: *visionem*, which means "vision," and *dom*, which signifies a "judgment or state." **So wisdom literally translates as "a state of vision"—a state in which we can truly see. To possess wisdom, therefore, requires that we abide in the consciousness of seeing, and live from a state of seeing.**

Here we aren't talking about seeing externally, but seeing within yourself. How can we see from within, in the unlit regions of your deepest being? What is that process like?

For a moment, imagine that you were in a completely dark room and wanted to see. What would you need? You would need a source of Light. With that source, you'd be able to easily see in the darkness. If you tried to navigate around that room without the light, you'd bump into everything.

So too we need a source of light to "see" deep within ourselves. **What is that source of Light? Where is the switch to turn it on? It is your own Heart-Wisdom that abides in the depths of your consciousness, that which we can call your "inner Light."**

Information does not illuminate.
It brings understanding or clarification, but not light.
Wisdom illuminates.
Information can be collected, but we can't collect wisdom.
Wisdom dawns from within.
It's the arrival of Light, not the collecting of Light.
It rises like the sun on the horizon of our heart.

Awakening the power of your own Heart-Wisdom turns on your own inner light and, therefore, unfolds your inner vision. That inner light helps you see everything with more clarity. You see yourself clearly. You see others clearly. You see your path clearly, and you see the world clearly.

Imagine that one day you wake up and discover that, by some kind of magic, a spectacular swimming pool has appeared in your own backyard. It looks so inviting and so exquisitely beautiful, and you are immediately drawn to enter the sparkling water. Immediately, you feel calm, expanded, and at peace.

As you rest in this enchanted pool, you realize that you're somehow able to see all aspects of your life with an expanded consciousness. Everything you contemplate seems illuminated by a state of profound wisdom. *"This is amazing!"* you conclude. *"Why didn't I know about this miraculous pool of clarity before? Has it been here all the time?"*

Although you probably don't have a mystical pool in your yard, you *do* have a magical pool that you haven't known about. It's not a physical pool, so you won't find it anywhere on the outside. **It's the pool of your own inner Heart-Wisdom, and it has always been there, because it is your true nature and true Source.** Why, then, haven't you been able to access it? The pathway to the pool has been blocked by obstacles, congested and cluttered with your patterns, your unresolved issues, your habits of unconsciousness, your frozen feelings, and your boulders of forgetfulness. All of these have prevented you from easily finding your way to that place of Inner Wisdom.

Your wisdom has always been there.
It's just that your access to it has been blocked
by your own internal clutter.
When you clear the path of vibrational and emotional debris,
finding the way to your Heart-Wisdom becomes effortless and inevitable.

TURNING ON YOUR COSMIC GPS SYSTEM

"Why do you read many books? It is of no use.
The great book is within your own heart. Open the pages
of this inexhaustible book, the source of all knowledge.
You will know everything."

— Sivananda

Heart-Wisdom is not about knowing things. When we know something, it means we have information about something, or have figured out something. Instead Heart-Wisdom is the experience of *knowingness*— **not a knowing of anything in particular, but a state of knowing: knowingness.** This knowingness has been described by many saints and sages—an inner state characterized by a lively stillness, a fullness rich with potentiality and the absolute presence of Divine Consciousness that pulsates with Infinite Intelligence.

It's natural when you read about knowingness to think of it as a higher, more enlightened version of your mind, and perhaps you're even visualizing it as an experience that is generated from your head or part of your brain. **You can't find knowingness in your mind. It reveals itself in the heart—not the physical heart, but the spiritual heart.**

Think about the times you've had an experience of knowingness, when a new level of wisdom rose up within you. That Higher Wisdom revealed itself in the depth of the spiritual heart as a knowingness that you somehow felt and sensed. It's not as if you received a text in your head that was sent by your Higher Self!

You've all had experiences of Heart-Wisdom. It's a still voice inside of you that doesn't speak in words, but in a knowing beyond words. Something prompts you from deep within your being. **You "know" something, without being given the information about something.** *"I just know I'm supposed to help this person." "I just know that it's time for me to move on from this job." "I just know something."*

The language of the spiritual heart is perfectly articulate
and yet it doesn't actually have a vocabulary.
In spite of that, and quite mysteriously,
everything gets said.

We often mistrust our knowingness because it doesn't seem logical or linear enough. We diminish it because it can't "prove its case" like the intellect, which comes in with a big entourage of lawyers and files, lays everything down in front of us, and can defend it all perfectly. **The irony, however, is that it's the mind that can't be counted on.** As strange as that sounds, we've seen throughout these pages that it's true. You can't really trust the mind because the mind is influenced by all kinds of things—your emotional programming, your inherited patterns, and so on.

When we believe that the information that comes from
the logical mind is more reliable than the knowingness
that emerges from deep within the invisible heart,
we can easily get lost on our journey.
The result is that we ignore our knowingness in favor of information,
not realizing that our insistent search for logical answers
may cloud our ability to really see clearly.

The mind loves information, and thinks that information will give it peace. The truth is that, when it comes to life's most important issues, *our peace doesn't come from gathering more information.* Information is very limited. How many times have you been in an emotional or spiritual crisis and told yourself if you could just find the correct information, you'd somehow be able to end your suffering? Trying to find the information to "fix things" can end up distracting you from listening to your knowingness.

Let's stop for a moment so I can clarify something: *I love information!* Information is wonderful, exciting, and useful when we make logistical decisions, such as getting information to help us decide whether or not we need to have a medical procedure, or what insurance policy to buy, or which food is healthiest to eat. **However, when we use information alone as our map and guide in all situations, and neglect our Heart-Wisdom, we often find ourselves in places we didn't intend to go, and in situations we wish weren't happening.**

Have you ever ignored your knowingness about something, only to discover later that your knowingness was correct? Perhaps you were hiring someone to work for you or help with a project. The information you had about the person looked good on paper. Your mind approved of it, but your knowingness was telling you something different. Maybe your knowingness was whispering, *"Don't trust that person,"* or *"They're saying the right things, but something is off."* You ignored your knowingness, hired the person anyway, and soon all of your inexplicable misgivings came true. *"I should have listened to my gut feeling,"* you scolded yourself.

This is why learning to open yourself to your Heart-Wisdom is so essential as you travel your path of transformation. Without consciousness and without knowingness, we can get tossed around by the whims of the mind, which may or may not perceive things clearly. *Knowingness acts like a compass, or in modern terms, a Cosmic GPS system.*

If you're driving a car, it doesn't matter what the destination is, or how often it changes. *What's important is that the GPS system in that car is working.* In the same way, it doesn't matter what you're going through in your life, whether it's a calm part of your journey, or a more difficult time with challenging twists and turns. What does matter is how can you make your trip smoother, less difficult, and avoid any preventable "accidents."

You have a Cosmic GPS system.
It is a standard feature of your human "vehicle."
This inner GPS system comes from your Heart-Wisdom
and not from your mind.

When you shift from trying to figure everything out by using only your intellect to instead accessing your Cosmic Knowingness GPS, your journey will be much more delightful, and you'll be able to reach all of your destinations with more ease and less "traffic"!

I've met so many people who ask me, *"Does everyone have an inner source of guidance, because mine seems to be broken?"* When we realize that our Heart-Wisdom *is* there within us, that question needs to change from "Do I have it?" to "How do I contact it?" The new, more accurate questions are *"How do I get to my knowingness? What can I be doing to clear the pathway?"*

This is the exciting work of personal transformation. The more you vibrationally recalibrate yourself by making the choice for love and practicing all we've discussed, the more of your own inner Heart-Wisdom will spontaneously be revealed.

TURNING BACK TOWARD KNOWINGNESS

"There is something beyond our mind which abides
in silence within our mind.
It is the supreme mystery beyond thought.
Let one's mind and one's subtle body rest upon that
and not rest on anything else."

— from the Maitri Upanishad

It's easy to miss experiences of Heart-Wisdom for the simple reason that Heart-Wisdom is very, very, very subtle! Your Higher Self, your expanded consciousness, doesn't speak in loud, aggressive, or frightening tones. It's quiet. It offers you truth in whispers.

The voice of the soul doesn't shout.
It reveals itself to us in subtle, sublime whispers.

If true Heart-Wisdom always whispers, then what is it that we often hear shouting at us from within? Why, the ego, of course!

"You blew it today—you'd better cover up your mistakes so no one sees."

"Don't trust anyone, and whatever you do, don't let them know how you feel!"

"Are you going to let them get away with that?"

"Make up a lie! If you tell the truth, they'll think less of you."

Recognize these? They're the voices of the ego. They're certainly not the voices of love, of wisdom, or of awakening. They're commanding and demanding. They overpower the subtle offerings of our knowingness. **If you ever hear something screaming inside of you (unless it's a strong warning of real physical danger), it's almost always your contracted self. Fear shouts. Judgment shouts. Anger shouts.**

Heart-Wisdom doesn't bellow at us through a cosmic megaphone. Imagine if your knowingness yelled these messages to you:

"Are you listening to me? I'm tired of repeating myself. How many times do I have to tell you that you're a child of God?"

"Pay attention this time: Call that person today, and you'll be offered an opportunity. Good fortune awaits you. And I don't want to hear that you're scared—just do it!"

Isn't it ridiculous to think about your Highest Self screaming at you? It does make the point! My experience is that the suggestions and messages of guidance will be offered like quiet, loving inner gestures, as if someone has left you a wordless gift of wisdom on the doorstep of your heart:

**Heart-Wisdom doesn't march into our mind like an
invading army of information, demanding we pay attention to it.
It moves into our awareness quietly,
like translucent clouds that suddenly appear in the sky,
or a graceful bird that suddenly soars into our vision,
or a soft breeze that suddenly blows in through the window.
It arrives without fanfare.
It just is.**

Heart-Wisdom is quiet. We need to become more silent in order to make space for it to emerge.

"Two people have been living in you all your life.
One is the ego—garrulous, demanding, hysterical, calculating.
The other is the hidden spiritual being,
whose still voice of wisdom you have only rarely heard or attended to.
You have uncovered in yourself your own wise guide."

— Sogyal Rinpoche

Imagine that for a long time, voices of your heart have been calling to you and trying to get your attention, sometimes about small things, and sometimes about crucial things, but your habit has been to ignore them. It's as if someone has been knocking on your door with an invaluable prize, and over and over, you've refused to let that person in. Imagine that this has gone on for months, years, and decades during which you didn't pay attention to your knowingness.

Now you can begin to understand another reason why, so often, we don't feel connected to our Highest, our Source, our true Self—even though we aren't conscious of it, we've *been snubbing it, and avoiding its communications for a long time!*

When we disconnect from or ignore our knowingness,
we're actually disconnecting from our true wisdom,
our true power, and our own Source.
We aren't strengthening the habit of
consistently connecting to our Highest.
Then, when it's time to access it,
we don't remember how to get there.

Have you ever driven somewhere that was a frequent destination, one you used to know by heart, only you hadn't been there for years? Perhaps it was a place in your childhood hometown, or a neighborhood restaurant you used to go to all the time but haven't visited since you moved. You tell yourself that you still know exactly how to get there, and certainly don't need a map or GPS. After all, you've done it hundreds of times. At some point, however, you realize the memory of the route that used to be so familiar and automatic has since vanished from your mind, and you're embarrassed to admit that you've forgotten the way.

This is exactly what happens when we don't take frequent trips to our heart, or answer its invitation and offer of wisdom: *we forget how to get there, and suddenly, when we need inner guidance or direction, we can't seem to tune in to a place of clarity inside of ourselves.*

MAKING SPACE FOR KNOWINGNESS

"Make time for quiet moments, as God whispers and the world is loud."
— Unknown

Turning back toward your Heart-Wisdom is actually quite simple. As we've seen, you don't have to search for it, or locate it. It's already there. It's the essence of who you are. It has never turned away from you.

You don't have to wait for your Heart-Wisdom to show up.
It's already been patiently waiting for you.
The moment you turn your attention within,
it will joyfully reveal itself.

The internationally renowned Brazilian novelist and author of *The Alchemist,* Paulo Coelho, writes with deep, mystical knowingness. I love what he says about making space for the whispers of the soul:

"Solitude is not the absence of company, but the moment when our soul is free to speak to us."

Isn't this an elegant and evocative description? You can imagine yourself at an enormous party called "your life," and at a certain moment, everyone has left, at least for the time being, and you're finally alone. All this time, your soul has been patiently waiting in the back room, anxious to approach you and share something important. Taking advantage of your solitude, your soul, relieved and thrilled to find you available, can finally speak to you.

When does your heart get your attention? When you are quiet, when you turn away from the constant calculations of your mind, and turn toward silence. Often when I work with people, all I have to do is say: *"Close your eyes, and allow your attention to turn within."* I guide them to open the door of their own inner silence, and within seconds, they can see things, feel things, and know things that they haven't been able to figure out or understand.

Of course, if we don't want to be bothered by our Heart-Wisdom, we keep ourselves very busy and keep our minds very active with no respite. We focus our attention outward, and not inward. **It's not that our knowingness doesn't keep trying to get our attention—it does. It's just that our consciousness is too noisy for us to hear anything that is quiet and subtle.**

Picture yourself standing in the middle of a crowded nightclub, or at a sold-out concert held in an enormous stadium, and imagine that you were trying to hear someone nearby whispering. You wouldn't even know they were speaking, let alone be able to hear their message. Even though the faint sound was there, the deafening noise would drown it out.

This is exactly what happens to us when our consciousness is full of vibrational commotion, crowded with roaming mental "gangs" of unruly thoughts. *The vibrational noise of our mind and emotions drowns out our knowingness.* We might complain that we don't have a connection to Spirit, to our higher wisdom, but we do. It's just not quiet enough for us to hear what's being offered.

The noise from our mental and emotional agitation
doesn't allow us to experience stillness and serenity within.
With that much vibrational commotion,
we can't hear the whispers of our own wisdom.

Wisdom is waiting to fill you, but you won't hear it or notice it if your attention is always being pulled elsewhere. The more you put all of the offerings on these pages into practice and make the choice for love, the easier it will be for you to turn back toward your knowingness.

DEEPENING YOUR RELATIONSHIP
WITH HEART-WISDOM

Here is a Recalibration Practice containing questions for contemplation. My suggestion is that you read each question below, and then access your knowingness before you answer. These instructions will help you have a more profound experience:

1. Hold the meaning of the question in your awareness, and then close your eyes. Instead of trying to scan your mind for the answer, feel into your heart space and be patient.

2. You may get an image in your mind of a person you know, or a situation in your life, as your knowingness points you in the right direction. You may suddenly have an awareness of a category, such as your health, or your finances, as your knowingness guides you toward a topic you need to explore.

3. Once you've opened your eyes, write down whatever comes to you, and then take some time to journal and explore what you've seen more deeply. You might want to contemplate these questions with another person, someone you're close to or who has also read *The Choice for Love*.

MY RELATIONSHIP WITH HEART-WISDOM

Where in my life right now is there some heart-knowingness I've been ignoring, something I've been sensing or feeling, or that I'm aware I need to address, but I've avoided it?

What has my heart been trying to talk to me about, but I've diminished its message because it didn't come with a big folder of logical facts and concrete evidence?

How do I cut off from and block my heart-knowingness?

(Examples: busyness; rescuing or fixing other people; never being alone)

What do I use to numb myself to the messages from my heart-knowingness?

(Examples: drugs; alcohol; food; TV; shopping)

How do I discount my heart-knowingness once I do become aware of it?

(Examples: Do I use my intellect to invalidate my knowingness because it doesn't offer "proof" of whatever it's trying to show me? Do I judge myself and decide I can't trust my inner guidance?)

Do I ever enlist other people to disagree with my knowingness so I have an excuse to ignore it? Does anyone in particular come to mind?

(Example: I know I can count on my sister to talk me out of doing anything that means I have to take a risk.)

When have I had strong experiences of heart-knowingness? What were the conditions that allowed my heart-knowingness to speak to me?

(Examples: walking in nature; after meditation or yoga; during prayer; in church)

Remember: *These aren't one-time questions.* Like all of the Recalibration Practices, they're designed as tools you can use whenever you are ready to gain more understanding and experience deeper transformation.

CHOICE FOR LOVE HEART PRACTICES

I'd like to teach you several Choice for Love Heart Practices. They're designed to help you connect with the powerful place of Heart-Wisdom inside of you, and to become familiar with how you feel when you've tapped into that inner Source. These are very simple but powerful emotional recalibration techniques. They're something I've practiced and taught my students for many years.

The first Choice for Love Heart Practice is called:
"Resting in the Heart"

When I guide my students in this meditation, their eyes are closed. However, you can begin to practice this with your eyes open as you read the instructions. Then, after you understand the technique and don't need the words, you can try closing your eyes.

᠗ **Resting in the Heart** ᠗

Take a few full, deep, slow breaths. Relax your eyes. Relax your shoulders. Relax all of the muscles in your body. Relax your heart.

Now, just have the intention of pointing your awareness within. Pointing your awareness within is just like diving into the water. If you just point and have the intention of going within and going deep, and then you let go and lean toward that inner direction, you'll begin to feel something very subtle pulling you, calling to you, embracing you, reaching out for you.

Try that now. *Have the intention of going deep within yourself. Feel that direction, and imagine leaning into that direction and just letting go.*

Allow yourself now to be drawn in and down toward that inner space, in the center of your heart area, as if you're being pulled deep, deep inside of yourself by a loving magnet.

Know that this inner space is actually always reaching for you. Feel it now, like a comfortable pillow; a soft bed; an inviting, warm blanket; a loving, safe embrace that's reaching out to you, calling to you. That inner space is welcoming you back to the Source, to the Quiet, to the essence of who you are underneath all the different masks and agitations and activities.

Let go, and know you're being called back into the spiritual heart, that place where your knowingness resides.

Just have the thought of pointing yourself toward that, and allow yourself to dive, to fall back into the inner space, to be caught, to be held.

Feel comforted. Feel safe. Feel recognized. Feel loved.

Have the thought:

> **"I'm going to sit for a few minutes
> and just rest in my own Love."**

Then, gently allow your awareness to rest in the area of your heart, not just inside of your body but moving out into the space a few inches in front of your chest.

You just have a very quiet intention of resting in your heart in the same way you would get into a pool of healing water, and just be in it.

You aren't doing anything. You're just resting.

Breathe in deeply, exhale, and let go even more fully into that space, where everything has melted into the peaceful pulsation of Knowingness.

There is only the Love.
You are Love.
You are home.

This is a wonderful practice to help you learn to "fall back" into the inner space of the heart, where revelation, wisdom, and knowingness await you. I designed it this way because it is our nature to think of trying to "get" somewhere, making an effort to go there, rather than allowing ourselves to simply *be* there. **After all, there really is no distance to travel, no journey to take. It's just a shift in your identification, from your limited Self to your Expanded Self.**

It's important to remember that you're not trying to know anything specific. You're *not* posing a question and then going inside and waiting to hear the answer. You're *not* trying to make something particular happen, or manufacture some experience you think you're supposed to have. *You're just resting in your heart.*

When you first begin working with this practice, I suggest you sit with your eyes closed, without doing anything, since this will help your awareness to focus within. If you like, you could offer a prayer first, or light a candle, or call upon what symbolizes the Highest for you—the Lord, Jesus, Buddha, Shiva, Allah, Mother Mary, the I Am Presence, and so on, although this isn't necessary.

Once you do that, however, you will need to let those thoughts go completely, *and not try to visualize any being or imagine anyone.* **You're just being with your own inner state of Heart-Wisdom.**

Can you see the difference between resting in your heart and trying to search for an answer to a problem? They're very different. **Trying to find an answer or acquire information has a specific goal. Resting in your heart has no goal other than what it sounds like—to just be in the space of your own heart with the intention of remaining open to whatever might emerge.**

You can practice *Resting in Your Heart* anywhere. As you become more familiar with taking the inward journey, you won't even have to be in a quiet or private place. My students have told me stories of practicing this technique in their parked car before going into a meeting, at their desk in the middle of a stressful work situation, and even in a restroom stall. Try *Resting in Your Heart* at night, when you're in bed with the lights out, right before you fall asleep. It will carry you gently and tenderly off into Dreamland.

The second Choice for Love Heart Practice is a very simple but powerful meditation that will very quickly recalibrate you to your heart. *It's designed to be used whenever you're feeling challenged, confused, worried, anxious, or stuck in your head.* It will help to shift your awareness from your mind back into your heart, and invite Heart-Wisdom to unfold.

It's called: **"The Heart-Wisdom Journey."**

Just like before, you can begin to practice this with your eyes open as you read the instructions. Then, after you understand the technique and don't need the words, you can try closing your eyes.

❧ The Heart-Wisdom Journey ❧

Allow yourself to become very quiet and close your eyes

Feel your awareness traveling down from your head, your eyes, down your face, down past your throat, down into your chest where your heart is.

Place one or both of your hands gently over the center of your chest in your heart area.

Breathe into the area around your heart, and when you exhale, imagine yourself melting into a space filled with shimmering light.

You are melting into the space of the heart.

Feel how expansive it is. Feel how full it is.

Then, whisper to yourself or have the silent thought:

"My heart knows. My heart knows."

You don't even have to understand what that means. Your heart just knows.

Breathe into your heart space. Breathe into your own knowingness.

Fill up with the peace it brings you.

Thank your heart for guiding you.

Thank your heart for its devotion to you and your freedom.

Thank your heart for not letting you forget your purpose and your path.

Smile, and feel what joy it brings you to remember that your heart knows.

Take a few moments just to be with the knowingness in your heart.

It is always there to serve you, if you just become still and listen.

"It is only when we silence the blaring sounds of our daily existence that we can finally hear the whispers of truth that life reveals to us, as it stands knocking on the doorsteps of our hearts."
— K. T. Jong

I love silence. To me, silence is not empty. It is full of everything. It pulsates with everything. It is the doorway to everything.

When I write, I crave silence and solitude. I don't leave my house. I go into total seclusion as much as possible. I can feel my unwritten words waiting impatiently to be drenched with silence so they can explode into what I hope will be magnificent blossoms, offered then to you, my reader.

In silence, I disappear, to make way for the Magic.

In silence, I run toward my Heart-Wisdom as one runs into the arms of their most cherished beloved.

Be still. Listen. Your Heart-Wisdom has been calling to you. It holds all of the answers you've been seeking, and all of the light you need to find your way home to awakening, to freedom, and to love.

Silence makes space for what is not silent to emerge.
When you become quiet,
you can be open.
When you become open,
you can be receptive.
When you become receptive,
you can be very soft.
When you become very soft,
you can feel your own heart.
When you can feel your own heart,
you can find your own astonishing knowingness.
Your heart knows . . .

❀ 10 ❀

Gateways Back to Love

*"The moment you have in your heart this extraordinary thing called love
and feel the depth, the delight, the ecstasy of it,
you will discover that for you the world is transformed."*

— J. Krishnamurti

No matter what challenges you face, no matter what unexpected obstacles suddenly arrive on your path, no matter how foggy the road ahead appears to be, *you can always make the choice for love.* Every true solution to every problem comes down to this—*more love, not less love.*

We courageously look for evidence of love in situations where we're sure there is none.

We compassionately find love for ourselves even when we're certain we don't deserve it.

We relentlessly search for the smallest, sparkling nugget of love in what appears to be only mud.

This is what the choice for love means—that we make the choice for love *instead* of choosing something else. Each time I haven't known what to do about something unwanted that's taking place in my life, each time I've felt overwhelmed by fear, dismay, or indecision, I've asked myself those Choice for Love questions:

**How can I bring the most love to this situation?
What would that look like right now?**

Every time, without fail, my heart would offer me the answers, and when I followed that auspicious map, it always led me to liberation.

**Only when we love do we truly triumph.
Only when we love do we truly ascend to our most awakened self.
Love is the only solution that resonates with
the highest purpose of life.
And that's why it is *always* the right choice.**

As we come to the final part of this journey of contemplation, we're ready to learn more about how to make love our chosen strategy for living—the compass that will guide us in the right direction to the right destination, and keep us from wasting time by getting lost on roads that will only lead us to more unhappiness.

> **There is never a good time for the unexpected.**
> **There is never a good time for disappointment.**
> **There is never a good time for loss.**
> **But it is always a good time for love.**

Look for Where Love Is

"Blessed are the pure in heart, for they shall see God."
— St. Matthew 5:8

One of my favorite things to do when I'm in San Francisco is to visit Chinatown, and I do my best to stop there every time I'm in the Bay Area. A few years ago, after finishing some business, I spent a delightful afternoon wandering up and down the crowded streets shopping for fabrics and gifts, and enjoying the sights and sounds of a culture I've always resonated with very strongly. I decided to find a restaurant where I could have a quick supper before heading back to my hotel.

As I began walking back up the hill, I saw two men standing on the sidewalk banging their fists loudly on a door. I immediately noticed that they were in front of a restaurant that was obviously closed—since there was a *"CLOSED FOR VACATION"* sign in the window, which a kind passerby pointed out to them—but that didn't stop these fellows from banging even more vigorously. I could hear them shouting: *"Come on, the guidebook said you'd be open! It's past five thirty! We came all the way from Dallas! Open up in there."*

An elderly Chinese woman approached and passionately gestured up and down the street to the at least two dozen other restaurants that were all open and ready for customers, but the men rudely waved her away and continued their insistent pounding on the one and only eating establishment that was very, very closed. An amused crowd of Chinese shopkeepers had now gathered across the street, talking and laughing in

Cantonese as they watched the strange, stubborn tourists, *who could only see the closed door that was keeping them out, and none of the many open doors that were inviting them in.*

That night, when I returned to my hotel room, I thought about this incident and felt grateful to the two bullheaded tourists for offering me a three-dimensional demonstration of one of the common ways that, instead of making the choice for love, we actually push love away and create suffering for ourselves:

We focus on where love isn't, rather than noticing where Love is.

We find a door that isn't going to open, and, like the two angry tourists, stand there banging on it with frustration. Meanwhile, all around us, other doors of love are open, and people are inviting us to enter. But we just *stubbornly stare at the one uncooperative door,* cursing it for not opening, bemoaning our fate for why it didn't open, and feeling sorry for ourselves because we are so unloved.

What is that closed door? It might be a friend or loved one who makes you emotionally chase them down and won't let you fully into their heart. It might be a business idea you just can't let go of even when it's apparent that it isn't going to work. Perhaps it's a work situation in which you and your talents have been unappreciated by people you realize aren't ever going to value you. Or it might be a relationship with one person that isn't giving you the love you need, and yet you don't allow yourself to even recognize, let alone receive, the support, caring, and kindness so many other people have been offering.

You've been standing at this closed door for a long time, but like the Texas Twosome, you refuse to leave because that was the door you wanted to enter. **You need to turn around and look for the doors that *are* open and waiting for you.**

**Instead of seeing where love isn't,
look for where love is.**

**When you're focused on how you're not getting love,
you won't even notice the love that's waiting
to come into your life.**

**When you keep chasing down people who aren't
ready or willing to love you,
you won't even see the people who are running after you
with offerings of love in their outstretched hands.**

Love is always available. *You just have to stop only focusing on where love isn't and begin to look for where it is revealing itself.* When you continue to beg for a few crumbs of love and appreciation from people who aren't prepared to or capable of giving much to you, you won't even realize how many other delicious cakes and pies of love the Universe is waiting to deliver:

Just because one door is closed doesn't mean all doors are closed.

Just because one person can't love you the way you hoped they would doesn't mean other people won't deeply love you.

Just because one company doesn't appreciate and honor your talents doesn't mean another company won't see your value.

Just because one friend has a difficult time letting you get close doesn't mean other new friends will also push you away.

Of course, it's human nature to want what we hoped we'd get and became attached to receiving. The tourists wanted to eat at that specific restaurant. It was closed, and they were angry. **All they could see was what wasn't available, and not what was available.**

There's always a restaurant open in Chinatown. *And there's always Love somewhere.*

The opportunity to experience Love is always available somewhere.
It might not be how you wish it would happen that day.
It might not be with the person you hoped
you could offer it to or receive it from.
But it *is* available.

Every day, the grace of love tries to offer us its gifts. Some we reject. Some we don't even recognize as gifts. Some we miss altogether. These gifts come wrapped in many forms: the phone call from an old friend that arrives at a time when we're feeling lonely and invisible; the business referral from a client that we receive in the middle of a depressing workweek; the compliment from a stranger delivered just when our partner seems distant and preoccupied. **Even though these may not be the sources from which we hoped to receive Love and caring, *it's still love.***

A few years ago, the last of my three fur angels left this earth. When my remaining dog, Shanti, passed on, it was the first time in 18 years that I was alone without my animal children. My heart was broken as I always knew it would be when that day came. How I missed the feeling of holding a warm little body in my arms, seeing their unabashed excitement when I walked into the room, or looking into those deep, dark eyes and experiencing the grace of pure, unconditional love.

As the days passed, something remarkable began to happen. Everywhere I went, dogs would pull their way over to me, dragging their owners clutching the leashes behind them. I'd be in the park and from 50 feet away, I'd see a little dog on its daily walk. Suddenly I'd realize the dog had seen me too, and as if on cue, it would start running toward me. I'd kneel down to receive it, and it would greet me with kisses and licks and so much delight.

The baffled owner would say things like, *"He usually doesn't like strangers. I'm sorry if he's bothering you,"* or *"I've never seen her pull that hard except to visit another dog."*

I'd smile and reply, ***"You don't understand—your dog just made my day. I recently lost my last one, and I feel like yours is offering me the love and affection I've really been missing. He must have known I needed it."*** Then I'd thank the dog for the surprise gift, and for doing such a wonderful job delivering its special postcard from heaven that I knew had been sent by my babies.

Day after day, for many months, I was showered with love by dogs, particularly smaller breeds like my own. Several cats even got in on the act, for although my kitty Luna had passed eight years earlier, I still missed her terribly. These cats began showing up at my house, walking in the door, and making themselves at home. One little guy in particular would run down to my office as if he knew just where to go, and jump up onto the love seat in the exact spot where Luna used to sit and keep me company. I would follow him downstairs and sit at my computer, so happy to hear the comfort of his purring, and see a little body curled up nearby.

Slowly, as I began to heal the most intense layers of my sadness, this emotional first aid—courtesy of the animal kingdom—tapered off. The cat visits stopped first, and even though an occasional dog would approach me in the park, most of them would just wag their tail as they passed me, and then go on their way.

I had absolutely no doubt about what had just taken place: Love had found me when I needed it. Even though it wasn't coming from the sources I wanted it to, from my Bijou, Shanti, and Luna, love was there nonetheless. These animal teachers had gently reminded me to focus on where love was, and not dwell on where love no longer was. Besides, I knew my three little ones had put them up to it!

No matter what's taking place in your life, love is always available somewhere, somehow. Every day, look for the open doors. Every day, notice and celebrate how Love *is* finding its way to you, through a friend, a flower, an animal, a song, a memory . . .

For a moment, just be still.
Think about all the areas in which Love is there for you.
Instead of cursing the doors that are not open,
look for the openings that exist.
Instead of cursing the Love that is not available,
look for where it *is* revealing itself to you.
Ask yourself: *"Where is the Love?*
Let me look for it.
I know it must be around here somewhere."

GATEWAYS BACK TO LOVE:
THE CHOICE FOR LOVE PRACTICES

I'm excited to introduce you to some more Choice for Love Practices. I designed these techniques and meditations to give you simple but powerful opportunities in which to make the choice for love every day.

᠀᠀ CALLING FORTH LOVE ᠀᠀

If you've read my book *Soul Shifts*, you're familiar with the powerful practice of "Calling in Light." I've created an adaptation of that technique called "Calling Forth Love." It's designed to help you call forth the vibration of love from within yourself. Whenever you're feeling stuck, not "juicy" enough, emotionally disconnected from your heart, in need of more compassion for yourself or others, or when you simply want to experience more love, practice Calling Forth Love.

~ ⌒⌒ CALLING FORTH LOVE ⌒⌒ ~

Close your eyes. Take a few deep, slow, full breaths.

Place your hands over your heart area, close to your body but not quite touching it, palms facing inward.

Now, imagine that infinite ocean of magnificent divine love deep within you, like a shining sea of light and delight. Feel your longing to be filled with that ocean of love, to become the ocean of love.

When you are ready, simply and tenderly have the thought:

"I CALL FORTH MORE LOVE."

If you'd like, you can softly say those words out loud: "I CALL FORTH MORE LOVE."

Don't try to see or visualize anything in your mind. Just be very still, surrendered, and open. Keep your awareness turned within. You're not calling forth love from above, or reaching for anything outside of yourself.

Take slow, deep, reverent breaths and feel yourself soaking in Love, drinking in the nectar of sweetness, compassion, and grace.

Continue to occasionally have the very quiet, subtle thought *"I call forth more love,"* and just open.

Sit for at least a few minutes like this, and whenever you feel ready to complete, fold your hands in a prayer position in front of your heart, bow your head slightly, and say, *"Thank you,"* out loud three times.

When you're finished, you can open your eyes.

Calling Forth Love is a very powerful practice to help you open to the love that is your true self and true source. It instantly uplifts your vibration and cultivates the experience of seeking inside of yourself for love, rather than looking for it externally.

After practicing this, you may notice more of a sense of peace, of sweetness and generosity of heart. You might experience a softening of harsh emotions such as judgment, anger, or worry.

THE CHOICE FOR LOVE INSTANT RECALIBRATION PRACTICE

Love expands our vibration more quickly than anything else. With that in mind, I've designed another easy-to-do practice: **The Instant Love Recalibration Practice.** This can shift your vibration *in a matter of seconds.*

As you'll see, **you can practice this when you realize you're having a difficult time feeling love or compassion—for a challenge or incident, for another person, or for yourself.** This technique "rewires" and recalibrates your brain to your own experiences of love so that you can more easily bring this expanded vibration into your current situation.

THE INSTANT LOVE RECALIBRATION PRACTICE

If you're having trouble finding anything to love about a challenging situation in any given moment, immediately look for something else to love around you: your dog, your cat, your plant, a show you really enjoy watching on TV—something that is not challenging you and is bringing you joy.

Just find something to feel love for, and hold it in your awareness for 15 seconds. Allow yourself to become saturated with the experience of loving that other thing (dog, new running shoes, etc.). Feel the vibration of that love. *It will recalibrate you to a more accepting, peaceful energy, and make your choice for love easier.*

*If you're having trouble feeling love, tolerance, or acceptance for someone, *think of another person in your life you really love*—a partner, a friend, a relative, a mentor—and hold them in your awareness with love for 15 seconds. You can also call or connect with them for a minute.

Once you've done this, feel the expansiveness created by focusing on the love with that person. Float in that sensation for a few moments. *This will recalibrate you to a more spacious, open energy and make your choice for love easier.*

*If you're having trouble loving yourself in a particular moment, *find something else about yourself that's easy to love*—recall a time when you were kind to someone, or did something helpful, or when you made a difference in someone's life. Say out loud: *"I am proud of myself for . . ."* and list at least one thing.

Once you've done this, feel the uplifting energy that honoring something else about you manifested. Savor it for a few moments. *This will recalibrate you to a more appreciative, generous energy, and make your choice for loving yourself easier.*

THE SEVEN ESSENTIAL CHOICE FOR LOVE DAILY ACTIONS

Is there something you can you do each day that doesn't take up much time but can help rewire you to the vibration of love? Yes, there is! I call these the **Seven Essential Choice for Love Daily Actions.** As you'll see, they are named *actions* because within seconds, they raise you to your highest vibration.

Ideally, you would have the intention of practicing all of them each day, which would take only a few minutes. I suggest you try doing that at least a few times so you can receive the full benefit of this technique. However, you can choose to practice any of the seven whenever you wish. **Just the process of looking for these opportunities itself will become a profound choice for love during your day.**

THE SEVEN ESSENTIAL
CHOICE FOR LOVE DAILY ACTIONS™

1. Thank someone you would normally not thank.

2. Express your love in a way that is unexpected, or to someone who is not expecting it.

3. Honor yourself for something you did today that reflects the best of who you are.

4. Forgive yourself for something you did today that reflects less than the best of who you are.

5. Feel compassion for someone you would normally judge.

6. Notice or experience something as miraculous that you would normally take for granted.

7. For one full minute, stop whatever you are doing and be deeply grateful for the gift of this day of your life. During this minute, contemplate the fact that yesterday, approximately 154,300 people on Earth passed from this world.

   Even while you are practicing this very exercise, 100 souls will leave their physical forms. Send them your prayers as they journey onward.

   Then, fold your hands in front of your heart, and with great gratitude, joy, and humility, proclaim these words out loud three times:

"TODAY, I AM ALIVE!

TODAY, I AM ALIVE!

TODAY, I AM ALIVE!"

HOW TO PRACTICE THE SEVEN ESSENTIAL CHOICE FOR LOVE DAILY ACTIONS

1. Thank someone you normally would not thank.

Who would you normally not thank? Perhaps it's one of your children who makes their bed every morning, but you haven't thanked them for a while. Perhaps it's somebody who is doing a service that you've paid them for, so you don't think that it's necessary to thank them. Instead of just telling your partner you love them, thank them for something you usually take for granted. Thank a stranger for wearing a colorful outfit that brightened your day. *It takes 15 seconds to practice this, but the impact will last much longer.*

2. Express your love in a way that is unexpected or to someone who is not expecting it.

Expressing your love in a way that is unexpected stretches you beyond your usual "love output." It allows you to begin to deliberately contemplate, *How can I express my love?* rather than just assuming at some point you will be loving.

Call someone. Text someone and just let them know you love them. Write an old high school friend and let them know you were thinking of them with gratitude. You must have 365 people in your life, so you can keep cycling through your list. Express your love in a new way to someone in your life—leave a note, buy flowers, say something you normally wouldn't say or do something you normally wouldn't do. Be creative!

3. Honor yourself for something you did today that reflects the best of who you are.

Normally we go through the day gathering evidence of our failures and overlooking our inner triumphs. *"I shouldn't have done that. I shouldn't have said that. I shouldn't have eaten that."* This is such an unloving thing to do. Honor yourself for something you did today that reflects **the best of who you are.** *"I was about to be sarcastic with someone, but instead I took a breath and said, 'I understand how stressful this has been.'"* *"I noticed that a woman dropped a shopping list on the floor of the store, so I picked it up and* *gave it to her." "I was stuck in traffic and instead of becoming grumpy, I used the time to listen to an uplifting recorded lecture."*

This will help recalibrate you to the highest.

4. Forgive yourself for something you did today that reflects less than the best of who you are.

Every day we each do things we wish we hadn't or that we realize we could have done better. Again, instead of using what you notice to criticize or punish yourself, consciously forgive yourself for it. Note what happened so you can improve, but offer yourself love and compassion for what took place. *Just hold the thought of whatever it is you're unhappy about, and have the intention of washing it with forgiveness.*

5. Feel compassion for someone you would normally judge.

During a typical day, you will inevitably encounter people who annoy you, irritate you, or anger you: the person driving too slowly in front of you, the less-than-articulate customer service representative on the phone, the grumpy co-worker. Just for one moment, try to find a compassionate place from which to view them. *Remember: You can feel compassion for someone and still not think that what they did was correct.* Simply think: *"I'm sorry for your unhappiness. May you find peace."* Of course, just by offering this thought, you will instantly raise yourself up to a more peaceful, loving vibration.

6. Notice or experience something as miraculous that you would normally take for granted.

There are a million everyday miracles we miss because we aren't paying attention. Choose just one, and experience it for the astonishing wonder that it is. Take 30 seconds to emotionally immerse yourself in it. Notice the beauty of the tall, graceful tree outside of your window; appreciate the fact that your hand that can move if you simply think, *"Move"*; watch a bird take flight and marvel at its freedom; walk through the supermarket and feel amazement at the abundance of food gathered there for you. *By placing your attention on the sublime hidden within the ordinary, you'll instantly lift up your own consciousness.*

7. For one full minute, stop whatever you are doing. Be deeply grateful for the gift of this day and of your life.

Even if you forget to do any of the other Choice for Love Daily Actions, I recommend you try practicing this one, which takes only about 30 seconds. You can do this any time you like. I enjoy doing this first thing in the morning to start off my day with the highest possible vibration. After all, each morning when we wake up, we *should* be grateful that we've been given another day of life and breath when hundreds of thousands of other people haven't.

Each time I proclaim, *"Today, I am alive!"* I'm recalibrated to the highest truth, and no matter how long my list of tasks, or what challenges await me, I've already put it all in perspective.

I invite you to begin practicing these Seven Essential Choice for Love Actions today! *Just the habit itself of looking for opportunities to put each one into practice will give you many experiences of instant, uplifting vibrational shifts.*

You might want to make a copy of these practices and have it available on your phone or tablet. If you suddenly realize that you've been having a difficult, stressful, self-indulgent, or angry day, take out the list and choose just one of these Choice for Love Daily Actions. In a few moments, you'll begin to feel your energy change, your mind settle, and your heart expand.

Love is not an attitude. Looking and sounding like we are loving is not the same as being in the state of love. Moment by moment, we need to do the real work, remembering that *each choice for love will make the next choice easier, and each choice for love is changing the world.*

When you are in a space of your own love,
it automatically uplifts the heart of anybody around you.

When you're in a space of your own peace, it vibrationally guides
the other person closer to their own peace.

Love is like a great, relentless light
illuminating whatever it touches,
kindling the light in each heart with its own.

The more you love,
the more you give others permission to do the same.
And that person can offer more love to the next person,
who can offer more love to the next person.

And this is how your love will heal the world.

❈ 11 ❈

Serving the World with Your Awakened Heart

"Behold, he spreads his light around him."
— Job 36:30

For thousands of years, people have sought the company of great beings whose very presence pulsates with the divine, and whose countenance seems to call forth the highest in us as human beings. Whether they've traveled to see an enlightened spiritual master, the Pope, the Dalai Lama, a renowned minister or rabbi, a wise monk, a Native American shaman, or a living saint, these pilgrimages were fueled by one purpose: **the longing to connect with someone who themselves was unwaveringly connected to the sacred and, by being in proximity to that vibration, the hope of experiencing its blessing.**

We gravitate toward individuals who radiate great *"soul light"* in the same way we gather around a blazing campfire in the darkness. There, we feel inspired, uplifted, and comforted. There, so much is illuminated, and the mysterious and unseen is not so frightening. Seen through our new teachings about the vibrational heart, we understand that *simply being near great masters of consciousness who are vibrating at such a high and pure level is what recalibrates our own vibration.*

There is a beautiful, ancient Sanskrit word for this phenomenon of being vibrationally uplifted by being in the presence of a powerfully loving and radiant being: *darshan*. I'm using the term here because it's the only word I know of in any language that articulates this phenomenon of how our heart and our love can transform others. In Western traditions, one might use the term *blessing*, although it has a different meaning.

Darshan originates from the Sanskrit word *darśana*, or "vision," derived from the root *Dṛś*—"to see." It literally means "sight" or "beholding." It is often used in the context of going to a saint or a great guru to receive their darshan, meaning to be in their presence, to behold their "Light," and to be uplifted by it. **To "have darshan" or "receive darshan" is to have the sight, glimpse, or experience of the highest in the presence of someone.**

I first heard this word many decades ago when someone told me they were going to visit a renowned Indian master because she was going to *"give darshan."* This was in the very early days of my spiritual path, when I was quite unfamiliar with these concepts. I remember wondering just what darshan was, guessing that perhaps it was some kind of gift, blessed object, or a special kind of lecture. Only when I had this experience myself did I understand *that darshan does, indeed, mean experiencing a gift, but it is the gift of the vibration of a High Being, a vibration that is pulsating with Light.*

Darshan is a sacred vibrational gift.
In the presence of someone, we experience that person's
high vibrational level, and it recalibrates us in that moment,
lifting our own vibration and raising us up to our Highest.

Since darshan has to do with presence and vibration, it transcends words and conversation. It can even transcend time and space. For example, a revered holy person might simply walk through a crowd, and someone who catches a glimpse of them will say, "I had the darshan of the Dalai Lama," or "I received the blessing (darshan) of the Pope." Someone else might share that, just by seeing a wise being on TV, reading a sacred book, or even seeing a photograph of someone they consider to be an awakened, elevated being, they felt an unmistakable opening happen in their heart. They aren't referring to the physical sighting of the person, but to the profound inner shift they experienced—the increase of Light. They say things like, *"The minute I saw him, I felt like I was embraced by an ocean of peace,"* or *"She looked at me and I felt someone was pouring love into my heart,"* or *"Just listening to him speak, I felt my whole being expand."*

Most of us will never have the unique opportunity to visit saints and masters. However, I'm sharing about this for a very important reason:

The truth is that, when people are in your presence, they're always receiving *your* darshan—meaning you're always "giving" them a vibrational experience of your own heart. They are "beholding" your vibration, experiencing the darshan of your consciousness. And, of course, you're always receiving the darshan of everyone else's heart.

Earlier we introduced the scientific knowledge that the heart gives off a powerful electromagnetic energy field. I'm sure physics has a scientific term for the energetic impact the waves of your energy field have on someone else's energy field, but you can see why I like the mystical term *darshan*, a concept that existed thousands and thousands of years before we knew about frequencies, quantum mechanics, and subatomic particles. *The quality of the vibration in your heart influences the energy of everyone around you. Your heart, and my heart, and all of our hearts are always in communication, giving each other darshan.*

Now we begin to understand how we are each literally transforming each other's vibrations, and what a truly life-changing impact making the choice for love has on ourselves and the world.

All of us are profoundly impacted,
not just emotionally but vibrationally,
by the inner coherence—or lack of coherence—of others.
When we sense another human being vibrating at a very high level
of harmony and love, our own heart recognizes this state,
whether we're conscious of it or not.
Something in us begins a process of remembering, and recalibrating.
Our own soul rises up to sing its most elevated melody
as it attempts to match and harmonize with the exalted vibration
of the other person's awakened heart.
We are receiving the *darshan*—the blessing—of love.

What this comes down to is that *you don't have a choice* about whether or not you want to make an impact on others. It's inevitable that you will! How, then, do you want to impact people? What kind of *darshan* are people experiencing in your presence?

Are they experiencing the darshan of your highest self, or the darshan of your limitations?

Are they experiencing the darshan of your love and compassion, or the darshan of your judgments and unresolved emotional issues?

Are they experiencing the darshan of your inner peace and harmony, or are they experiencing the darshan of your anxiety and agitation?

I know that I've always wanted to give people the *darshan* of my love, of my light, and of the highest when they are in my presence. Isn't this what we all long for—to have people feel better and higher and happier because of who we are?

Living in the vibration of love, you become a walking blessing to others. You don't even have to say anything, impress, perform, or fix. You might be shopping in the supermarket, or sitting with friends, or passing strangers on a crowded street. The *darshan* of your open heart *will* bless everyone in your path in invisible and mysterious ways.

Making the choice for love,
you become a powerful, pulsating field of love.
That love will be a vibrational blessing and benefactor.
Your own state of love will vibrate others into their love.

Your choice for love will have profound consequences—it will show up in how you work, live, and behave toward everyone. This is not the same as an attitude that says, *"I should be loving."* Authentic love cannot contain itself and doesn't need to be coaxed out. It will be abundant. It will not economize. It will insist on overflowing.

"When angels visit us, we do not hear the rustle of wings,
nor feel the feathery touch of the breast of a dove;
but we know their presence by the love they create in our hearts."
— Mary Baker Eddy

Once during my weekly radio show, a caller told me that she'd spent her entire life trying to contact angels. She was desperate to know who her angels were, and how she could receive their blessings and protection. While there are some beautiful, gifted people who have the destiny to vividly enjoy these otherworldly relationships, most of us do not. Meanwhile, from what she told me, this caller had pulled away from her own humanity, shut off to doing any other work on herself, and had very unhealthy interactions with others.

"I keep looking and looking!" she complained, *"but I just can't find any angels, even when I pray or meditate. I think they're rejecting me. What should I do?"*

The answer rose up from my heart without any prompting from my intellect or expertise, and I heard myself reply:

"Maybe it's time to stop looking for angels, and become one instead."

These words struck such a powerful chord in my own consciousness. (Who knows—perhaps it was one of my own angels who gave me that message!) Whatever the source, this is an important wisdom offering for us all:

I do believe we are here to embody the highest love, compassion, and wisdom for one another, and to assist in raising the vibration of our planet to one of peace and harmony. This reinforces our unwavering commitment to continue to make the choice for love, moment by moment, and transmute our own vibration to the highest possible frequency. This, then, is how we each serve.

You are here to be the manifestation of divine love,
to be a living bridge from the heavenly to the human.
When you awaken and abide in your own field of love,
you become a blessing to others, and to the world.
Don't look for an angel.
Become one.

HEALING THE HEARTBREAK OF THE WORLD

"At times like this, I feel so far from Home."
— Barbara De Angelis

Have you ever had days when you feel like you must be on the wrong planet? Perhaps you've wondered if people from some other, much less evolved world than ours have been deliberately placed here for the purpose of annoying you, exasperating you, and upsetting you. You collide with people's small-mindedness, prejudice, insensitivity, ignorance, cruelty, and crudeness. You witness or hear about horrible things happening that are utterly incomprehensible and think, *"Surely there must be some mistake. How could I have been put in the same cosmic classroom as these horrible beings?"*

Several years ago, during a day when I was having just such an experience, I saw a poster on a bulletin board at my local health-food store that read:

"Seriously, I don't know when exactly that UFO landed and dumped all these stupid people, but they apparently aren't coming back for them."

As amusing as this sign was, the issue it addressed is one that many of us on a path of personal and spiritual transformation regularly wrestle with.

We are visionaries, and for as long as we can remember, we've dreamed of helping to build a better world.

We are idealistic.

We have a fervent desire for truth, for freedom, and for the upliftment of ourselves and the planet.

However, these ideals constantly collide with disappointment and disbelief in the failings of others, as well as our own. *"What is wrong with people?"* we wonder. Something in us, some ancient part of us or higher part of us, *knows* it's supposed to be different, and so we live with a kind of spiritual heartbreak and homesickness. *We do feel so far from home.*

In my life, I've cried many tears for myself as well as for things and people I'd cherished and lost. But often my most heart-wrenching tears have been those I cried because of the cruelty and harshness of this world.

**There are tears we cry for ourselves,
and then there are tears we cry for our world.
There is personal grief, and then there's what I call
cosmic grief, when our heart breaks not just for ourselves,
but for the planet.**

Some of my earliest memories are of experiencing waves of cosmic grief, a knowingness that the world could be, and should be, so much better. **As I grew older and began my own conscious spiritual journey, I realized that *I was* part of that world, and was not meant to be *apart from it.*** I needed to focus on how *I* could be become as loving and enlightened as possible.

In spite of our commitment to make a positive difference, all of us who are helpers and healers and uplifters—including me—have moments when we look around at the overwhelming suffering and ignorance of much of the planet and think: *"Can't I just run away and live on an island and leave everyone who's ruining everything to destroy one another? Haven't I done enough good already? Why am I the one who has to fix things?"* Throughout history, even great saints, masters, humanitarians, and visionaries have become frustrated and burdened by the force of darkness that does exist in this world.

As I write this, we are in very turbulent and frightening times on our planet. It's shocking to realize that, as I've been working on this book and contemplating the choice for love, compassion, and the power of healing the heart, I've seen the level of darkness around all of us rising. Just about every day in the past few weeks when I've taken a break, I've ended up standing in front of my television witnessing reports of the latest massacre, attack, murder, or explosion, and weeping in disbelief at the next new nightmare that's taken place. I keep asking myself the same questions that are probably familiar to every conscious seeker:

How can people descend into such hatred and violence?

How can people be so cruel and unfeeling to other human beings?

How can people sit back and allow terrorism, tyranny, corruption, and inhumane acts to take place?

The words that have poured forth onto these pages have offered me the answer: **It's the denial of the "we" that allows evil to exist in the world.**

**All delusional separation and disowning of our ultimate
spiritual and vibrational relationship with one another
is the cause of all that is dark in the world,
from the smallest act of unkindness or prejudice toward others
all the way to every war, every atrocity,
every unthinkable expression of inhumanity.**

The denial of the "we" proclaims:

"You and I are not connected, and therefore you are no part of me or anything I am. You are not me or mine, and therefore I denounce you. Because there is no common thread binding us, I can persecute you, abuse you, and slaughter you, and it means nothing to me, because you are nothing to me."

It's chilling to read this, isn't it? It was chilling for me to write it. Of course, none of you fall into this category. It's a good sign if you cannot fathom darkness—it means that you've been evolving from ME consciousness into WE consciousness, and so the concept of dehumanizing others seems utterly impossible to you. Still, we each must resist the temptation to close off our hearts and collapse into *much subtler, less lethal, but still unhealthy forms of detachment* from what is happening around us *and* within us.

What does this mean? We must be brave enough to look at all of the ways we are *not* making the choice for love.

Our *stubborn insistence on the illusion of our separation from one another* is the way that even advanced spiritual travelers and seekers of the truth can unconsciously drift away from love. We may not go so far as to run away to that desert island, but by disconnecting from and discounting the WE, we give ourselves an out: *We don't have to care as much, or behave as compassionately, not just with the world in general, but with the people we love, the people with whom we work, and with our family and friends.* What possible enlightened or awakened result does that bring?

"The heart of humanity has strings in all hearts."
— Eliphas Levi

Last week I was teaching about this topic to my students during our weekly phone call, and one remarked: *"All of this negativity in the world is too much for me. I've decided to just stay out of it."* When I heard this, I laughed and replied, ***"But, my dear, that will be impossible, because there is no OUT."***

You can't *not* be one with Spirit/Source/God.
You can't *not* be part of the whole.
You can't *not* be from the same one source, which is Love.
You cannot *not* be IN all of this.
This is ALL there is. There is no OUT.

I want to share some deeply insightful, poetic, and poignant words written by the humorist and author Andrew Boyd:

"When you feel connected to everything, you also feel responsible for everything. And you cannot turn away. Your destiny is bound with the destinies of others. You must either learn to carry the Universe or be crushed by it. You must grow strong enough to love the world, yet empty enough to sit down at the same table with its worst horrors.

"To seek enlightenment is to seek annihilation, rebirth, and the taking up of burdens. You must come prepared to touch and be touched by each and every thing in heaven and hell.

"I am One with the Universe and it hurts."

There is such wisdom and grace in these eloquent words. *"I am one with the Universe and it hurts."* It does hurt. And yet, what is the alternative? For me, there has never been one. I can't not care or serve or be touched by it all. The truth is, none of us can.

I believe that the remedy for this aching heartsickness is a recipe we've already been cooking in our Choice for Love journey. It contains three main ingredients: *Love, Compassion, and Humility.*

We find ways to offer love to ourselves and others.
We hold ourselves and the world and its suffering with compassion.
And we remember the immeasurable privilege
of being a soul that is alive and awake,
and humbly honor our responsibility to serve others.

"See God in each other."

— Swami Muktananda

Swami Muktananda was one of the great saints of the 20th century and the founder of the Siddha Yoga spiritual path who came to the west from India in the 1970s. Baba, as he was known to his devotees, was part of the lineage of spiritual teachers with whom I've had the privilege of studying. Many years before that, when I was still a teenager, I committed to my own spiritual growth and became a teacher of meditation. At that time, I first heard Baba's famous teaching: *"See God in each other."*

I loved this concept, but often it would collide with my direct experience. In moments when something had angered or upset me, I would feel very guilty. *"I'm certainly not seeing God in that person. I'm seeing unconsciousness. I'm seeing stubbornness. I'm seeing selfishness. I'm seeing stupidity. I guess I'll know I'm enlightened when I don't see those things anymore."*

Of course, as I matured spiritually, I understood that to see God in each other didn't mean to only see the highest and ignore everything else. **My experience is that when we are established in our expanded consciousness, we will spontaneously perceive how the highest in someone—God/Light/pure spirit—has gotten covered over, bent, blocked, or twisted into a different shape that's not allowing its pure essence to shine through.**

The choice for love means the choice to see everything.
"See God in each other" doesn't mean to see *ONLY* God in each other.
It means don't forget to see God *along with*
whatever else you're seeing.

LOVE, ONE DROP AT A TIME

"Ours is not the task of fixing the entire world all at once,
but of stretching out to mend the part of the world that is within our reach.
Any small, calm thing that one soul can do to help another soul,
to assist some portion of this poor suffering world, will help immensely."
— Clarissa Pinkola Estes

Here's my retelling of a short Native American fable that I've always loved.

One day, a fire suddenly erupted in what had been a peaceful and vast forest. The flames roared through the trees, and the terrified and panicked animals left their homes and fled the forest away from the raging blaze. They ran and ran, and finally, panting and trembling, they arrived at a river. They stood together, looking back in grief at the fire destroying their habitat.

Then they noticed a little hummingbird hovering near the water, dipping down and collecting a tiny drop in its beak, then flying off back toward the blaze, where he'd drop the water into the flames. *"Stop!"* some of the animals cried out in an attempt to warn the hummingbird. *"Your wings will get scorched, and you will die."*

"What's wrong with him?" others laughed. *"What a fool! Does he really think he can make a difference?"*

Over and over again, the hummingbird flew back and forth, carrying tiny drops of water and ignoring the cries and jeers of the other animals.

On his next trip to the river, the hummingbird saw a great eagle swoop down next to him. *"Little bird, what are you doing?"* the eagle asked.

The weary hummingbird looked up at the eagle and replied: *"I'm doing what I can."*

I love this story. It contains many lessons for us as we contemplate how to serve others and the planet. **So often, we judge ourselves and our offerings to the world as small and unimportant.** I meet wonderful people all the time who feel unsuccessful because, even though they have a satisfying career that benefits others, they aren't well known. I encounter people who are contributing their caring to their family, a small group of individuals, or an organization, but feel as if they've somehow failed because their love and service aren't reaching tens of thousands.

We live in a time that many researchers and psychologists see as the age of digital narcissism, complete with reality shows that churn out instant celebrities, overnight Internet sensations from the talented to the bizarre, each with their own YouTube channel, obsession with selfies, social media, and online status. **The prevalent attitude is that if someone isn't watching what you're doing, it doesn't have much value.** Perhaps the old philosophical query *"If a tree falls in the forest and no one hears it, does it make a sound?"* has been replaced by *"If I do something and I don't post it/tweet it/Instagram it/upload it/share it, did it even happen and does it even matter?"*

The digital age is miraculous. It has created so many unfathomable possibilities that are changing the world in profoundly beneficial ways. **However, the focus on constant measurement based on massive external acknowledgment has influenced all of us, and I fear it has contributed to an epidemic of emotional and psychological insignificance.**

Just because it's not a thousand people, why isn't it meaningful and significant for you to shift one person? Just because you didn't write a book about your efforts, or become renowned for it or wealthy because of what you offer, why isn't it significant if you've helped a friend open up and heal her heart, or nursed a relative back to health, or volunteered to teach one child how to dance or play ball?

Measuring the impact of your service in linear ways diminishes your service, and robs you of the pure joy that should come from doing something with a pure and giving heart. You may never know how profoundly your acts of love, caring, and compassion transform those who are the recipients of these gifts.

Do what you can. One drop at a time.

**Think in big ways and serve in small ways.
Everything you do *does* count.
Just because it doesn't fix everything
doesn't mean it didn't do something.
When you bring big love to small acts of
caring, compassion, and service,
those acts become enormous.**

DEFYING THE DARKNESS WITH YOUR LOVE

"There are no passengers on Spaceship Earth—we are all crew."
— Marshall McLuhan

As we each evolve into a "spiritual grown-up," we must face the unfortunate reality that, while there are many ways we can serve, there are even more ways in which nothing we can do will help. The more we grow in compassion not only for ourselves but for others, we become better at knowing the difference. **There is one thing we can *always* do, however, no matter what the circumstance: *We can always offer our blessings.***

One of the ways I practice this is by watching the news every day. Some people are quite taken aback when they hear this. *"You're a spiritual teacher. Aren't you exposing yourself to a lot of negative energy?"* they ask me. Others explain: *"I don't want to ruin my mood or my inner state by getting depressed or angry about all of the terrible things that are happening, so I avoid reading the news or watching it on TV to protect myself."*

I respect each person's freedom to make choices about how to live their life. **However, I do not believe that the choice to close ourselves off to what is happening around us is a choice for love—many times, it is a choice for *avoidance*, a choice for *denial*, and a choice for *indifference*.** And there is no protection, benefit, or benevolence in that.

Every day, I choose to know what is taking place in my own country and in the world because I feel an obligation to learn about what's happening to my spiritual relatives everywhere. I see where people are hurting or frightened, where they are in grief or heartbreak or facing unthinkable calamities that, God willing, most of us will never be forced to endure. *Knowing what is happening informs me of where my "service" is needed—my compassion, my prayers, and my love.*

What do I do in these moments? How do I serve?

First, I open my heart and allow myself to fully feel the impact of what I am watching or reading, no matter how uncomfortable it feels.

Next, I close my eyes and visualize the people involved—one person or hundreds or thousands—and imagine holding them in an enormous embrace of the most tender, compassionate love. I cry with them and for them. I whisper, *"I am so sorry,"* over and over again. I pour as much caring and comforting energy into them as I can, envisioning it like golden light penetrating deep into their being.

Finally, I offer prayers for them, for the souls of those who have been slaughtered or wounded, or lost their homes to fires, floods, famine, earthquakes, or accidents, or those who've lost loved ones to natural or unnatural deaths and are suffering in grief. I ask for blessings, that they may be comforted, that they may be guided to peace and merciful healing, that they be wrapped in divine love and showered with grace.

I do believe these offerings energetically reach people, in some small way. They are a *vibrational care package* we send from our heart, carried by the mysterious network of invisible threads that intimately connect us all.

Of course it would be more "pleasant" to go about our own life
and not allow the horrors on the planet to disturb our
supposedly "peaceful" state of mind, or taint our "serenity"
with that pesky thing called *reality*.

But how steady is your own state of consciousness if
you have to keep it sheltered from the winds of truth?

How genuinely expanded is the ocean of your heart if
there's no room in it to hold and dilute the suffering of a stranger
for even five minutes?

How bright and unwavering is your light
if you're terrified to gaze, even for a moment, at the darkness?

This planet is our home. We are, as we've seen, all vibrationally connected, and whether or not we want to admit it or are even conscious of
it, we are feeling the waves of pain from all over the world. We are an
intrinsic part of what is happening to everyone, because the "We" *is* real.
As the late Marshall McLuhan said in the quote I shared above: *"We are
all crew."*

What about the teaching in some spiritual circles that, if you're feeling happy and uplifted, you shouldn't "bring yourself down" by exposing
yourself to the darkness going on around you? **My answer is, if you're a
conscious being, and you're blessed with any kind of comfort, safety,
and good fortune,** *you're even more obligated to offer your blessings to
those who are not experiencing these things.*

If you're having a good day, your prayers are needed by someone
who's not having a good day.

If your life is currently smooth and fulfilling, your prayers are needed
by someone who is in the midst of brutal storms.

If you're feeling centered and peaceful, your prayers are needed by
someone who can't remember what peace feels like and is drowning in
fear and pain.

If you were suffocating in your own suffering, wouldn't you want
someone, somewhere, to be praying for you, blessing you, loving you?

"If you're a sensitive person, just stepping outside can be heartbreaking."
— Lykke Li

Last week I received a letter asking me to renew my membership to Amnesty International, the wonderful global movement dedicated to ending abuses of human rights around the globe, freeing prisoners of conscience, stopping violence against women, and speaking up and out for anyone whose dignity or freedom is threatened. One of their most touching activities are the notes of hope they find ways to deliver to political prisoners who are often locked up for years and fear no one remembers them. These messages can be all that sustains someone who has been detained for speaking out or fighting for justice.

There was a line in the Amnesty letter that really moved me:

"We deeply believe that the free must remember the forgotten."

If you are free, if you're feeling any kind of strength or hope or light, you must not forget the hopeless, the lost, or the forgotten.

Do not turn away from the darkness in this world.
Bravely turn toward it.
See it. Feel it.
And then defy it with your choice for love.

LOVE IS THE HIGHEST SERVICE

"When we grow in spiritual consciousness,
we identify with all that is in the world—there is no exploitation.
It is ourselves we're helping, ourselves we're healing."
— Dr. Govindappa Venkataswamy

The greatest service you can offer to others and to the world is to learn to live in your own Highest Vibrational state. *For this reason, making the choice for love is the most powerful form of service.* You make the choice for love in each situation and in every moment. You can be having a good day in business, or a bad day in business, a good day at home, or a bad day at home. In spite of that, there is always an opportunity for you to live your highest purpose.

From that place of love, you can truly know and connect with the love and goodness in yourself. From that place of truth, you can see the love and goodness in others. *When you see someone in their Highest, they instantly rise up, and you have served them in the highest way possible.*

How can you offer your service to the world each day?

Your service to the world is to keep your heart open.

Your service to the world is to meet the pain and suffering of others and yourself with compassion.

Your service to the world is to live in the vibrational space of Love and bring that divine field of Love wherever you go, so you become a channel for that Love, *an ambassador of Love in each and every moment.*

Love is the Highest form of Service.
Your source of power and true influence is your love.
Your source of power and true influence is your ability to uplift people.
Your source of power and true influence is your ability
to be a safe harbor and sanctuary for all those you meet.
This is how you can serve.
There's no greater gift you could give to the world
than walking around with an open heart.

This is one of my favorite Choice for Love Practices and one of the first techniques I teach my students. It is simple, but very powerful. You can use this in any situation with anyone. I created it with very specific wording so that it will instantly and automatically help you make the highest choice for love.

Choice for Love Practice:
How Can I Serve with Love?

When you're with someone and want to make sure you are making the choice for love, ask yourself:

"Right now, how can I serve this person with Love?"

Tune in to your Heart-Wisdom and listen for the answer. This might be easier if you take a moment to close your eyes. It's important to remember that the correct answer won't come from your intellect, which poses a different question: *"What can I **do** for this person?"* When you ask this question precisely as I've written it—making sure to include the "with love"—you'll be surprised at the response you receive.

EXAMPLE: Your husband seems very irritable and tight when he arrives home after a very difficult day at work. *"Right now, how can I serve my husband with love?"* You may hear the voice of your heart say, *"You can leave him alone and can give him some quiet time,"* when your head would have instructed you to try to engage him in conversation, get the details, and offer suggestions for how he could feel better. Even though it may feel counterintuitive to not "help" in that moment, you will be serving him more by just being there and not pressuring him to explain it all.

EXAMPLE: Your employee has been taking care of her elderly parent and is under a lot of stress. She makes a mistake handling an account, and you're very upset. *"Right now, how can I serve my employee with love?"* You may hear the voice of your heart say, *"Point out her mistake and ask her to rectify it, but make it brief. She's too emotionally overloaded today to take in much feedback. Wait a few days."* Your logical mind might have told you to let her know how unhappy you are and give her an ultimatum, but it won't serve the situation and may create even more drama.

At first, you may have to ask yourself this question several times. When you receive the correct guidance, it will resonate with something deep inside of you—that knowingness we've talked about.

There are an infinite number of ways to serve others with love. Sometimes serving someone with love takes the form of listening, or seeing their highest even when they have lost sight of it. Sometimes serving someone with love means telling them how much it hurts you to see them allowing another person to hurt or disrespect them. Sometimes serving with love means doing an errand for them, or laughing with them, or crying with them.

How will you know the best way to serve someone with love? *Your heart will know. That's why you need to ask it.*

Even in those times when we know we can't make the kind of difference we long to make, and there's nothing specific we can *do*, we remind ourselves that we can always simply hold and radiate a high vibration of Love. We offer the darshan of our most compassionate, awakened heart. This is the most sacred form of service.

**The choice for love is the choice to pass our love on
in small ways, big ways, and any ways.
We may not be able to do something for everyone,
but we can do something for someone.
Each day, in some small way,
we can leave the world a better place than the day before.**

"Sometimes our light goes out, but is blown again into instant flame by an encounter with another human being."

— Albert Schweitzer

Last year a couple going through a challenging time came to one of my seminars. "My wonderful wife has been battling an illness," the man stood up and shared. "And I feel frustrated and helpless. She's a very spiritual person and has been leaning on her faith to get her through this. She spends a lot of time praying to God for strength and healing, but I'm just a simple man and don't have anything miraculous like that to offer. *I'm afraid that only God can give her what she needs and that there's nothing she needs that I can give her as her husband. What can I do?"*

"You can do something God can't do," I answered. "You can hold your wife in your arms. You can bring her coffee. You can brush her hair. You can kiss her cheeks. You can dry her tears when she's sad. You can say words that she needs to hear. God or Spirit can't be that kind of companion to her. You are needed to do that.

"Isn't this a beautiful way to think about it?" I continued. "**To ask yourself, if God could talk to my wife, what would God say? If God could do something for my wife, what would God do? You have to be the deliverer of God's love to your wife. Isn't that a beautiful job?"**

The man and his wife tearfully embraced. All she wanted was her husband's human love. All he wanted was to find a way to serve her. *He just needed a reminder that he didn't have to be a perfect container to contain the perfect love.*

Love will always be your salvation.
It will lift you beyond a limited experience of yourself
and expand you to your highest.
It will connect you to that source of love that wants to use you
as a miracle for somebody.

THE WORLD IS WAITING FOR YOUR LOVE

"Love knows that nothing is ever needed but more love.
It is what we do with our hearts that affects others most deeply.
It is not the movements of the body or the words
within our minds that transmit love.
We love from heart to heart."

— Maharishi Mahesh Yogi

Right now, someone, somewhere is waiting for your Light. Someone is waiting to be moved by you. Someone is waiting to be healed by you, to be transformed by you, uplifted by you and inspired by you. They're not waiting for you to be perfect. They're not waiting for you to impress them. ***They're waiting for your presence. They're waiting for your love.***

For their sake, you are reading these words. For their sake, you are being brave enough to heal and open your heart. For their sake, you are learning what it means to make the choice for love.

Love wants to use you as its messenger. Who are you to disqualify yourself? Accept this cosmic job offer and say:

"I am ready for service. Use me wherever I am needed. May I be the voice and the hands of Spirit, and the heart of L`ove."

What would happen if each day, you made just one commitment:
that no matter what else occurred,
or what else was on your to-do list,
you were going to make the choice for love,
again and again and again?

If you did just that one thing,
you would find yourself and the people around you
miraculously shifting.

Remember: *You are not here for yourself alone.*
The world is waiting for your love.

❀ 12 ❀

Love, Now More Than Ever

*"The moment you have in your heart this extraordinary thing called love
and feel the depth, the delight, the ecstasy of it,
you will discover that for you the world is transformed."*

— J. Krishnamurti

We all have moments in our life when nothing makes sense, moments in which we wonder if there's any kind of order or meaning to everything, or if we're simply being randomly tossed around in a crazy cosmic game. Then there are moments of grace, of clarity, of revelation, and of love, when we're given a glimpse of the intricate, miraculous workings of the divine play of consciousness, and suddenly, everything makes sublime sense.

One Wednesday during my weekly show on Hay House Radio, I took a call from a woman named Tanya from Nova Scotia. All of the lines were full with listeners waiting to speak with me, but something drew me to go to Tanya first. *"I'm calling to thank you for saving my life,"* she began in a trembling voice.

I assumed she meant this as a figure of speech, a way of letting me know how much she'd been impacted by my teaching, but I was wrong. **"I mean, you literally saved my life,"** she continued, and then she shared a story that I will never forget.

Tanya explained that one year earlier, she was in an excruciating spiritual crisis. She felt totally lost, depressed, hopeless, and alone. Everything she did to try to understand the source of her paralyzing despair failed and left her even more distraught. *"And so," she said, "I decided to end my life.*

"I was very clear about what I was going to do," Tanya told me. "I took care of all of the business I needed to so everything would be prepared when I was gone, and I planned out exactly how I would die. The day arrived, and I drove up the mountain to a deserted lookout spot I'd chosen to jump off of. I walked to the ledge, and for a moment, I just stood there gathering my courage, thinking about what I was about to do. *I knew in my heart that I was ready. I wanted to be free.*

"Suddenly, out of the corner of my eye, a flash of something red caught my attention. I can't tell you why, but for some reason I turned my head to see what it was. When I looked over, I realized somebody had left a book on a bench. From where I stood on the ledge, I could see that the red flash I'd noticed was the book cover. **And I can't explain why, but in that moment I felt drawn to climb off the ledge that I'd just been about leap off of, and go over and look at the book."**

Tanya paused in her story, and I could hear her take a big breath. **"When I walked over, Dr. Barbara, the first thing I saw was your face smiling at me. There in the middle of nowhere, right next to where I was about to commit suicide, someone had left your book *Soul Shifts* with its beautiful red cover on a bench.**

"I felt completely overwhelmed and didn't understand what was happening, but I felt I had to pick up this book and open it. And the first lines I read were:

'My Highest welcomes your Highest to this great journey of awakening! I'm overjoyed that you remembered our appointment with each other, and, even more important, that you kept your appointment with yourself and with the unfolding of your own emotional and spiritual freedom.'

"Dr. Barbara, when I read those few words, I felt like I'd just been lifted out of darkness, and I immediately knew that, not only was I not supposed to kill myself, but that by some miracle I had found a guide and a teacher. Some angel who I'll never know had placed that book there for me to find."

Tears poured down my face as I sat in my Santa Barbara office listening to this astonishing story. Later I received posts and messages from other listeners all around the world sharing about how they, too, were weeping.

Tanya went on to tell us that she sat down on the bench and began to read *Soul Shifts*, only leaving when it began to get dark. She drove back down the mountain with the book, and for the next few weeks read it over and over again. She had never heard of me before, but learned about my radio show and began listening.

"It's been one year," she said softly, **"and I am a completely transformed person. Just those first few pages of the book gave me the answers I'd been looking for and explained the spiritual battles I didn't understand.** *Dr. Barbara, if that book had not been there, I would have jumped."*

It's difficult to describe how I felt in that moment listening to Tanya. That book, just like this one, was made up of more than words. It was an offering of love, a vibrational invitation to a certain kind of healing and awakening. When I write, I pour all of my heart into every word, every graphic design, and every detail. Then I let go. I don't know where each copy of the book will end up, or who will find it. *But I pray that whoever does see it, or touches it, and certainly whoever reads it, will feel the waves of healing love it contains.*

Tanya received it. Somewhere on a deserted mountaintop in Nova Scotia at dusk, that book was miraculously there waiting for her. It called to her as she stood on the edge of the cliff, and pulled her away from death and back to life.

I can say with absolutely no reservation that what saved Tanya's life was my choice for love. It was the choice for love that spoke to me from within and guided me to choose *Soul Shifts* as my next book. It was the choice for love that made me fight for my words to remain as they were, and for my stories to not be edited out.

It was the choice for love that gave me the inspiration for the book cover and somehow instructed me to design it myself late one night, using fabrics and objects in my home, and to spend days choosing that exact shade of deep red that Tanya said caught her eye. It was the choice for love that compelled me to push my wonderful publisher as hard as I did to use my cover design.

I didn't know who Tanya was when I wrote *Soul Shifts*, but I knew she was out there, and could feel her and everyone else waiting for my words as I wrote, just as I have been able to feel you in writing *The Choice for Love*. Each time I finish a book, I hold the manuscript close to my heart, charging it with as much grace as I can, and I pray that it be a vehicle for the highest energy of love and awakening for each person who finds it. *I ask for blessings—for their freedom, their fulfillment, and their enlightenment.*

The night I finished *Soul Shifts*, I said that prayer for the Tanya I didn't know yet, and for everyone who would ever receive the book. And in a few hours, when I'm finally done with these last pages, I will say those same prayers for you.

Tanya felt I gave her a priceless gift, but I actually feel she did the same for me. Her story reminded me of a high truth that, as seekers, we all need to continually remember:

**None of us can ever know the end result of what we offer in life.
We can't see it. We can't fathom it.
It's part of the mystery of creation.
In spite of that, we're asked to give, to serve, to love,
and then to let go.**

There was something so unconditional about somebody leaving that book on the bench. It was such a perfect component of this magical story, *because love in its truest form is always unconditional.* It rises up within us and moves out from us because it must, because its purpose is to bless. **It's what raises us up to our most elevated humanity, because it inspires us to love not for credit or to receive something in return, but because *whenever we love, we are reunited with our essential divinity.***

Soon after I spoke to Tanya that day on the radio, she sent me this message, which I will always cherish:

*"In one precious moment, you changed my life for good. My wings and heart were broken, but like a moment of divine magic, your words healed my wings enough to stop my fall. **My heart filled with enough warmth to make a different choice in my life . . . a choice for my life.** Since that moment, I have submerged myself in your teachings and wisdom, pulling back all my layers, and reconnecting to a place that is the truth of who I am. I love you for eternity. You are my guardian angel."*

I received Tanya's exquisite message as a message not only for me but for you, my dear reader:

When you make the choice for love, your words, too, will help heal other people's broken wings.

When you make the choice for love, your love, too, will help remind people of the love in their own hearts so they can make life-affirming choices for their highest.

When you make the choice for love, you, too, will be a messenger of love to others, their guardian angel, and the living proof for them that the world makes sense.

I share all of this in honor of courageous Tanya, and in honor of the anonymous stranger who doesn't know, wherever they are, that they saved a life, doesn't know that their act of leaving the book on the bench touched me in the deepest part of my heart, doesn't know that tens of thousands of people all over the world who listen to my radio show have heard about their part in this miracle, doesn't even know I am writing about them now. Maybe they will never know.

Here is my last, and perhaps most important Choice for Love offering:

LEAVE YOUR BOOK ON THE BENCH.
Leave your love everywhere.
Offer it anywhere.

What is your "book"? It's a vibrational gift that emerges from deep within you in each moment—*the book of your kindness, the book of your appreciation, the book of your wisdom, the book of your compassion, the book of your forgiveness, and always the book of your love.* Leave it on the bench of someone's heart. They may find it right away, or they may not notice it. It may save them, or just comfort them, or do nothing. It doesn't matter. Leave it anyway.

Leave your love on the bench of as many hearts as possible.
No offering of love is ever wasted.
Eventually, it will find its way into somebody's heart and soul,
even if you're not there when they open the package.

PREPARE FOR LOVE AND PREPARE TO LOVE

Awake, my dear.
Be kind to your sleeping heart.
Take it out into the vast fields of Light
and let it breathe.
Say,
"Love,
Give me back my wings.
Lift me,
Lift me nearer."

— Hafiz (tr. Ladinsky)

I have a beautiful, very large, carved stone fountain from India that sits in the center of my backyard. It was a gift from some of the long time students in my community, and I cherish it. From where I sit at my computer, I can see the fountain and hear the soothing sound of the water splashing into the bowl.

My yard is a popular gathering spot for birds of all kinds, partly because I put out birdseed for them every morning, but also because I have a very intimate, mysterious relationship with birds and believe we serve each other in magical ways. As I'm writing this, I'm watching a small flock of doves fly in and land on the table; I can see the hummingbirds sipping nectar from the flowers; I can hear the happy songs of dozens of little starlings that are relaxing in the big tree on my patio. A pair of red-tailed hawks gracefully soars overhead.

The birds love my fountain and enjoy drinking from it. I always do my best to keep the fountain full of clean water, but when the days are warm and the winds are especially strong, the liquid evaporates more quickly. At these times, I see the birds perched on the edge staring quizzically down into the stone container. They know the water is there. They can see it. But the urn is no longer full, and the water level has dropped below where their little beaks can easily reach.

Once in a while, an adventurous bird hoping for a drink leans over too far and accidentally falls in, angrily splashing his wings against the water until he gets his bearings and flies away. Mostly, however, the birds wait, perhaps not understanding how it will happen, but hoping that soon, the fountain will once again be full so they can drink.

Who knows who will come along one day and need a drink from the fountain of your heart?
Who knows what thirsty soul will look to you for comfort or compassion?

Keep your heart filled up to the brim with your love.
Do not make people strain to reach you.
Make your heart so full that it overflows onto everything,
everyone, everywhere.
Prepare yourself to love.
Prepare yourself for love.

Each time you heal and relinquish an old pattern, you are not only making the choice for love but you're preparing for more love.

Each time you practice one of the techniques I've offered, you're preparing for more love.

Reading these words, you have been preparing for more love.

Prepare for love and prepare to love, reminding yourself that *somewhere, love is preparing for you.*

What footprint will you leave upon this world?
When your time on earth has come to an end,
how will you have changed it,
contributed to it, uplifted it, blessed it?
Walk the Path of the Heart.
Leave only Love.
Choose only Love.

"I will be walking in the middle of your soul."
— Oklahoma Cherokee love incantation

Now it's time for me to leave my book on the bench of your heart.
I leave it here with the deepest, sweetest fulfillment that it came through me and found its way to you, its longed-for destination.

I leave it here with my deepest respect for your commitment to wake up in this lifetime, and to heal the world with your beautiful, expanding heart.

I leave it here with my most sincere blessings for your courageous soul journey.

I leave it here with the utmost gratitude for giving me this sacred opportunity to love you.

Now more than ever, your love is needed.

Now more than ever, the only possible choice is the choice for love.

Now more than ever, may you find the courage to hold firmly on to the torch of love, and may it light your path to awakening and freedom.

Now more than ever, may our prayers, our light, and our love heal the world.

You are a brave, shining, magnificent wave of love.
Thank you for keeping your promise.
Thank you for not turning away.
Thank you for listening to your Heart-Wisdom, and finding this, and me.

Thank you for allowing me to serve you with my words, with my heart, and most of all, with my love.

There is only one Field of Love.
There is only one Ocean of Light.
There is only one Infinite Heart that contains all of our hearts.
We are all walking in the middle of each other's souls.
In the radiant, eternal Field of Love,
our hearts are always One,
and we are Home, together.

Acknowledgments

I am honored to share the names of those who have loved me, inspired me, and supported me while I birthed this book.

Deepest gratitude to my spiritual teachers, guides, and protectors in this world and beyond:

His Holiness Maharishi Mahesh Yogi and *Gurumayi Chidvilasanda* for the priceless and prayed-for gifts of awakening, liberation, and unending grace, without which I would not have been able to fulfill my promise in this lifetime.

My beloved mother, Phyllis Garshman, for being the embodiment of love and devotion while you were alive, and for your unmistakable guidance and protection from the Other Side.

My precious animal companions now in heaven, Bijou, Shanti, and *Luna,* for being my forever angels and teaching me about unconditional love.

All those divine invisible ones whose names I do not know, but whose presence I feel with me always. I am humbled to be a vehicle for your timeless wisdom.

Deepest gratitude to honored supporters, healers, and heart family:

Lenna Wagner, beloved friend, sister, mother, and student, for being my safe harbor and steadfast, precious heart companion.

Marisa Morin, for being my bridge to the highest love and light, and always reminding me of the eternal truth.

Rose and Jack Herschorn of *The Sacred* Space, for always welcoming me and my students, and being my treasured Santa Barbara family.

Dr. Wayne Dyer, davidji, Anita Moorjani, and *Aviv and Relli Siegel,* for special gifts of support, friendship, and shared vision.

Anita Fisher, Pek Lee Choo, and *Nina Bregyin,* for 10 years of unconditional, uninterrupted love and service as my original pillars.

Bill Gladstone and Waterside Productions, for your steady, wise counsel and belief in me, my books, and my mission.

Dr. Monika McCoy, D.C., for your intuitive, loving support for my body, mind, and spirit.

Dr. Weidong Henry Han, for your humble care and brilliant, healing gifts until the incomprehensible crime of the death of you and your family.

The wonderful people at Hay House Publishing for your dedication to serving the world, especially *Reid Tracy* for once again giving me the opportunity to share the message and transmission of this book with so many people, *Patty Gift* for honoring my words and wisdom, *Margarete Nielsen* for her deeply appreciated support and enthusiasm, *Perry Crowe* and *Riann Bender* for your editorial and design magic and for being delightful to work with, and *Louise Hay* for your overflowing heart that has changed the world.

Everyone who works for and with my company, Shakti Communications, for the treasure of your love and devotion, and for always walking the path forward right alongside of me—especially my dear ones *Deanne Rymarowicz, Justine Murray, Linda Prain,* and *Diane Johnston* for bringing your whole hearts to our mission, and blessing me with your loyalty, integrity, and invaluable service.

My Gateway Journey family, for allowing me to be your spiritual mother, guide, and teacher, for being my greatest delight, and for keeping your promise to me and allowing me to keep mine to you.

And most of all, deepest gratitude to my beloved students and readers, past and present, from all over the world. It is for you that I am here. It is for you that I explore, teach, write, and serve. It is because of you that my heart rejoices.

ABOUT THE AUTHOR

Dr. Barbara De Angelis is one of the most influential teachers of our time in the field of personal and spiritual transformation. As a renowned author, speaker, and media personality, she is legendary as one of the first people who helped popularize the self-help movement in the 1980s, and for over four decades has reached tens of millions of people with her inspirational messages about how to create a life of true freedom, mastery, and expanded consciousness.

Dr. De Angelis has written 15 best-selling books that have sold over 10 million copies and been published in 25 languages, including four #1 *New York Times* bestsellers. She has starred in her own television shows on CNN, CBS, and PBS, and has been a frequent guest on *The Oprah Winfrey Show*, the *TODAY* show, and *Good Morning America*. She was the creator and producer of the award-winning infomercial *Making Love Work*, which was seen throughout the world by hundreds of millions of people and was the most successful program about love and relationships of its kind.

Dr. De Angelis is known for being one of the most moving and inspirational female speakers in the world, and is one of only five women ever honored as one of the most outstanding speakers of the century by Toastmasters International. She has been a featured presenter at countless conferences along with such luminaries as His Holiness the Dalai Lama, Sir Richard Branson, Deepak Chopra, Wayne Dyer, Louise Hay, and many other great teachers.

Dr. De Angelis credits her dedication and unrelenting commitment to her own personal journey as the source of all that has come through her to millions of people. She is a serious seeker who has deeply immersed herself in spiritual practice and study from the age of 18, and spent many years in residence with several of the most renowned spiritual masters of our time.

Dr. De Angelis is president of Shakti Communications, Inc., dedicated to bringing enlightened messages to the world through her work. She offers seminars, retreats, online courses, and training programs to all those longing to live a life of love, fulfillment, and authentic awakening. She is delighted to be a resident of Santa Barbara, California.

More from
Dr. Barbara De Angelis

Live Seminars, Retreats & Online Courses

Barbara De Angelis is delighted to offer live *CHOICE FOR LOVE seminars and retreats*, as well as many other workshops throughout North America, for those interested in having a deep, in-person, transformational experience.

In addition, her many *online courses and live tele-seminars, all taught personally by Barbara*, are a convenient way you can work with her from anywhere in the world to gain more valuable wisdom and practical support to create the awakened life you deserve. **Please contact us or visit Barbara's website to see a list of courses and to learn more.**

www.BarbaraDeAngelis.com

Listen to Dr. De Angelis on Hay House Radio

Tune in each week to hear Barbara live on *Hay House Radio*, streaming on the Internet 24/7. For more information, and to instantly listen to past programs, visit:

HayHouseRadio.com

Speaking Engagements

Over the past 35 years, Dr. De Angelis has been a highly sought-after motivational speaker, giving hundreds of presentations to major corporations, conferences, conventions, hospitals, and churches. Recently she was honored with the prestigious Toastmasters International Golden Gavel Award as one of the outstanding speakers of the century, and is known for sharing her eloquence, passion, and inspirational presence with her audiences.

To inquire about booking Dr. De Angelis, please contact us at:

Booking@BarbaraDeAngelis.com